The Icelandic Concrete *Saga*

TO MY PARENTS

The Icelandic Concrete *Saga*

Architecture and Construction
(1847–1958)

Sofia Nannini

jovis

Sofia Nannini, PhD, is an architectural historian specializing in the relationship between building materials, society, and culture in nineteenth- and twentieth-century Europe. She is the author of *Icelandic Farmhouses: Identity, Landscape and Construction (1790–1945)*, published in 2023, and is currently an assistant professor at the Politecnico di Torino, Italy.

Acknowledgments	8
Foreword	12

INTRODUCTION 17
A COLLISION

CHAPTER 1 29
A BUILDING EDUCATION:
LEARNING FROM DENMARK (1847–95)

Inhabiting and Exploring Iceland: Between Turf and Pozzolana	34
Cement, Lava, and Lime: Education and Production	37
The Icelandic Invention of Concrete	47

CHAPTER 2 63
STEINSTEYPUÖLDIN:
BUILDING THE AGE OF CONCRETE (1899–1915)

A Survey on Building Techniques	67
"Cement Was a Magic Cure": Concrete Cast Stones and Aalborg Portland Cement	70
The Icelandic War: The Battle Against Cold and Humidity	78
Reinforced Concrete Moves North	87
The Foundation of the Icelandic Engineers' Society	99
Public Buildings in the Home Rule Years	102
Concrete and Fire Regulations	115
Steinsteypuklassík: Icelandic Concrete Classicism	122

CHAPTER 3 137
ICELANDIC STATE ARCHITECTURE:
HOW CONCRETE BUILT A NATION (1916–50)

Concrete to Mold the Icelandic Landscape	143
Geology and the Surface of Concrete: The Origins and Decline of *Steining*	162
After 1944: The Americanization of Icelandic Architecture	174

EPILOGUE 189
WHEN ICELAND BECAME INHABITABLE

References	202
Image Credits	216
List of Names	220
Imprint	224

> WITH THE HELP OF THE
> SLOW DICTIONARY
>
> Jorge Luis Borges

> WHO ARE YOU? AND WHAT ARE YOU
> DOING IN THESE PARTS,
> WHERE YOUR SPECIES WAS UNKNOWN?
>
> Giacomo Leopardi

Acknowledgments

This book is only the last step of a long journey which I embarked on years ago, when I first listened to Sigur Rós' album *Ágætis Byrjun* and I thought, "If only I could understand the lyrics!". Almost twenty years have passed, and the sad part of the story is that I still struggle to make myself understood in Icelandic. The uplifting part is that, with the help of the dictionary, I learned how to slowly read this beautiful but annoyingly complex language.

This book originates from my PhD thesis and the research conducted as a PhD student at the Politecnico di Torino between 2017 and 2021. First and foremost, I am indebted to my supervisors: Sergio Pace, who welcomed me with open arms into the Politecnico di Torino; Atli Magnus Seelow, who enthusiastically accepted to oversee my work and provided me valuable support and knowledge, for which I am infinitely grateful; Alberto Bologna, for his constant advice on our shared interest in the aesthetics and production of concrete. My gratitude goes to all members of the board of the PhD course in "Architecture. History and Project" at the Politecnico di Torino, who contributed to my work with precious insights, especially Edoardo Piccoli, Marco Trisciuoglio, Filippo De Pieri, Francesca Frassoldati, and the members of the Construction History Group. I am also indebted to the members of my PhD defense committee for their valuable comments: Antonello Alici, Michael Asgaard Andersen, Mario Bevilacqua, Guðmundur Hálfdanarson, and Thomas Leslie. My work also benefitted from valuable conversations with: Marta Bacuzzi, Michele Francesco Barale, Francesca Favaro, Marianna Gaetani, Tullia Iori, Mari Lending, Federico Marcomini, Chiara Monterumisi, Monica Prencipe, Rafico Ruiz, Sofia Singler, the DocTalks collective, and the editorial team of *in_bo*.

The book draws on years of research conducted in many archives and institutions. I am particularly grateful to the staff at the National Archives of Iceland, namely Benedikt Eyþórsson, Helga Hlín Bjarnardóttir, Kristjana Vigdís Ingvadóttir, and Kristinn Valdimarsson. I would also like to thank the staff at the National and University Library of Iceland and Andrés Erlingsson and Margrét Hildur Þrastardóttir at the Reykjavík City Archives. I am grateful to the staff at the Einar Jónsson Museum, particularly Sigríður Melrós Ólafsdóttir and AlmaDís Kristinsdóttir. A warm thanks to the staff at the National Museum of Iceland, especially Kristín Halla Baldvinsdóttir of the Photographic Collection and Gróa Finnsdóttir of the National Museum Library; Unnur Björk Lárusdóttir and Guðrún Þóra Garðarsdóttir at the Icelandic Road and Coastal Administration; Valdís Einarsdóttir at Byggðasafn Dalamanna; Andri Guðmundsson and Ívar Gissurarson at the Skógar Museum; Elín Guðjónsdóttir at the National Gallery of Iceland.

My thanks also go to Laila Zwilser and Louise Karlskov Skyggebjerg at the Technical University of Denmark.

This book was written with the help of many library collections: the British Library and the RIBA Library in London; the Danish National Art Library and the Royal Library in Copenhagen; the Kunsthistorisches Institut and the Architecture and Technology University Library in Florence; the Bibliotheca Hertziana in Rome; the "Roberto Gabetti" Architecture Library in Torino; the "Giovanni Michelucci" Architecture Library and the library of the Istituto Storico Parri in Bologna. The last drafts were completed at the Canadian Centre for Architecture, Montréal.

This work benefitted from many interesting conversations with several colleagues in Iceland. I would like to thank Gunnar Óskarsson and his wife Guðfinna for our talks and dinners in Reykjavík; Pétur H. Ármannsson for having generously shared his knowledge with me on the work of Guðjón Samúelsson; Már Jónsson for his assistance during my stay as a visiting PhD student at the University of Iceland; Guðmundur Guðmundsson for sharing with me his knowledge on cement production in Iceland; Massimo Santanicchia for his time during my first research stay in Reykjavík; Bjarni Reynarsson and Haraldur Sigurðsson for their time and suggestions; Óskar Örn Arnórsson for his kind support and suggestions, and the time he dedicated in writing the foreword to the book; the board of The Icelandic Concrete Association, especially Børge Johannes Wigum, as well as Erla Margret Gunnarsdóttir and Guðbjartur Jón Einarsson. I am particularly grateful to Erla Dóris Halldórsdóttir, my guardian angel at the archives, who always cheered me up through long conversations. I would like to thank Silvia Cosimini for her enthusiasm and precious reading advice. My endless gratitude goes to my Icelandic teachers, who made the most difficult language accessible and fun: Ólafur Guðsteinn Kristjánsson and Gísli Hvandal Ólafsson, *takk kærlega*.

Iceland has gifted me with many friends and great memories of fantastic people, especially Arlène Lucianaz, Iván Pelegrín, Nicholas Borbely, Louise De Vries, Maarit Intke, Carolina Weps, and Sonja Greiner. More friends, in Italy and beyond, shared the joys and sorrows of my research: I am particularly indebted to Lorenzo Fecchio, Luca Gullì, and Suzanna Reiss-Končar. Warm thanks to Giulia Gabrielli, Silvia Pizzirani, and Alessio Santoro for having traveled around Iceland with me.

This book would not be physically possible if it weren't to the institutions, companies, and associations who generously supported this project: Steinsteypufélag Íslands/The Icelandic Concrete Association, Vegagerðin/The Icelandic Road and Coastal Administration, Aalborg Portland Íslandi, and Federbeton Confindustria. Thanks also to the

National Museum of Iceland, which generously allowed me to reproduce the photographs of its collection free of charge.

I am grateful to the team at jovis Verlag for having enthusiastically embraced the idea of this book from the very beginning. Warm thanks to Franziska Schüffler for her amazing work as editor, to Bianca Murphy for copyediting the texts to the tiniest detail, and to Floyd Schulze for the beautiful graphic layout. Finally, I would like to thank all my friends, family, and loved ones for the experiences we share and the time we spend together. Unna, your paws are within each line. This book is dedicated to my parents, Maria Cristina Masarà and Roberto Nannini, who have always made it possible for me to write in a room of my own.

Foreword

T
H
E

PERIOD FROM 1915 TO 1940 WAS CHARACTERIZED
BY A SYSTEMATIC DEVELOPMENT,
THE PROCESSING OF EXPERIENCE, AND THE ADAPTATION
OF INTERNATIONAL PERSPECTIVES TO
ICELANDIC CONDITIONS.
SOME OF THE MOST INTACT URBAN AREAS
IN ICELAND ARE FROM THIS PERIOD.
BUT AS ICELANDIC BUILDERS WERE
COMING TO TERMS WITH THE TASK OF HOW TO ERECT
SUITABLE HOUSING FOR THEIR NATION,
MASTERING MATERIAL, TECHNOLOGY, AND ART,
THE TRIAD OF ARCHITECTURE,
THE [FOREIGN] OCCUPATION OF ICELAND RODE ROUGHSHOD AND DISRUPTED THE PRIOR PREMISES. HOWEVER,
THAT IS ANOTHER STORY NOT TO BE TOLD HERE.

Hörður Ágústsson, *Íslensk byggingararfleifð: Ágrip af húsagerðarsögu 1750–1940*, 1998[1]

Although this lament appears only three quarters through Hörður Ágústsson's monumental *Íslensk byggingararfleifð* [Icelandic architectural heritage], it is effectively its argument. According to Hörður Ágústsson, it was only during this brief interregnum between Danish Empire and American cultural and political hegemony, when the rest of Europe was in the throes of revolution, depression, and war, that Icelandic builders were in true control of their destiny, having shed the triad of the prior age's building materials—turf, timber, and stone—to get their hands on concrete, with which they could mold a true Icelandic architecture.

Hörður Ágústsson's is only the second book-length systematic study of Icelandic architecture, and he organizes it comparably to the first, Guðmundur Hannesson's pioneering *Húsagerð á Íslandi* [Construction in Iceland]. In these two works, the country's building materials of turf, timber, and stone serve as ordering elements according to which their authors arrange builders, buildings, and technologies before concrete supersedes them and renders them obsolete.[2]

But beyond serving as ordering elements, materials conjure imaginaries, both structuring and rendering visible aspects of history, culture, and politics. This is why reading works like those by Hörður Ágústsson and Guðmundur Hannesson is such a fascinating exercise. Materials tell a story of their own. In this story, turf is the autochthonous material of the backward, though fiercely independent, yeoman sheep farmer, extracted by his hand from the soil of his own land. Turf is his blessing and curse—a material that provides insulation for him and his family against the cold outdoor environment, but does so at the cost of an unsanitary and ill-ventilated indoor environment, and, to some extent, his self-respect.

In this story, timber is the material of commerce and, later, entrepreneurial capitalism. It is the material of the fisheries and, hence, the coast and the contact with the outside world, imported from abroad, and often entirely prefabricated. It is the material of nascent villages and thus urbanity, of unrooted populations, whether foreign merchants or temporary workers sent by the farmers to the coast during the winter when there was no work in the countryside.

And in this story, stone is the material of both the Enlightenment and the Danish Empire, the knowledge of which the Danish Crown exported to its furthest reaches through the drawings by its finest architects, who simultaneously designed its palaces in the metropole. These drawings materialized in Iceland as buildings for a modern colonial administration, cutting across the domains of turf and timber, the rural and the urbanizing—the state treasurer's residence

(Viðeyjarstofa, 1752–55), a cathedral (Hóladómkirkja, 1763), a prison (Lækjargata, 1761–71), and a residence for the director of public health (Nesstofa, 1761–67). It represented state power and ultimate foreign imposition—even though the stone was Icelandic, the techniques and labor required were impossible to obtain locally. The material itself was too hard to quarry and a poor match for the climate, while the Crown had to send to Iceland the tools, binding agents, and the masons themselves.

The two latter materials in this story roughly correspond to what Eric Hobsbawm refers to as the "Dual Revolution" between 1789 and 1848, that of the British industrial revolution, with its technologically and entrepreneurially infused capitalism (timber), and the French revolution, with its ideological and political underpinnings (stone), with turf representing what has yet to be revolutionized, the regime of primitive accumulation.[3] All three materials were used simultaneously from about 1752–1908, each in their domain, when concrete ended the use of all three in one fell swoop at the end of the nineteenth and the beginning of the twentieth centuries. Two where rendered obsolete by disasters—the turf house by earthquakes, most notably that of 1896 in the south of Iceland, and the timber house by fire, most notably that of 1915 in Reykjavík. The beginning of Icelandic Home Rule rendered stone buildings obsolete, thereby abandoning the architecture of the Danish Empire in Iceland.

The Icelandic word for story is, of course, *saga*. The present work, *The Icelandic Concrete Saga: Architecture and Construction (1847–1958)*, charts the rise of concrete as the successor to all three materials and, simultaneously, as the material to lead Icelanders into modernity. Its unique contribution to Icelandic architectural history is that it takes the materiality as its protagonist around which other historians have organized this history. One can only hope for further monographic treaties on the other three materials and the worlds that they conjure—of turf, timber, and stone—, studies that might serve as counterfactuals to the *Concrete Saga*.

Óskar Örn Arnórsson
Assistant Professor, Iceland University of the Arts

ENDNOTES

1   Hörður Ágústsson, *Íslensk byggingararfleifð: Ágrip af húsagerðarsögu 1750–1940* (Reykjavík: Húsafriðunarnefnd ríkisins, 1998), p. 325. Translated from Icelandic by Óskar Örn Arnórsson.

2   Guðmundur L. Hafsteinsson follows a material schema that is succinct but comprehensive. "Ágrip íslenskrar húsagerðarsögu fram til 1970" in *Skrá yfir friðuð hús og hús í vörslu safna: lög, reglugerðir og samþykktir: ágrip íslenskrar húsagerðarsögu 1750–1970* (Reykjavík: Húsafriðunarnefnd ríkisins, 2000). This work is available for download on the website of the Cultural Heritage Agency of Iceland, lending it a character of a state-sanctioned history. Hörður Ágústsson never uses the word architecture, preferring the Icelandic synonyms *byggingarlist*, literally "building art", and *húsagerð*, the term preferred by Guðmundur Hannesson.

3   Eric Hobsbawm, *The Age of Revolution: 1789–1848* (New York: Vintage Books, 1996 [1962]).

FOREWORD

Introduction

A Collision

"OUR BUILDING MATERIALS ARE AS MUCH AS A THIRD CHEAPER THAN THE STUFF YOU'LL GET IN VIK," CONTINUED THE CO-OPERATIVE MANAGER. "WE GOT A WHOLE CARGO OF CEMENT DIRECT FROM ABROAD LAST SUMMER." ... "OH, TO HELL WITH IT ALL," CRIED BJARTUR ANGRILY, FOR HE WAS EXASPERATED BEYOND MEASURE AT THE THOUGHT OF HOW MUCH THIS GAPING CEMENT MONSTER HAD ALREADY COST HIM IN READY MONEY. ... IT WAS A RELIEF TO BREATHE FRESH AIR AGAIN AFTER THE SMELLS OF CEMENT AND DAMP IN THE HOUSE. PROBABLY IT WAS AN UNHEALTHY HOUSE. WHAT THE DEVIL HAD HE BEEN THINKING OF TO GO AND BUILD A HOUSE?

Halldór Laxness, *Independent People*, 1934–35[1]

I first visited Iceland in winter 2016, taking part in a ten-day photographic journey with talented photographers and enthusiastic travelers from Italy. My trip was prompted by an interest in the Icelandic language and Jorge Luis Borges's poems on Iceland, which I had read since I was in high school, and by an almost legendary idea of the island as the *Ultima Thule*. In my mind, Iceland was a land yet to be discovered in the remote North Atlantic Ocean, full of monsters and wonders as in Abraham Ortelius's *Theatrum Orbis Terrarum*. Back then, Icelandic architecture was not on my mind—all I sought were snow-capped mountains, endless horizons, and the possibility to practice my basic Icelandic. If I had to imagine Icelandic buildings, however, I would have envisioned some red wooden cottages, like the ones I had seen in the Lofoten archipelago or on the island of Gotland; or perhaps low, grass-covered turf houses like those populating the Shire in the world of J. R. R. Tolkien.

The first days we spent in the western part, between the Snæfellsnes peninsula and the national park of Þingvellir; we visited neither towns nor villages. Architecture was scant, and we slept in squared, modern cottages, covered with corrugated iron. We ate in restaurants near gas stations. For a while I had the impression of being in North America. However, while traveling along the southern coast of the island, I started

INTRODUCTION

A COLLISION

Fig. 1
Viðborðssel farmhouse,
Sveitarfélagið Hornafjörður.

Fig. 2
Sigurður Pjetursson, House in Fjölnisvegur, Reykjavík (1931).

Fig. 3
Guðjón Samúelsson, Verkamannabústaðir [Workers' Houses], Hofsvallagata, Reykjavík (1931–32).

noticing an increasing number of farmhouses along the road, either inhabited or in ruins and sharing a common trait—they were all in concrete. Fig. 1

My eyes were drawn to these buildings drowned in the snow, rather than by the surrounding mountains and glacier lagoons. As a result, while my travel companions were taking photographs of waterfalls and cliffs, I usually turned the other way, picturing farms, stables, and lighthouses. At the end of the journey, I spent a weekend in Reykjavík, where I found evidence of my impressions about local building traditions: except for a few timber houses in the city center, covered with colored corrugated iron and resembling my memories of Scandinavia, Icelandic architecture was wholly in concrete. This was evident in both public and residential buildings, in the center and on the outskirts of the city. Fig. 2–3

I came back to Iceland six months later to attend a course in Icelandic at the University Centre of the Westfjords. The course took place in the former school of Núpur, along the coast of the Dýrafjörð fjord, which I now know was one of the first concrete *héraðsskólar* [district schools] built in the late nineteen-twenties. Back then, my attention was focused on learning the language. However, before going home, I remember visiting the imposing Hallgrímskirkja in Reykjavík and thinking that I wished to know more about its bizarre concrete architecture: I googled it in search for quick information and found almost nothing. Feeling disappointed, I thought to myself that it would be fascinating to

Fig. 4
Guðjón Samúelsson,
Hallgrímskirkja, Reykjavík (1937–86).

start a research project on Icelandic concrete architecture. I knew nothing about Icelandic history and my first readings were the novels by Nobel laureate Halldór Laxness (1902–1998). Reading about the modernization of the Icelandic countryside in Laxness's *Independent People* made me realize the importance of concrete in Iceland in the first half of the twentieth century. Fig. 4

Three years later, during my research stay in Iceland in 2019, I visited the beautifully preserved Bustarfell Museum, near the Vopnafjörður fjord, in North Iceland. Fig. 5

It is a traditional turf farm, with wooden gables and soft, green grass covering the roof. Its rooms are full of objects that belong to another era—photographs of its inhabitants, farming tools, buckets full of toys made of sheep bones and old wool. The timber floors creak as the visitors walk on them, and although everything is now clean and in good order, it is not hard to imagine those same rooms full of people working and bending below the thick smoke rising from the burnt peat. After a tour around the sleeping rooms and the stables, our guide showed us what used to be the old kitchen and laundry room: a humid, dark, and cold room with the floor made of wet soil, and walls made of—as are all the other walls in the farm—several layers of turf blocks, one stacked on top of the other. Before continuing our visit, the guide stopped at the entrance of this room and said that this was the very spot in the house where one could grasp the clash of the times that had occurred in Icelandic history. She used, if I remember correctly, the Icelandic word *árekstur*, meaning collision. She was standing in the threshold of a doorway, and that doorway was halfway between a thick, wet wall of turf blocks and a thinner but damp concrete wall. Among all the objects that she could have picked to explain the drastic transformation that took place in Iceland in the first decades of the twentieth century—she could have chosen the children's toys, the pieces of peat that were used as fuel, an old photograph of a young woman emigrating to America, she chose those two walls, one standing next to the other, one representing the long past of weak and vulnerable housing, the other symbolizing a promise for a better and more durable future. Turf and concrete were still standing together, and that was possible thanks to the fact that the farm had been under the protection of the National Museum of Iceland since the nineteen-forties. Fig. 6

Turf farms needed restoration work at every generation. A turf wall of an abandoned turf house would have lasted only a few years. This almost unnatural comparison between turf and concrete was the silent explanation of the century-long struggle that the Icelandic society faced in order to improve their housing conditions and, not less importantly, to create a national architecture for twentieth-century Iceland. In opposition to the intrinsic weakness of turf and grass, the durability of concrete in the harsh Icelandic landscape made it possible to create something that had never existed before—a lasting architecture for its inhabitants. Turf houses make no ruins: if unused, they collapse, and are soon swallowed by the green landscape that surrounds them.

This book seeks to be a historical narration of the people and events that changed the Icelandic building tradition between the mid-nineteenth and the mid-twentieth century. Iceland's centuries-long physical and social isolation, paired with its rigid climate, is mirrored in a very peculiar architectural history. For a long time, Iceland was perceived by dismissive foreign visitors as a country without its own distinct

INTRODUCTION

A COLLISION

Figs. 5, 6
Bustarfell Museum, Vopnafjörður.

urban culture, to the point that, when British poet Wystan Hugh Auden (1907–1973) visited Reykjavík in 1927, he claimed: "There is no architecture here".[2] Since the mid-nineteenth century, the Icelandic society had experienced a slow and non-violent political struggle for autonomy and independence from the Kingdom of Denmark, together with abrupt processes of urbanization and the industrialization of its fishing industry. An essential debate was introduced into the country: how and what to build in order to overcome the perceived backwardness of traditional turf architecture, and to create an architecture able to represent Iceland as a politically autonomous country. The difficulties in obtaining timber, due to a general lack of forests, the fire hazards, and the hardness of Icelandic rocks, which hindered the development of stonemasonry techniques, indicated that a new material should be used for the needs of the island—and that material, or process, was concrete.[3]

The Icelandic Concrete Saga focuses on more than a century of Icelandic history of construction, architecture, and technology. The book deals with the reception and development of concrete as a building method, as well as its role in reforming Icelandic architecture. This is a history made up of several limited events; however, the spread of technical novelties and their impacts on Icelandic society and culture can only be perceived and analyzed in a long-term timeframe. The essence of this book is placed on Icelandic architectural, construction, and cultural history, and yet the boundaries of this research were not limited to the manifest geographical isolation of the island. The book highlights economic and commercial connections linking Iceland to the rest of Europe and placing the island in closer contact with the Continent.

The Icelandic Concrete Saga is also concerned with issues of tradition and modernization: the underlying theory is embodied in the idea that anonymous or amateurish concrete construction could be seen as one of the driving forces behind architectural and social transformation, as well as behind the eradication of centuries-long traditions which concrete contributed to wipe out. Icelandic historiography defined the emergence of concrete in the country's history as *steinsteypuöldin*—"the age of concrete." This term clearly promoted a new kind of temporality for Icelandic history, inextricably tied to the all-pervading presence of this building technique in the built environment. First coined in 1911, *steinsteypuöldin* was a way to label the growing popularity of concrete in Icelandic construction, and at the same time it was a wish towards the shapes and materiality of its future.[4]

It may be also argued that the ubiquitous applications of concrete did not simply result in a self-evident concrete age for Iceland, but they may also have bridged the geographical gap which had for centuries separated the island from European building traditions. The arrival of cement and concrete into Iceland could be interpreted as a step towards the homogenization of global architectural practices—an architectural "homogenocene", to borrow a term made popular by Charles Mann.[5] Concrete was the building technology which mostly unified the ways of doing architecture at a global scale and contributed to eradicate local specificities and vernacular traditions. As Anselm Jappe puts it, analyzing this phenomenon from a political perspective, concrete may be considered as "capitalism's weapon of mass production".[6] In the case of Iceland, concrete completely replaced all local forms of construction: it became a material mirror of the country's industrial development and of the increasing commercial connections to and from Europe. Icelandic architectural history can also be interpreted through the lens of the energy framework proposed by Barnabas Calder.[7] While traditional turf architecture had been the result of specific climate and material conditions, the establishment of Icelandic concrete architecture was strongly intertwined with the new energy system of coal and steam. It was the emerging network of maritime transportation sustained by fossil fuels which turned cement into an available commodity to be employed in all corners of the island.

The book also explores the technical and political relationships between Iceland and Denmark regarding construction matters. It touches upon the Icelandic quest for political independence and the country's need to convey its own cultural identity through public buildings. Over the years, construction was simultaneously a tool for asserting political and technological power of the Danish government in Iceland, a field for sharing professional expertise, and a realm for self-determination and nation-building by the Icelandic society. Not only was concrete a key agent of change for the country's history, but it also became an embodied metaphor of Iceland's collective struggle against the natural elements and towards the construction of an independent nation.

The book is divided into three chapters, ordered chronologically from 1847, when Portland cement was first used in the country, to 1958, the year when the first and only cement plant of the country was inaugurated. Chapter 1 traces the early developments of stone and concrete architecture in Iceland throughout the nineteenth century, laying the foundations for understanding how and when cement and concrete became available building materials and techniques in the country. Chapter 2 focuses on the first generation of Icelandic civil engineers, active in the first decades of the twentieth century. It discusses their pioneering work in research, trade, and design, which was at the core of a new age in Icelandic construction history. In those years, turf as a construction material was swiftly being abandoned, resulting in dramatic changes in the building tradition of the island. Chapter 3 focuses on Icelandic architecture after the Act of Union with Denmark in 1918. It deals specifically with the architectural achievements of Iceland's first state architect, Guðjón Samúelsson (1887–1950), and his peculiar approach to concrete as a technical means to reach aesthetic and symbolic results. The epilogue recollects the inauguration of Iceland's cement plant in 1958, which was praised as the symbol of the country's fully reached material independence. Furthermore, it briefly considers the all-pervading presence of concrete in Icelandic architectural culture in the second half of the twentieth century, to the present day.

The Icelandic Concrete Saga follows the process of transformation which characterized Icelandic construction and architecture, and it focuses on the intersection between the country's technological development and its social and political changes. From the perspective of an increasingly popular building technology, the book explores Iceland's struggle for better living conditions, which included the contributions of professionals and common people alike. More than architects, designers, or town planners, the real protagonists of this book are builders, farmers, engineers, and tradesmen, who personally contributed to the material construction of twentieth-century Iceland. Despite the large number of people directly involved in this collective process, the book, just like many other Western architectural histories, narrates the history of men and of male-dominated professional worlds. However, this research aimed at giving voice to lesser-known figures of Iceland's history of architecture and building techniques. History of construction can be interpreted as a social history and, as Robert Carvais suggests, its development is shaped by the key role of anonymous actors.[8] As Antoine Picon puts it, the study of construction history may be a bridge between the history of technology and "the material dimension of culture".[9] *The Icelandic Concrete Saga* aims at adding another geographical and cultural piece to the global history of construction and architecture and its ever-changing relations to human societies throughout the centuries.

NOTES ON ICELANDIC PRONUNCIATION

Á/á – "ou" as in "house"
Ð/ð (eð/eth) – "th" as in "the", "weather"
Þ/þ (þorn/thorn) – "th" as in "thin", "thick"
Æ/æ – "i" as in "Hi"

Icelandic persons are always referred to with their full names, the last name usually being a patronymic [*–son, –dóttir*]. Unless otherwise specified, all translations from Icelandic and other languages are by the author.

ABBREVIATIONS

BR = Borgarskjalasafn Reykjavíkur – Reykjavík City Archives
Lbs = Landsbókasafn Íslands – National and University Library of Iceland
ÞÍ = Þjóðskjalasafn Íslands – National Archives of Iceland
ÞMÍ = Þjóðminjasafn Íslands – National Museum of Iceland

GLOSSARY FOR ARCHIVAL DOCUMENTS

askja = box; *bréf* = letter; *flokkur* = group; *geymsla* = storage; *mappa* = folder; *örk* = file; *skúffa* = drawer; *teikning* = drawing; *verkefni* = project

ENDNOTES

1   Halldór Laxness, *Independent People*, trans. J. A. Thompson (New York: Alfred A. Knopf, 1946), pp. 421, 431, 444.

2   Wystan Hugh Auden and Louis MacNeice, *Letters from Iceland* (London: Faber and Faber, 1937), p. 109.

3   On concrete as a process: Adrian Forty, "A Material without a History," in *Liquid Stone: New Architecture in Concrete*, edited by Jean Louis Cohen and G. Martin Moeller Jr. (Basel: Birkhäuser, 2006): pp. 34–45.

4   This term was first used by Jón Þorláksson in: Jón Þorláksson, "Hvernig reynast steinsteypuhúsin?," *Búnaðarrit* 25, no. 1 (1911): p. 207. Historiography largely employed the term: Lýður Björnsson, *Steypa lögð og steinsmíð rís. Sagt frá mannvirkjum úr steini og steypu* (Reykjavík: Hið íslenska bókmenntafélag, 1990), p. 65; Páll V. Bjarnason, "Icelandic Architecture in the Concrete Era," in *XIV. Nordic Concrete Congress & Nordic Concrete Industry Meeting, 6–8 August 1992* (Reykjavík: Icelandic Concrete Association, 1992), pp. 251–58. More recently, "the age of concrete" was the subject of a five-episode documentary series for The Icelandic National Broadcasting Service RÚV, edited by Egill Helgason and Pétur H. Ármannsson: "Steinsteypuöldin" (2016).

5   According to Mann, homogenocene is the biological era inaugurated by the Columbian Exchange. Charles C. Mann, *1493: Uncovering the New World Columbus Created* (New York: Alfred A. Knopf, 2005). See also: Charles C. Mann, "The Dawn of the Homogenocene," *Orion Magazine* 30, no. 3 (2011): pp. 16–26.

6   Anselm Jappe, *Béton. Arme de construction massive du capitalisme* (Paris: Les Éditions L'échappée, 2020).

7   Barnabas Calder, *Architecture: From Prehistory to Climate Emergency* (Harmondsworth: Penguin Books, 2021).

8   "Comme pour l'histoire des sciences et des techniques, il faut s'intéresser aux petites gens, aux inventeurs anonymes, aux découvreurs d'astuces, aux personnages relais de trouvailles." Robert Carvais, "Plaidoyer pour une histoire humaine et sociale de la construction," in *Édifice & Artifice. Histories constructives*, edited by Robert Carvais, André Guillerme, Valérie Nègre, and Joël Sakarovitch (Paris: Picard, 2008), p. 38.

9   Antoine Picon, "Construction History: Between Technological and Cultural History," *Construction History* 21 (2005–2006): p. 17.

Chapter 1

A Building Education: Learning from Denmark (1847–95)

THE SAID THULE IS THE ISLAND CALLED ICELAND BECAUSE OF ITS ICE WHICH MAKES THE SEA SOLID. ABOUT THIS ISLAND PEOPLE TELL AMONG OTHER THINGS THE FOLLOWING REMARKABLE FACT: THE ICE IS SO BLACK AND DRY BECAUSE OF ITS HIGH AGE THAT IT WILL BURN IF ONE SETS IT AFIRE. HOWEVER, THE ISLAND IS SO BIG THAT IT IS THE HOME FOR MANY PEOPLE. THEY LIVE EXCLUSIVELY FROM LIVESTOCK FARMING AND DRESS IN ANIMAL SKINS. THERE IS NO CEREAL THERE AND ONLY SPARSE LUMBER. THEY LIVE IN SUBTER-RANEAN PITS AND ENJOY SHARING HOUSE, FOOD AND COMPANY WITH THEIR ANIMALS. ... THE MOUNTAINS ARE THEIR CITIES AND THE SPRINGS THEIR HAPPINESS.

Adam of Bremen, *Gesta Hammaburgensis ecclesiae pontificum*, late eleventh century[1]

A FARM HOUSE LOOKS MORE LIKE A VILLAGE THAN A SINGLE HABITATION. SOMETIMES SEVERAL FAMILIES LIVE ENCLOSED WITHIN THE SAME MASS OF TURF. THE COTTAGES OF THE LOWEST ORDER OF PEOPLE ARE WRETCHED HOVELS; SO VERY WRETCHED, THAT IT IS WONDERFUL HOW ANY THING IN THE HUMAN FORM CAN BREATHE IN THEM.

George Steuart Mackenzie, *Travels in the Island of Iceland*, 1811[2]

More than 700 years divide the descriptions of Iceland and of its living conditions by German chronicler Adam of Bremen (before 1050–1081/85) and Scottish geologist George Steuart Mackenzie (1780–1848). Both texts fall into a large number of travel descriptions and reports written by foreign visitors on the society and landscape of Iceland, creating what Karen Oslund has aptly described as "Iceland Imagined".[3] Evidently, Iceland's severe environmental conditions did not seem to have led to almost any changes in local construction habits for more than seven centuries. Cold winters and the almost complete absence of forests had allowed the inhabitants to use only what was available—turf, driftwood, and quite a lot of patient resilience towards an almost uninhabitable territory. When Mackenzie visited Iceland in the early eighteen-tens, he was negatively impressed by the poor living standards in the countryside, and yet he admired the human strength hiding behind an architecture made of earth. Figs. 1–2

Although the permanence of Icelandic turf construction would be the standard until the early twentieth century, the first steps towards a change in Icelandic construction history were indeed taken in the decades following Mackenzie's travel. After centuries of economic and social hardship, caused by the island's intrinsic isolation and many natural disasters, the nineteenth century was a moment resounding with debates of Icelandic nationalism and political autonomy. Under the Kingdom of Denmark since the Kalmar Union, established in the late fourteenth century, the status of Iceland within the Danish kingdom was often blurred, and the island was usually referred to as a dependency [*biland* in Danish, *hjálenda* in Icelandic]. The island was generally given a preferential status compared to other Danish colonies, such as Greenland.[4] However, Icelandic history was recently examined through the lens of the colonial and postcolonial discourse, highlighting the different nuances of coloniality at the edges of the Continent.[5]

Fig. 1
Kaldárhöfði, near Sog, Grímsnes, ca. 1900.

Fig. 2
In older Reykjavík.
House covered with chamomile, ca. 1900.

The most evident act of colonial power was the establishment of the trade monopoly in 1602, which was abolished in 1787 and wholly lifted in 1855.[6] These decades were particularly troublesome for Icelandic history: in 1783–84, Iceland was tragically hit by a series of volcanic eruptions in the craters of Laki—the *skaftáreldar*—in the southern part of the country. The event caused the death of approximately a quarter of its population due to poisoning and the resulting famine.[7] The news of this eruption and of Iceland's severe living conditions spread around the world; it is not a coincidence that Italian poet Giacomo Leopardi (1798–1837) included an Icelander as the protagonist of the difficult dialogue between mankind and nature.[8] Since the early nineteenth century, there had been an increasing interest in Icelandic language and culture, which resulted in the foundation of the Icelandic Literary Society (1816) and the *Fjölnir* journal (1835–47), published in Copenhagen by Icelandic scholars.[9] From this cultural movement emerged a quest for more political autonomy, whose leader was Icelandic scholar Jón Sigurðsson (1811–1879). These claims led to an increasing wave of Icelandic nationalism, prompting a gradual and somewhat peaceful separation from the Danish state in the following decades.[10] A key change in Iceland's politics soon unfolded: in 1843, the Danish kingdom established the Icelandic consultative assembly, named Alþingi after the name of the assembly founded in the tenth century by the first generations of Icelandic settlers. The assembly originally met in the fields of Þingvellir, in south-west Iceland.[11] When restored in the nineteenth century, it was relocated in Reykjavík. In the wake of the 1848 European revolutions, the Danish kingdom adopted a constitution in 1849, thus ending its status as an absolute monarchy. Following these recent changes, the national assembly was held in Reykjavík in 1851: while Danish authorities invited Iceland to accept the recent Danish constitution, Icelandic representatives demanded Iceland's full autonomy in union with Denmark. The meeting ended with a collective protest from the Icelandic side, yet it was dissolved with no further results. Iceland was granted its first constitution only in 1874, according to which the parliament had legislative power on internal affairs.[12]

Icelandic history is usually associated with some important dates, which acted as key watersheds for the political history of the country—the almost mythical year 874, long considered the exact date of arrival of the first settlers, the Kalmar Union in 1397, the national assembly in 1851, the first constitution in 1874, the beginning of home rule in 1904, the Act of Union in 1918, the declaration of independence in 1944. As a result, many underlying processes are overshadowed by a shared political narrative. As Guðmundur Hálfdanarson argues, while economic and social developments in Iceland are usually regarded as factors depending on political changes, this correlation should be analyzed conversely.[13] It was the increasingly substantial economic and social changes, occurring since the mid-nineteenth century, which convinced both Icelandic representatives and Danish authorities that Iceland should act as a fully independent state. This change of perspective gives a great historical importance to technical progress in Iceland, which promoted the establishment of modern infrastructures and shared professional knowledge on technical matters.[14] In particular, historiography has often highlighted the pivotal role played by the industrialization of the country's fishing industry.[15] When it comes to construction and building traditions, the roots of this material development can be found in the very decades when the independence movement emerged. On the one hand, at the core of the growing nationalist movement was the idea that the Danish kingdom was liable for Iceland's poverty and backwardness, and that only a greater political autonomy would eventually free Iceland from its impoverished status.[16] At the same time, as the next chapters will show, the actors of Iceland's shift in building matters were rarely imbued with extreme nationalist visions. On the contrary, they were eager to strengthen their island's connections with Denmark and other European countries in order to improve local building techniques. Adopting a rhetoric that blended a promotion of higher hygiene standards and sharp accusations of the vernacular tradition, engineers and building experts contributed to an increased awareness of the living conditions of rural Iceland, until they managed to wholly transform the country's built environment. This rhetoric could be explained as a pivotal ingredient of the nineteenth-century independence movement, which strived to detach Icelandic society from the seemingly backward conditions and—the narratives of—its past.[17]

The nineteenth century thus became the stage for a slow yet steady material progress. However, throughout the century, only a few built projects proved that Iceland was renewing its seemingly unalterable building traditions and moving towards what Icelandic historiography would later call *steinsteypuöldin*—"the age of concrete". With the exception of a few buildings, it was a number of geological explorations, local master masons, construction techniques, and amateurish productions that performed as true actors enabling a deep change in Icelandic construction and architectural history. This chapter will deal with the main stages of this process. It will analyze several discoveries, results, and failures in order to understand how an architectural tradition of scattered turf farms was quickly abandoned in a matter of a few decades and replaced by the building technology of an increasingly globalized world.

INHABITING AND EXPLORING ICELAND: BETWEEN TURF AND POZZOLANA

Since the times of the settlement, Icelandic building traditions had revolved around the only building materials available in the country: mostly turf, gravel, and driftwood. The island did not offer sufficient clay resources for brick production, and it had also experienced a decrease of its forests due to human activities and sheep grazing.[18] For almost a thousand years, most farmhouses and churches had been built according to the traditional procedures of turf construction.[19] Iceland was made inhabitable only through a seemingly inalterable architecture that disappeared in the landscape. Over the centuries, however, vernacular Icelandic architecture had produced different variations of the same typology: the *baðstofa*—the turf farm.[20] By the early nineteenth century, the most common typology was that of the *burstabær* [gabled house], which consisted of a series of timber gables in front of the turf cluster.[21] Figs. 3–4

Turf construction provided some benefits, as it employed building materials that were available in all corners of the island, and it also offered insulation against the cold weather. Nevertheless, while thick walls with very few windows retained the heat inside, they created bad respiratory conditions, as heating was obtained by burning manure and the inhabitants often shared the living spaces with cattle and sheep. Furthermore, turf houses needed almost constant renovation, with an average lifespan of no more than a few decades.[22] This endless need of refurbishment was considered a "public and national issue" at the turn of the century.[23] As recent literature shows, turf construction is not inherently unhealthy and has little sway on indoor air conditions.[24] However, the urge to renovate the vernacular construction in turf was

Fig. 3
Grund (in Skorradalur), ca. 1900.

Fig. 4
Reykholt
(Borgarfjarðarsýsla, Iceland), ca. 1900.

often imbued with colonial positions shared by many nineteen-century Icelandic intellectuals, who considered turf buildings as remnants of an underdeveloped past—a past to be forgotten in order to make space for progress.[25]

Continental timber architecture appeared no earlier than in the sixteenth and seventeenth centuries, mostly as headquarters for European merchants on a few coastal outposts.[26] The presence of trade centers increased rapidly since 1602, when the Danish kingdom issued a decree that imposed a monopoly on all commerce. Trade was coordinated by Danish citizens in specifically designated commercial harbors along the Icelandic coast: until the mid-nineteenth century, timber houses were thus a prerogative of the Danish trading class.[27] However, final abolition of the Danish monopoly in 1855 and the growing number of Icelandic carpenters and builders resulted in an increase of both private and public wooden structures in Icelandic villages.[28] In the late nineteenth century, entirely prefabricated timber houses became available on the island. Known as *katalóghús*—"catalogue houses"—they were produced in Norway and exported to the Icelandic centers.[29] The main drawback of timber construction in Iceland was its high cost, due to constant dependence on skilled carpenters, imported wood for structures, and corrugated iron for cladding.[30] Although timber houses did play an important role within Icelandic construction, and still characterize some of Iceland's quaint town centers today, timber was not only expensive, but it was also constantly threatened by fires. As Chapter 2 will show, by 1915 new timber buildings were entirely banned from the city center of Reykjavík, thus bringing Icelandic timber architecture to an end. Fig. 5

Icelandic concrete history dates back to the eighteen-forties. However, the debate on Iceland's geological resources and their exploitation for building purposes had already started in the late eighteenth century. The first reference to binders in Iceland can be located in an essay on lime written by Icelandic scientist and physician Sveinn Pálsson (1762–1840), published in the journal of the Icelandic Society for Learned Arts in 1788.[31] The essay can be considered a brief treatise on limestone and lime production written in Icelandic. In the first two paragraphs, Sveinn Pálsson mentioned the chemistry and geology of limestone deposits; then he highlighted the methods for burning lime and using it for stonemasonry. Acknowledging that limestone deposits had not been discovered in Iceland, he alluded to the possibility of obtaining lime from seashells as raw material.[32] Sveinn Pálsson also referred to the existence of hydraulic binders, such as Roman cement and hydraulic lime, and claimed that deposits of "clay or red earth" could be found in many places in Iceland.[33] Between the lines, Sveinn Pálsson might have

been suggesting that Iceland could offer deposits of pozzolana, one of the most coveted earth products in modern construction history.

Throughout the eighteenth century, Italian pozzolana deposits were largely exploited, until new deposits were discovered outside the historical boundaries of the Gulf of Naples and the Roman countryside.[34] This prompted a rush for pozzolanic materials among the European states in order to sustain the increasing demand for hydraulic infrastructures. In line with these geological explorations and material needs, although with considerable delay if compared to France or Spain, in the early nineteenth century, Denmark also started promoting the geological analysis of its territory, both in Europe and overseas. The main actor behind these explorations was Johan Georg Forchhammer (1794–1865), student of renowned physicist Hans Christian Ørsted (1777–1851) and a pioneer in Danish geological studies. As a result of his research, Forchhammer published several essays on the geology of the island of Bornholm, of the Faroe Islands, and of the whole Danish territory.[35] Although these printed sources do not directly refer to geological surveys conducted in Iceland, there are archival references to Forchhammer's focus on Icelandic geology and, specifically, concerning the presence of pozzolana deposits.[36] The presence of Icelandic pozzolana had already been mentioned in the eighteen-twenties, and by

Fig. 5
Reykjavík, Vesturgata, ca. 1900.

the early eighteen-thirties, Forchhammer resumed research, appointing his colleague Ögmundur Sigurðsson (1799–1845, usually referred to as Ögmundur Sivertsen) to lead geological explorations on the Snæfellsnes peninsula.[37] Given the fact that there were no further mentions of pozzolana deposits in Iceland until local cement production started in the late nineteen-fifties, when the debate emerged again in contemporary terms, these investigations seemed to have resulted in a failure. No matter how unsuccessful Forchhammer's survey might have been, it was nevertheless a sign of the geological importance of Iceland during Denmark's golden age of scientific inquiry. Since the late seventeenth century, Iceland had already become particularly famous for its deposits of Iceland spar, or Iceland crystal. Until the first decades of the nineteenth century, Iceland's geological curiosities were still in the hands of Danish scientists and explorers, who did not consider them as elements for improving the living conditions of the Icelanders but were rather interested in extraction activities. These two worlds collided only after the eighteen-forties, when Icelandic nationalism started to emerge in the shape of an independence movement. It was then acknowledged that the vernacular world of turf farms could be transformed only through the exploration of the geologically rich country. These were, in fact, the premises on which the Icelandic concrete *saga* began.

CEMENT, LAVA, AND LIME: EDUCATION AND PRODUCTION

Icelandic stonemasonry and concrete construction largely developed throughout the second half of the nineteenth century, and its advancement was marked by two distinct events: the first application of Portland cement in the country in 1847 and the first cast-in-place concrete building completed in 1895. During these decades, Iceland experienced a wave of nationalism that eventually set the political agenda towards an increasing autonomy from the Kingdom of Denmark. In spite of the growing movement that argued for Iceland's full independence from Denmark, the development of Icelandic construction was very much dependent on Danish technical knowledge. This interdependence could be seen as a bridge connecting Iceland to the Continent with a twofold consequence. On the one hand, it tightened the economic and social connections to Denmark, in the very moment when Danish authorities were loosening their grip on the island. On the other hand, it also allowed more commercial and scientific relations with other countries, such as Germany and the United Kingdom, resulting in the importation of the latest technical expertise to Iceland.

According to Icelandic historiography, cement was first used in Iceland in 1847 to plaster the outer walls of Reykjavík's recently enlarged cathedral. This information has been reported many times by historians throughout the twentieth century, and its origins can be linked to the comprehensive 1942 volume on Icelandic construction history written by physician, urban planning and building expert Guðmundur Hannesson (1866–1946).[38] Claiming that "the history of concrete is like an adventure", Guðmundur Hannesson's included a short outline of the discovery of Portland cement.[39] He proudly asserted that the Icelanders "soon paid attention to cement and concrete", and he marked 1847 as the year when cement was first used on the walls of Reykjavík's cathedral.[40]
By 1847, the whole country hosted only a handful of stone buildings, all commissioned by Danish authorities and consequently designed by Danish architects. The first was Viðeyjarstofa, designed by Nicolai Eigtved (1701–1754) and built between 1753–55 as the residence of Skúli Magnússon (1711–1794).[41] Viðeyjarstofa was soon followed by a number of small churches and residences in the south-western part of the country; among them was the cathedral of Reykjavík.[42] Fig. 6

Despite its small dimensions, the history of Reykjavík's cathedral was long and troublesome.[43] The presence of a cathedral in Reykjavík is, in fact, rather recent: until the late eighteenth century, Reykjavík did not serve as the bishop's seat. Since the Middle Ages, Icelandic bishops had resided in Skálholt. After the 1784–85 earthquakes that destroyed most of the settlements in the Árnessýsla and Rángarvallasýsla counties, the Danish kingdom prompted the transfer of the parish church to Reykjavík, which had already become Iceland's main trading center.[44] The new cathedral was designed by Danish carpenter and architect Andreas Kirkerup (1749–1810). The final outcome was a small church, with one single hall and no apse, located in the area of Austurvöllur between the harbor and Tjörnin, the pond located south of the city center. The main structure was built of local stones bound together with lime, covered by a timber roof. The works started in 1787 and were carried out by Danish master masons; the cathedral was inaugurated almost ten years later, in 1796.[45]

A few decades later, Kirkerup's cathedral had become too small for Reykjavík's growing population.[46] Thus, in 1846, the Danish treasury invited the young Danish architect Laurits Albert Winstrup (1815–1889) to travel to Iceland and draw up a proposal for the renovation of the cathedral: this invitation made Winstrup the first Danish architect ever to visited the country.[47] Winstrup's proposal resulted in some essential transformations of the church's layout. A brickwork level was added on top of the original stone walls, a second row of windows was installed,

34. Domkirken i Reykjavík.

CHAPTER 1

A BUILDING EDUCATION

Fig. 6
The Church and Stiptamtmann's House (Viðeyjarstofa), Viðey.

Fig. 7
Severin Worm-Petersen, Domkirken i Reykjavík [The Cathedral in Reykjavík].

and the choir, the sacristy, and a projecting entrance were added. There were two main technical novelties: flagstones were used for the roof, and all outer walls were finished with a cement render. Bricks, lime, and cement were imported from Denmark.[48] The works proceeded quickly, and the renovated cathedral was inaugurated in 1848. Fig. 7

Soon, however, Winstrup's renovation came under criticism from local inhabitants and master masons. As it was evident that plastered masonry structures were not suitable for the cold and humid Icelandic climate, in 1867, some Icelandic masons raised their voices for more autonomy regarding the construction of public buildings. They sent a letter to the Þjóðólfur newspaper: they criticized most of the cathedral's renovation project, such as the absence of foundations under the new sacristy and the use of seawater within the lime, which severely damaged the walls. The authors claimed that the low construction quality of the cathedral was due to a lack of knowledge that Danish builders exhibited regarding the Icelandic context and weather.[49] For the first time in a newspaper, Icelandic building professionals demanded to be considered as an autonomous body of experts for the construction of the island's public buildings. This article was one of the few episodes when Icelandic master masons emerged as a unanimous voice in the national debate. From then onwards, the political aims of autonomy and technical innovations in construction were often intertwined.

Although it is nearly impossible to validate, the assumption that cement was first used for the renovation of Reykjavík's cathedral is rather likely. Before 1847, no Icelandic newspapers mentioned Portland cement or its derivatives.[50] The first remarks on the use of modern cement in Icelandic printed sources are dated a few years after the inauguration of the enlarged cathedral, which most likely served as an example for the use of cement. Apart from a few technical suggestions, cement soon came to embody social meanings for a country that was seeking better living conditions. During the National Assembly of 1851, the candidate Björn Jónsson (1802–1886) stated that within Iceland there was "everything needed to build a house, there is cement, gravel, flagstones, and lime".[51] Thanks to a few reports on imported goods, it is possible to conclude that cement was increasingly used by the population since the eighteen-sixties.[52] However, it was only in the eighteen-seventies that a public debate on cement, lime, and concrete started to echo in Icelandic newspapers and journals. For more than a decade, most Icelandic builders devoted their attention to lime and, in line with the national struggle towards economic and material independency, they tried to promote local production near the city of Reykjavík.

In 1852, in the pages of the *Ný félagsrit* journal, physician Jón Hjaltalín (1807–1882) underscored one of the greatest challenges of the Icelandic independence movement: the desire for better housing solutions and greater autonomy in construction matters:

> Where are those who can teach people how to cut stone and build a house out of it? ... Is there anyone who can produce lime? No, absolutely no one in the whole country: people learn Danish, Latin, Greek, Hebrew, German, French, and English, but there is no one here who knows how to make lime ... .[53]

The decades leading to the construction of the house of parliament in 1881 were pivotal because they prompted the growth of a working class of trained master masons and the local production of building materials.[54] This process highlighted an increased transfer in building expertise from the Continent to Iceland, with a preeminent Danish influence. One of the main actors in Iceland's building education was Sverrir Runólfsson (1831–1879), among the first Icelanders ever to get a formal training as a stonemason.[55] Fig. 8

Fig. 8
Portrait of Sverrir Runólfsson.
Photograph by Sigfús Eymundsson,
ca. 1860–75.

Sverrir Runólfsson acted as an important link between Danish and Icelandic industrial activities, especially in the building field.[56] Sverrir Runólfsson moved to Denmark in 1856. First he trained as a stonemason in Copenhagen, then he moved to Bornholm in the Baltic Sea, where he "learned how to produce lime, cement, and bricks".[57] In particular, his accounts indicate that he worked both in the villages of Rønne, Bornholm's largest harbor, and Allinge. The island of Bornholm is characterized by a complex and unique geology, with northern granite formations and a number of limestone deposits along the southern coast.[58] Both features transformed Bornholm into a mining and production site for Denmark. At the beginning of the nineteenth century, Bornholm's geological peculiarity was researched by Danish scientists.[59] By the eighteen-fifties, the island had become the country's center for lime and cement production.[60] A number of limestone quarries were opened on Bornholm, later followed by the construction of almost a dozen cement factories between the eighteen-forties and the nineteen-twenties.[61] These plants produced what was known as Roman or natural cement, either red or gray in relation to the presence or absence of burned ironstone.[62] Fig. 9

Bornholm's granite and sandstone deposits were also exploited, and several former quarries can still be found on the island. Such ubiquitous availability of stones had been a feature of the island's architecture since way before the beginning of the modern mining season: several

Fig. 9
Cementfabrikken Phønix, Rønne, ca. 1900.

historical buildings made with stone ashlars have been part of the local landscape for centuries, such as the Romanesque churches of Østermarie and Aa.[63]

It is not possible to know exactly what kind of activity Sverrir Runólfsson was involved in while in Bornholm. However, he must have been exposed to both the island's natural cement production and its peculiar stone architecture. One experience was of particular importance: he visited the village of Allinge-Sandvig while the construction of the harbor was taking place.[64] The harbor's piers were entirely made of coarse, flat stones, most likely held together by thick layers of lime mortar. Similarly, several rural houses and farms were made with coarse granite or sandstone ashlars, usually bound together with lime. It was a technique that could not have escaped the attention of Sverrir Runólfsson or any expert visitor. Once back to Iceland in 1860, he engaged in a number of activities directly connected to the Baltic island: he experimented with coarse stone structures, and he was one of the active protagonists of Iceland's first lime production.

In Iceland, Sverrir Runólfsson led the construction of two important buildings: the church at Þingeyrar in northern Iceland (1864–77) and the former prison on Skólavörðustígur in Reykjavík (1871–73).[65] Like many of his works, these projects shared the same building technique. Figs. 10-12

The double walls were made of coarse basalt or volcanic ashlars of different dimensions, bound together with lime mortar, and without any surface render.[66] If compared to the contemporary turf heritage, both the church and the prison must have stood out in the Icelandic landscape. Sverrir Runólfsson's stonemasonry technique could take advantage of Iceland's natural resources, yet added almost no extra costs related to stone cutting—which would have been particularly expensive due to the hardness of Icelandic volcanic rocks and the lack of specialized labor. Thanks to his experience gained in Bornholm, Sverrir Runólfsson innovated Icelandic construction like no one before him, to the point that he was later considered "Iceland's first architect".[67] Although stone buildings were still rather uncommon in Sverrir Runólfsson's time, it is necessary to remember that coarse rocks and gravel were largely used for the lower parts of the walls in turf farms. The real difference in the master mason's works was not merely the use of stone within the main structures, but the key ingredient that could bind them all together, despite the lack of smooth-cut edges: lime mortar. Sverrir Runólfsson must have learned quite a lot about lime and natural cement while in Bornholm: this key piece of information became one of the most debated topics in Reykjavík throughout the eighteen-seventies.[68]

Fig. 10
Sverrir Runólfsson, Church at Þingeyrar (1864–77).

Fig. 11
Sverrir Runólfsson, Church at Þingeyrar (1864–77). Detail of the basalt ashlars.

Fig. 12
C. Klentz, with Sverrir Runólfsson, Former prison on Skólavörðustígur, Reykjavík (1871–73).

Lime mortar was not a complete novelty in the Icelandic context, as it had already been employed for the construction of the few Danish residences and public buildings since the mid-eighteenth century. Thanks to the contribution of Sverrir Runólfsson, the demand for lime increased considerably in the eighteen-seventies, while several new stone structures were built around the country. As Sverrir Runólfsson had noted while working at the church at Þingeyrar, lime was the most difficult building material to obtain and to safely transport to remote building sites.[69] In some cases, the absence of lime was compensated by using other earth products. This is the case with *smiðjumór*, a binding material based on wet clay.[70] It might have already been in use for turf constructions, and since the eighteen-fifties it had also been employed for stone buildings.[71] One example is the small warehouse built in 1875 at Sómastaðir, along the eastern shore of the Reyðarfjörður fjord: the walls were made with coarse dolerite ashlars, bound together with clay.[72] Fig. 13

Common lime was mainly imported from abroad, most likely from Denmark. However, as noticed by Lýður Björnsson, the amount of imported lime decreased in the years between 1873 and 1877.[73] This trend highlighted a specific chapter of Icelandic construction history,

Fig. 13
Warehouse at Sómastaðir, Reyðarfjörður (1875).

that is, the short-lived yet much discussed enterprise of lime production in Reykjavík.[74] The pioneer of Icelandic lime production was Jón Hjaltalín, physician and member of the parliament. He was particularly concerned with sanitary and health issues, and most of his battles were fought in the *Heilbrigðistíðindi* journal, which he founded and edited in the eighteen-seventies. As early as 1863, the doctor claimed to have found a limestone deposit on Esja, the main mountain range north of Reykjavík.[75] The issue was approached by a number of local experts, including Sverrir Runólfsson, and by 1874, a lime production company was founded.[76] First the company opened a small lime kiln near the Rauðará river, on the outskirts of the city; then another kiln was opened in the area of Arnarhóll.[77] The production did not last long: limestone mining stopped in 1879, and so did the operations of the lime kiln. It has been suggested that the reasons behind this failure were related to the product's high costs and relatively low quality. The whole process faced a number of obstacles that undermined its amateurish production—from the quarrying of limestone using gunpowder to the difficult transportation of the goods on horses.[78]

Despite its short life, Reykjavík's lime adventure left some traces both in local printed sources and in the city's architecture. As a matter of fact, this local production prompted some of the first systematic self-reflections on Icelandic construction and its improvement. Throughout the eighteen-seventies, Jón Hjaltalín wrote extensively on the necessity to change Iceland's building traditions, and his positions echoed the widespread "anti-turf house discourse" shared by many Icelandic doctors, artists, and thinkers.[79] In his articles, he used to refer to traditional turf farms as "the worst cancer for Iceland".[80] He promoted the construction of stone houses with local sources, claiming that suitable housing conditions were directly linked to an improvement of people's health. According to Jón Hjaltalín, newborn babies were at a higher risk of an early death if living in turf farms than in timber or stone dwellings.[81] In order to foster stonemasonry, Icelanders needed to get easier access to binding materials such as lime. Jón Hjaltalín often mentioned his own discovery of limestone deposits on Mount Esja and the production that followed.[82] He even went so far as to propose to the parliament a bill to ban the export of Iceland's most valuable product: Iceland spar. Fig. 14

Also known as Iceland crystal or *silfurberg*, pure pieces of Iceland spar mainly consist of crystallized calcium carbonate: in theory, it could be the perfect ingredient for producing lime. Thanks to the pioneering studies by Danish physician Rasmus Bartholin (1625–1698), Iceland spar had been largely studied in relation to the fields of optics and

crystallography, and until the first decades of the twentieth century, the Icelandic quarry at Helgustaðir, at Reyðarfjörður, was the main mining site in the world. Iceland spar had become one of Iceland's rare export goods, which supported the global industry of optical lenses and a great number of scientific studies.[83] In 1875, Jón Hjaltalín suggested ceasing the export of crystals so that all Icelandic calcium carbonate resources could be used for producing lime for building purposes.[84] Quite interestingly, he also claimed that Iceland—a volcanic island "just like Sicily"—could offer the necessary earth products to make "hydraulic cement", and consequently concrete.[85] Despite an extensive debate among parliamentarians, this proposal must have sounded controversial in economic terms and was soon discarded. However, the very presence of this bill in the parliamentary records highlights the extreme measures that some Icelandic politicians were willing to suggest with the only aim of improving local living conditions—especially in a moment of intense emigration to North America triggered by economic needs, cold winters, and the eruption of the Askja volcano in 1875.[86]

THE ICELANDIC INVENTION OF CONCRETE

Sverrir Runólfsson's specific knowledge and Jón Hjaltalín's political battle did leave their marks on the future development of Icelandic construction. Iceland's "age of concrete" had its roots in these very years and originated from several construction experiments that soon

Fig. 14
Rasmus Bartholin, *Experimenta Crystalli Islandici Disdiaclastici: Quibus mira et insolita refractio detegitur* (Hafinae: Sumptibus Daniel Paulli, 1670). Book cover.

followed. From an architectural point of view, an increased availability in lime mortar prompted the construction of a few stone buildings in Reykjavík and on its outskirts. As claimed by Lýður Björnsson, the lime produced in the city was mainly sold in small quantities to several masons. The smaller the quantity, the greater the likelihood that lime had been used only to paint the walls.[87] However, lime mortar was also progressively employed as a binding agent for stone structures. In particular, one building was by far the most interesting technical accomplishment of this decade, combining personal and technical knowledge with a bit of rural adaptation. Built between 1876 and 1881, the little house at Garðar, near Akranes, was considered by Guðmundur Hannesson "the first concrete house in Iceland and possibly in the Nordic countries".[88] The construction was supervised by mason Sigurður Hansson, who had previously worked with Sverrir Runólfsson.[89] Perhaps because the building site lacked suitable stone ashlars, Sigurður Hansson took advantage of the materials available in the area: sand, gravel, and ground rocks. He built the structure with cast stones produced on site, while the small gable was cast within formwork.[90] Sigurður Hansson was a client of Reykjavík's lime kiln: his concrete mixture was mainly composed of lime, with a very small quantity of cement. Due to the vast presence of lime in the casting mix, this method is usually referred to as *kalksteypa*, or lime conglomerate.[91] It must have been the large quantity of lime within the mix that delayed the hardening phase, thus explaining the long construction time for such a tiny building.[92] Fig. 15

Despite the historical importance of the experiments in lime conglomerate at Garðar, Guðmundur Hannesson's assumption that the building could be the first concrete house "in the Nordic countries" seems to be too far-fetched. At the time of Iceland's first experimentations, several other Nordic countries had extensively experimented with concrete for infrastructural and architectural works. By the early eighteen-seventies, cement was largely produced in Denmark. Cement factories were located in Bornholm, Sjælland, Fyn, and northern Jutland.[93] As a result, cement was used in fortification works in the harbor of Copenhagen—such as the Prøvestenen Fortress (1859–63) and in the expansion of the Trekroner Fortress (1865–68)—, as well as in residential buildings in the eighteen-sixties. By the early eighteen-nineties, reinforced concrete was already in use.[94] On the other side of the Baltic Sea, Portland cement had been available in Finland since the mid-eighteen-fifties; by the end of the century, concrete had been used in many infrastructure projects such as harbors and lighthouses.[95] Cement was available in Sweden at least since the early

eighteen-seventies, when the first cement plant was founded.[96] Similarly, Portland cement had been in use in Norway since the eighteen-seventies, and in 1888, the first Portland cement factory was established at Slemmestad, near Oslo.[97] It is therefore clear that cement, and subsequently concrete, were already quite widespread in the Nordic countries in the last decades of the nineteenth century, and they reached Iceland as a direct consequence of what was happening on the Continent—especially in Denmark. A written mention to the house at Garðar, published as early as 1883, described it as a "concrete" building, and it used two terms simultaneously—the Icelandic *steypusteinn*, meaning "cast stone", and the German/French *beton*.[98] This linguistic hint undoubtedly shows that all local experiments with concrete did originate overseas, most likely in continental Europe, and reached Iceland in a timeframe spanning from the late eighteen-forties to the early eighteen-eighties.

Throughout the eighteen-eighties, cast conglomerate became progressively embedded in Icelandic building traditions, and it subsequently spread all over the country. In the last two decades of the century, three key plot lines emerged: the importance of the house of parliament as an open-air building school for Icelandic master masons, the progressive popularization of European cement and concrete knowledge in the Icelandic press, and the debated acceptance of these building materials by farmers and city dwellers.

Fig. 15
Garðar House, Akranes (1876–81).

Since the early eighteen-forties, the meetings of Alþingi, the restored Icelandic Parliament, had taken place in Reykjavík. However, the debates were held in the Latin School. By the end of the eighteen-seventies, this temporary location was finally replaced with the project of a new parliament house, built next to the cathedral on the Austurvöllur Square in the city center of Reykjavík. The design was entrusted to Ferdinand Meldahl (1827–1908), one of Denmark's most prominent architects and professor at the Royal Danish Academy of Fine Arts.[99] Meldahl drafted a two-story structure, with a double row of rounded windows on a rusticated facade. He envisaged Iceland's new parliament house as a neo-Renaissance *palazzo*, with evident references to Florentine models.[100] Figs. 16–17

Until today, the building is one of Reykjavík's most important landmarks.[101] However, the parliament house was more of a technical turning point than a stylistic one, and it was a key moment for the future of Icelandic construction. Construction works were carried out between 1880 and 1881, supervised by Danish master mason Fredrik Anton Bald (1845–1909), who acted as Meldahl's delegate. Since 1866, Bald had worked on many Danish public projects in Iceland.[102] Thanks to his expertise in the Icelandic context, Bald was the first choice to supervise the building site, and he acted as a bridge between Meldahl, located in Copenhagen, and a mixed team of Danish and Icelandic masons at work in Reykjavík.

The choice of Bald as supervisor of the building site was not straightforward. When it was first discussed among members of parliament in 1879, most representatives declared that they wished the house of parliament to be built by local workers and supervised by local experts: "I choose an Icelandic man to build an Icelandic house of parliament", claimed Einar Ásmundsson (1828–93) during the debate.[103] This request was also followed by another wish: that the location of the parliament had specific cultural and national meanings. The parliament house was first thought to be located on Arnarhóll, a small hill at the eastern edge of the city center of Reykjavík. Arnarhóll was said to be the location of the farm of Reykjavík's first settler, Ingólfur Arnarson, and thus it held—and still does nowadays—particular significance as a place of historic importance. Nevertheless, with much dissatisfaction in the press and in the parliamentary debate that followed, Bald chose to locate the building on a less steep lot, and the house of parliament was eventually built close to the cathedral.[104] Fig. 18

There are two reasons that made the construction of the parliament house so important: the building techniques that were employed and its sheer size, which required many workers. Despite the rusticated facade,

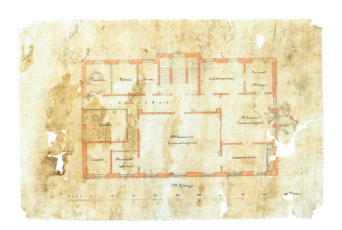

Fig. 16
Ferdinand Meldahl, Altinget [parliament house], Reykjavík. North elevation, 1879.

Fig. 17
Plan of first floor, 1879.

the structure was not entirely made of stone ashlars. The walls were composed of a double layer of dolerite ashlars, made with a sequence of two pieces placed longitudinally and one transversally as a connecting element; the inside core was filled with a mixture of sand, lime, and cement.[105] With the exception of the small house at Garðar, this was undoubtedly the first time that concrete was used at such a vast scale in Iceland. And this very scale was pivotal for the spread of the technique around the country: Bald's building site became a two-year crash course in stonemasonry and concrete construction for all Icelandic workers that contributed to the project.[106]

Guðmundur Hannesson pointed out that all building tools were sold after completion of the works, and this meant that "Icelanders, who had learned to work with and cut stones, then got their hands on proper tools and could start building stone houses by themselves", to the point that this process "later repaid all building costs".[107] This development may not have occurred by chance. Contemporary sources point out that this was a more or less intended consequence of the building process. In

Fig. 18
The Cathedral and the Parliament House, Reykjavík, ca. 1890–1900.

November 1880, the *Þjóðólfur* newspaper claimed that the work on the parliament house were Iceland's "best technical school".[108] In January 1881, the same journal asserted that Icelandic masons were going to learn much more under Bald's supervision than in technical schools abroad, at a much lower cost.[109] When the members of parliament first met in the new building in 1881, criticism still was at the center of the debate. Jón Jónsson (1841–1883) lamented the choice of Bald as supervisor of the works, not only because he was a foreigner, but also because "it would have been easy to employ a local builder to work for a lower salary".[110] Many parliamentarians were still disappointed that the house of parliament had not been located on Arnarhóll. However, when they discussed whether to give Bald a monetary reward for his contribution, most of them approved, and parliamentarian Eiríkur Kúld (1822–1893) even claimed that Bald had done more than merely construct a building: he had also taught Icelanders how to build.[111]

While general attention focused on spreading stonemasonry techniques among Icelandic workers and on how to exploit Icelandic resources of dolerite and basalt, the spread of stone construction after the inauguration of the parliament house was, however, rather limited. In Reykjavík, for example, the direct architectural influence of the parliament house is evident in a few buildings, including a new elementary school in Pósthússtræti, built in 1883, and in a printing house in Bankastræti, built in 1885.[112] It is likely that ordinary stonemasonry did not take root in the country due to its high costs. Nevertheless, another technique applied by Bald was transferred with much greater success to all corners of the island: ever since the early eighteen-eighties, concrete became the solution that Icelandic master masons experimented with the most, thanks to its flexibility, affordability, and growing coverage in the local press.

It was only a few years after the inauguration of the parliament house that concrete became a matter of discussion in Icelandic journals. The increasing acceptance of this technique was mirrored in the terms used to label it: the first remarks on concrete referred to the building method, usually adding the word *beton* in brackets, but soon the Icelandic translation as *steinsteypa* emerged as the most common and recognizable term—from the noun *steinn* [stone] and the verb *að steypa* [to cast]. Two articles were the main sources for a local scientific debate on concrete: Helgi Helgason's "Um steinsteypu" (1883) and Georg Ahrens's "Um sementsteypu" (1885).[113]

Helgi Helgason (1848–1922) was a tradesman and carpenter from Reykjavík.[114] In his article, he described the procedure in very simple terms, suggesting a mixing ratio of 1 : 3 : 6. He strongly advised against the use of sea sand and particularly suggested the casting of concrete stones for building purposes. Although Helgi Helgason was located in Reykjavík, his article was published in the northern village of Akureyri. This may attest to the fact that print sources played a key role in the spread of technical information all around the island. Georg Daníel Edward Ahrens (1852–1911) was an Icelandic carpenter of German origins. According to his article on concrete construction published in the *Þjóðólfur* newspaper, he had visited Germany and England and collected technical details on how concrete was used there. Throughout the eighteen-seventies, both countries were experimenting with above-ground concrete constructions, which the Icelandic author might have seen during his travels.[115] Georg Ahrens' suggestions on the use of concrete for building purposes were more scientific than those of Helgi Helgason. For example, he largely commented the use of formwork. Furthermore, Georg Ahrens pointed out a very precise setting time of 7 to 28 days, instead of the general advice of "two days" proposed by Helgi Helgason. He also mentioned the use of concrete for underwater infrastructures and made a clear distinction between Portland cement and other kinds of cement.[116] Despite their differences, both articles represented an important step for Icelandic construction: as building techniques entered into the realm of print sources, the spread of information could move faster through the national press.

Cement was first used in Iceland in the late eighteen-forties, and conglomerates of all sorts had been largely used since the eighteen-seventies. Yet, the building that launched Iceland's "concrete age" was raised only at the very end of the nineteenth century. In 1895, Sigurður Hansson built the farmhouse at Sveinatunga in the valley of Norðurárdalur, in partnership with the owner Jóhann Eyjólfsson (1862–1951). Fig. 19

Guðmundur Hannesson described this farm as the first Icelandic construction made with cast concrete walls, whose mixing ratio was 1 : 2 : 3.[117] The farmhouse is the proof that such literature had made an impact on local building traditions; however generic, the debate around concrete in Icelandic journals made it possible for builders to experiment with this technique. The novelty of the Sveinatunga farmhouse was its cast-in-place walls, accomplished with the help of moveable timber formwork.[118] The peculiarity of this system was that only three timber planks were used at a time, fastened onto the outer supports with timber wedges, and then moved upwards as soon as the concrete below had set. This undoubtedly reduced the amount of timber needed on site, which had to be spared considering the scarcity of wood on the island.

Thanks to Guðmundur Hannesson's 1942 volume on Icelandic construction, the farmhouse at Sveinatunga became the symbol of a founding myth for Icelandic construction history: that unexpectedly and without any foreign influence, concrete was "invented" there. The author claimed that Iceland's first concrete experiment did not originate from "educated men, who could read foreign languages", and neither from

"those who had traveled and seen foreign models". On the contrary, Guðmundur Hannesson wrote that "there were an Icelandic farmer and a builder, who were making some attempts on their own and they *discovered concrete*!".[119] The history of concrete is indeed made up of "many, small, consecutive, or even temporally parallel inventions".[120] As Adrian Forty points out, "the early development of reinforced concrete in the nineteenth century was not attached to a particular time or place; rather it was invented several times, in slightly different ways and in different places."[121] According to Guðmundur Hannesson, Iceland might have been one of these "different places", even though this chapter has so far highlighted the sheer number of foreign influences from other

Fig. 19
Sveinatunga farmhouse, ca. 1929.

geographies. His opinion regarding the Icelandic invention of concrete was surely influenced by a nationalistic attitude that re-read and re-imagined Icelandic social and technological accomplishments. Guðmundur Hannesson's book was published on the verge of Iceland's declaration of independence, and it contains some myths that aimed at underpinning Iceland's autonomous role in technical matters. The Sveinatunga farm was soon followed by several concrete structures built all across the country, particularly in Reykjavík. Their presence, together with the emergence of Iceland's professional class of trained engineers, greatly influenced the development of Icelandic construction and inaugurated the country's "concrete age".

ENDNOTES

1 "Haec itaque Thyle nunc Island appellatur, a glacie quae occanum astringit. De qua etiam hoc memorabile ferunt, quod eadem glacies ita nigra et arida videatur propter antiquitatem, ut incensa ardeat. Est autem insula permaxima, ita ut populos infra se multos contineat, qui solo pecorum fetu vivunt eorumque vellere teguntur; nullae ibi fruges, minima lignorum copia, propterea in subterraneis habitant speluncis, communi tecto ... Nam et montes suos habent pro oppidis et fontes pro deliciis." Adam of Bremen, *Gesta Hammaburgensis ecclesiae pontificum*, edited by Johann Martin Lappenberg. Second edition (Hannover: Impensis Bibliopolii Hahniani, 1876), p. 184. English translation by B. Wallace, https://www.canadianmysteries.ca/sites/vinland/vikinglife/emigration/iceland/4116en.html, accessed June 7, 2023.

2 George Steuart Mackenzie, *Travels in the Island of Iceland* (Edinburgh: Thomas Allan and Company, 1811), p. 115.

3 Karen Oslund, *Iceland Imagined: Nature, Culture, and Storytelling in the North Atlantic* (Seattle: University of Washington Press, 2011). See also: Haraldur Sigurðsson, *Ísland í skrifum erlendra manna um þjóðlíf og náttúru landsins. Ritaskrá* (Reykjavík: Landsbókasafn Íslands, 1991); Sumarliði R. Ísleifsson, ed., *Iceland and Images of the North* (Sainte-Foy: Presses de l'Université du Québec/Reykjavík: The Reykjavík Academy, 2011); Sumarliði R. Ísleifsson, *Deux îles aux confins du monde. Islande et Groenland. Les représentations de l'Islande et du Groenland du Moyen Âge au milieu du XIXe siècle* (Québec: Presses de l'Université du Québec, 2018).

4 Guðmundur Hálfdanarson, "Iceland: A Peaceful Secession," *Scandinavian Journal of History* 25, no. 1–2 (2000): p. 88; Guðmundur Hálfdanarson, "Iceland Perceived: Nordic, European or a Colonial Other?," in *The Postcolonial North Atlantic. Iceland, Greenland and the Faroe Islands*, edited by Lill-Ann Körber and Ebbe Volquardsen (Berlin: Nordeuropa-Institut der Humboldt-Universität, 2014), pp. 39–66. For an overview of the Danish empire and its history, see: Michael Bregnsbo and Kurt Villads Jensen, eds., *The Rise and Fall of the Danish Empire* (Cham: Palgrave Macmillan, 2022).

5 Íris Ellenberger, "Somewhere Between 'Self' and 'Other': Colonialism in Icelandic Historical Research," in *Nordic Perspectives on Encountering Foreignness*, edited by Anne Folke Henningsen, Leila Koivunen, and Taina Syrjämaa (Turku: University of Turku, 2009), pp. 99–114; Gavin Lucas and Angelos Parigoris, "Icelandic Archaeology and the Ambiguities of Colonialism," in *Scandinavian Colonialism and the Rise of Modernity: Small Time Agents in a Global Arena*, edited by Magdalena Naum and Jonas M. Nordin (New York: Springer, 2013), pp. 89–104; Kristín Loftsdóttir, *Crisis and Coloniality at Europe's Margins* (Abingdon/New York: Routledge, 2019).

6 Gísli Gunnarsson, *Monopoly Trade and Economic Stagnation: Studies in the Foreign Trade of Iceland, 1602–1787* (Lund: Ekonomisk-historiska föreningen, 1983).

7 Gunnar Karlsson, *The History of Iceland* (Minneapolis: University of Minnesota Press, 2000), pp. 177–81.

8 *Dialogo della Natura e di un islandese* [Dialogue of Nature and an Icelander], written in 1824, was included in Leopardi's *Operette Morali*, first published in 1827. Giacomo Leopardi, *Poesie e prose*, Vol. 2 (Milano: Arnoldo Mondadori Editore, 1988), pp. 76–83.

9 On the development of a national debate regarding Icelandic cultural and political autonomy, see: Gunnar Karlsson, *The History of Iceland*, pp. 200–04. On the Icelandic language as a cultural cornerstone for Iceland, see: Guðmundur Hálfdanarson, "From Linguistic Patriotism to Cultural Nationalism: Language and Identity in Iceland," in *Language and Identities in Historical Perspective*, edited by Ann Katherine Isaacs (Pisa: Pisa University Press, 2005), pp. 55–67. On the Icelandic Literary Society, see: Sigurður Líndal, *Hið íslenska bókmenntafélag 1816–2016: Söguágrip* (Reykjavík: Hið íslenska bókmenntafélag, 2016).

10 Guðmundur Hálfdanarson, "Iceland: A Peaceful Secession."

11 As the location of the historical national assembly of Iceland, Þingvellir was turned into a National Park in 1930 and it is often labelled as a *lieu de mémoire*: Guðmundur Hálfdanarson, *Íslenska þjóðríkið: uppruni og endimörk* (Reykjavík: Hið íslenska bókmenntafélag, 2001), pp. 173–90; Guðmundur Hálfdanarson, "Þingvellir: An Icelandic 'Lieu de Mémoire'," *History and Memory* 12, no. 1 (2000). In 2004, Þingvellir became Iceland's first UNESCO World Heritage site, which makes it a controversial place where national history and mass tourism collide: Kristín Loftsdóttir and Katrín Anna Lund, "Þingvellir: Commodifying the 'Heart' of Iceland," in *Postcolonial Perspectives on the European High North*, edited by Graham Huggan and Lars Jensen (London: Palgrave Macmillan, 2016), pp. 117–41.

12 On the Icelandic independence movement and its origins, see: Gunnar Karlsson, *The History of Iceland*, 200–23; Gunnar Karlsson, "Upphafsskeið þjóðríkismyndunar 1830–1874," in *Saga Íslands* IX, edited by Sígurður Lindal and Pétur Hrafn Arnason (Reykjavík: Hið íslenska bókmenntafélag, 2008), pp. 167–376. See also: Guðmundur Hálfdanarson, "Social Distinctions and National Unity: On Politics of Nationalism in Nineteenth-Century Iceland," *History of European Ideas* 21, no. 6 (1995): pp. 763–79; Guðmundur Hálfdanarson, *Íslenska þjóðríkið*, pp. 45–96.

13 Guðmundur Hálfdanarson, "Severing the Ties – Iceland's Journey from a Union with Denmark to a Nation-State," *Scandinavian Journal of History* 31, no. 3–4 (2006): pp. 246–47.

14 On the industrial and agricultural revolution which took place in Iceland in the first decades of the twentieth century, see: *Iðnbylting á Íslandi. Umsköpun atvinnulífs um 1880 til 1940*, edited by Jón Guðnason (Reykjavík: Sagnfræðistofnun Háskóla Íslands, 1987); Ólafur Ásgeirsson, *Iðnbylting hugarfarsins* (Reykjavík: Bókaútgáfa menningarsjóðs, 1988).

15 David Gordon Tucker, "The History of Industries and Crafts in Iceland," *Industrial Archaeology* 9, no. 1 (February 1972): pp. 5–27; Sigfús Jónsson, "The Icelandic Fisheries in the Pre-Mechanization Era, C. 1800–1905: Spatial and Economic Implications of Growth," *Scandinavian Economic History Review* 31, no. 2 (1983): pp. 132–50; Gunnar Karlsson, *The History of Iceland*, 239–42.

16 Guðmundur Hálfdanarson, "Iceland: A Peaceful Secession," p. 90; Guðmundur Hálfdanarson, "Severing the Ties," p. 242.

17 Alyson Bailes, Margrét Cela, Katla Kjartansdóttir, and Kristinn Schram, "Iceland: Small but Central," in *Perceptions and Strategies of Arcticness in Sub-Arctic Europe*, edited by Andris Sprūds and Toms Rostoks (Riga: Latvian Institute of International Affairs, 2014), p. 92.

18 Michael J. Kissane, "Seeing the Forest for the Trees: Land Reclamation in Iceland," *Scandinavian Review* 86, no. 1 (1998): pp. 4–7.

19 Hjörleifur Stefánsson, *Af jörðu: Íslensk torfhús* (Reykjavík: Crymogea, 2013). English translation: *From Earth: Earth Architecture in Iceland* (Reykjavík: Gullinsnið, 2019).

20 Hörður Ágústsson, *Íslensk byggingararfleifð I: Ágrip af húsagerðarsögu, 1750–1940* (Reykjavík: Húsafriðunarnefnd ríkisins, 2000), pp. 31–94; Hannes Lárusson, "The Icelandic Farmstead," *Almanach Warszawy* 10 (Warszawa: Muzeum Warszawy, 2016), pp. 523–43; Sofia Nannini, *Icelandic Farmhouses: Identity, Landscape, and Construction (1790–1945)* (Firenze: Firenze University Press, 2023), pp. 23–29.

21 Hjörleifur Stefánsson, *Af jörðu*, pp. 53–55.

22 Nannini, *Icelandic Farmhouses*, pp. 34–40.

23 Þ. B., "Sigurður Pjetursson og byggingarannsóknirnar," *Búnaðarrit* 1 (1901): p. 5.

24 Joost van Hoof and Froukje van Dijken, "The Historical Turf Farms of Iceland: Architecture, Building Technology and the Indoor Environment," *Building and Environment* 43 (2008): pp. 1023–30.

25 Sigurjón Baldur Hafsteinsson, "Icelandic Putridity: Colonial Thought and Icelandic Architectural Heritage," *Scandinavian Studies* 91, no. 1–2 (Spring/Summer 2019): pp. 67–70.

26 Hjörleifur Stefánsson, Kjell H. Halvorsen, and Magnús Skúlason, eds., *Af norskum rótum: gömul timburhús á Íslandi* (Reykjavík: Mál og menning, 2003); Hörður Ágústsson, *Íslensk byggingararfleifð I*, pp. 95–132; Atli Magnus Seelow, *Die moderne Architektur in Island in der ersten Hälfte des 20. Jahrhunderts. Transferprozesse zwischen Adaption und Eigenständigkeit* (Nürnberg: Verlag für moderne Kunst, 2011), pp. 45–49.

27 Until the late nineteenth century, Danish merchants boasted their status also through the use of the Danish language and culture. Auður Hauksdóttir, "Language and the Development of National Identity: Icelanders' Attitudes to Danish in Turbulent Times," *Made in Denmark: Investigations of the dispersion of 'Danishness'. KULT* 11 (2013): pp. 71–72.

28 One example is the Latínuskólinn [Latin School] in Reykjavík, built in 1843–46, since 1937 known as Menntaskólinn í Reykjavík. Heimir Þorleifsson, ed., *Saga Reykjavíkurskóla: Historia Scholæ Reykjavicensis* (Reykjavík: Menningarsjóður, 1975–84); Guðný Gerður Gunnarsdóttir and Hjörleifur Stefánsson, *Kvosin. Byggingarsaga miðbæjar Reykjavíkur* (Reykjavík: Torfusamtökin, 1987), pp. 238–40.

29 Kjell H. Halvorsen, "Forsmíðuð hús – norskt handverk, iðnaður og útflutningur," in *Af norskum rótum*, pp. 68–89.

30 Corrugated iron was very popular in Iceland between the nineteen-seventies and the first decades of the twentieth century. Hjörleifur Stefánsson, ed., *Bárujárn. Verkmenning og saga* (Reykjavík: Minjavernd, 1995).

31 S.P. [Sveinn Pálsson], "Um kalkverkun af jørdu og steinum með litlum viðbæti um tilbúning skelia-kalks; samanlesit úr dønskum, þýðskum og ødrum ritum," *Rit þess (konunglega) íslenzka Lærdómslistafélags* 9 (1788): pp. 91–143. Hið *íslenzka Lærdómslistafélag* [The Icelandic Society for Learned Arts] was founded in 1779 by Icelandic scholars in Copenhagen, and its journal was published between 1781 and 1798. The society was one of the actors that fostered the promotion of Enlightenment ideals in the Icelandic context: its effects were to be seen throughout the whole nineteenth century. See: Ingi Sigurðsson, "The Icelandic Enlightenment as an Extended Phenomenon," *Scandinavian Journal of History* 35, no. 4 (December 2010): pp. 371–90.

32 The author particularly refers to two different methods employed in Bremen and in Holland. Lýður Björnsson, *Steypa lögð og steinsmíð rís*, pp. 38–41. On lime production from seashells by Dutch manufacturers, see also: Roberto Gargiani, *Concrete from Archeology to Invention: 1700-1769. The Renaissance of Pozzolana and Roman Construction Techniques* (Lausanne: EPFL Press, 2013), pp. 78–80.

33 "[…] at í vatnskalk skuli brúka járnleir eða rauða þann, nóg er af viða í leirholltum á Íslandi." S.P. [Sveinn Pálsson], "Um kalkverkun," p. 131. The author also commented on the experiments on Roman conglomerate and hydraulic lime carried out by Antoine-Joseph Loriot (1716–1782). On Loriot, see: Gargiani, *Concrete from Archeology to Invention*, pp. 342–51.

34 In particular, Jean-Baptiste Labat (1663–1738) discovered the presence of pozzolana, or "red earth", in the volcanic islands and French colonies of Guadalupe and Martinique. Gargiani, *Concrete from Archeology to Invention*, pp. 41–61.

35 See: Johann Georg Forchhammer, *Om Færöernes geognostiske Beskaffenhed* (Copenhagen: Martv. Frid. Popps Bogtrykkerie, 1824); *Danmarks geognostiske Forhold* (Copenhagen: Schultz, 1835); *Om de bornholmske Kulformationer* (Copenhagen: Videnskabernes Selskab, 1837); *Skandinaviens geognostiske Natur* (Copenhagen: C. A. Reitzel, 1843).

36   Þĺ, Rentukammer. Bréfasafn, 1928 – B24/0005. Bréfadagbók 20 [*Islands Journal* 20]. 1841–1842. Örk 18. The documents span from 1806 to 1842. The first set of documents is composed of letters and reports regarding the nature of pozzolana, written by scholars such as Gregers Wad (1755–1832) and Gottfried Becker (1767–1845), in relation to some geological inquiries on Icelandic soil and pozzolana carried out by Charles Teilmann (n.d.) in 1820. The correspondence was resumed by Forchhammer in 1833, when a discovery of coal in the Skagafjörður area prompted new scientific inquiries on Iceland's geology.

37   Sivertsen researched the areas of Búðir and Ingjaldshóll, at the slopes of the Snæfellsjökull volcano on the western coast, and the area of the Skagafjörður on the northern coast. Þĺ, Rentukammer. Bréfasafn, 1928 – B24/0005. *Bréfadagbók 20* [*Islands Journal* 20]. 1841–1842. Örk 18. See the expense sheet signed by Sivertsen, October 20, 1835.

38   Guðmundur Hannesson, *Húsagerð á Íslandi* (Reykjavík: Prentsmiðjan Edda H. F., 1942), 241; Lýður Björnsson, *Steypa lögð og steinsmíð rís*, p. 42; Hörður Ágústsson, *Íslensk byggingararfleifð I*, 291; Seelow, *Die moderne Architektur in Island*, p. 70. On Guðmundur Hannesson, see: *Aldarspegill. Samtal við Guðmund Hannesson*, edited by Ásdis Hlökk Theodórsdóttir and Sigurður Svavarsson (Reykjavík: Hið Íslenska Bókmenntafélag, 2016); Nannini, *Icelandic Farmhouses*, pp. 47–51.

39   "Sagan um steinsteypuna er æfintýri líkust". Guðmundur Hannesson, *Húsagerð á Íslandi*, p. 240.

40   "Það verður ekki annað sagt en að Íslendingar færu snemma að gefa sementi og steinsteypu gætur." Guðmundur Hannesson, *Húsagerð á Íslandi*, p. 241.

41   Skúli Magnússon was Iceland's *landfógeti* between 1749 and 1793. The *landfógeti* (*Landfoged* in Danish) was the representative of the Danish king regarding the finances of Iceland. On the residence at Viðey, see: Þorsteinn Gunnarsson, *Viðeyjarstofa og kirkja* (Reykjavík: Reykjavíkurborg, 1997).

42   Some of the early stone buildings are the cathedral in Hólar (1757–63), the church of Viðey (1766–74), the prison of Reykjavík, now headquarters of the Cabinet of Iceland (1765–70), the church in Heimaey on the Westman Islands (1773–78), the church in Bessastaðir (1777–78), the Amtmann's residence at Bessastaðir (1761–67), and the Nesstofa residence in Seltjarnarnes (1761–63). See: Helge Finsen and Esbjørn Hiort, *Gamle Stenhuse i Island fra 1700-tallet* (Copenhagen: Arkitektens Forlag, 1977); reprinted in Icelandic as *Steinhúsin gömlu á Íslandi*, trans. Kristján Eldjárn (Reykjavík: Iðunn, 1978); Hörður Ágústsson, *Íslensk byggingararfleifð I*, pp. 271–83.

43   Þorsteinn Gunnarsson, "Dómkirkja," in *Fornar kirkjur í Reykjavík. Dómkirkjan, Fríkirkjan, Kristkirkja* (Reykjavík: Þjóðminjasafn Íslands, 2012), pp. 30–82.

44   Esbjørn Hiort, "Andreas Kirkerup's islandske kirke. Af Reykjavík Domkirkes bygningshistorie," *Architectura. Arkitekturhistorisk Årsskrift* 2 (1980): pp. 126–28.

45   Esbjørn Hiort, "Andreas Kirkerup's islandske kirke," 139–43; Þórir Stephensen, *Dómkirkjan í Reykjavík*, pp. 56–80.

46   Þórir Stephensen, *Dómkirkjan í Reykjavík. Byggingarsagan. Vol. 1* (Reykjavík: Hið íslenska bókmenntafélag, 1996), p. 131.

47   The Danish treasury—Rentekammeret—was the department of the Danish kingdom that managed its economies and taxation. It was abolished in 1848 and substituted by the ministerial system. Winstrup had trained as an architect and master mason and was mainly active in Denmark. See: Þórir Stephensen, *Dómkirkjan í Reykjavík*, pp. 134–35. Winstrup left notes and sketches of his Icelandic voyage: Ida Haugsted, "L.A. Winstrups rejse til Island," *Architectura* 20 (1998): pp. 71–85.

48   "Helluþökin í Reykjavík," *Þjóðólfur* 1, no. 5 (January 13, 1849): pp. 23–24; Þórir Stephensen, *Dómkirkjan í Reykjavík*, pp. 146 and 153.

49   "Það væri lengi...," *Þjóðólfur* 19, no. 14–15 (February 8, 1867): pp. 58–61. The cathedral underwent major renovations already in 1879. See: Þórir Stephensen, *Dómkirkjan í Reykjavík*, pp. 190–99.

50   This claim stems from research on the online database Tímarit, which includes the majority of journal and newspaper articles published in Iceland since the eighteenth century. Lbs, Tímarit.is.

51   "… að helzt væri nauðsynlegt til húsabygginga, var cement, múrgrjót, hella og kalk". Statement by Björn Jónsson, in *Tíðindi frá þjóðfundi íslendinga árið 1851*, edited by Pétur Pétursson, Jens Sigurðsson, and Gísli Magnússon (Reykjavík: Prentsmiðja landsins, 1851), p. 374.

52   In 1864, at least one barrel of cement was imported: "Vöruskrá," *Norðanfari* 3, no. 30–31 (1864): p. 62; in 1870, cement was listed among the imported goods coming from Denmark and other countries, under the name of *múrlím*: "Verzlan á Íslandi árið 1866," *Skýrslur um landshagi á Íslandi* 4 (1870): p. 334. For a comprehensive analysis on the quantity of imported cement in the last decades of the nineteenth century, see "Table IV" in: Lýður Björnsson, *Steypa lögð og steinsmíð rís*, p. 49.

53   "Hvar eru þeir, sem geta kennt manni að höggva steina, og byggja hús úr þeim? … Er þá enginn, sem kann að brenna kalk?—nei, alls enginn á öllu landinu; dönsku, latínu, grísku, hebresku, þýzku, frakknesku og ensku læra menn, en hér er enginn sem kann að brenna kalk … ." Jón Hjaltalín, "Fjórða bréf," *Ný félagsrit* 12 (1852): p. 66. The *Ný félagsrit* journal was published in Copenhagen between 1841 and 1873, after an idea by Jón Sigurðsson, as a platform to discuss the developments of Icelandic society.

54   The word master mason or mason is here used to translate the Icelandic term *smiður*, which generally represents a craftsman. The combination with other terms adds more meanings to the word: *trésmiður* [carpenter], *húsasmiður* [builder], *húsgagnasmiður* [cabinet maker].

55   Most sources assert that Iceland's first trained stonemason was Þorgrímur Þorláksson (1732–1805), who trained in Denmark and worked at the building sites of Bessastaðastofa, Nesstofa, and of the churches at Viðey and Bessastaðir. See: Lýður Björnsson, *Steypa lögð og steinsmíð rís*, p. 43; Gunnar Bollason, "Ágrip af sögu minningarmarka og steinsmíði á Íslandi frá öndverðu fram á 20. öld," *Árbók hins Íslenzka fornleifafélags* 100 (2009): p. 22.

56   Most information about his life can be found in an autobiography written during the eighteen-seventies and published only in 1909, and his name is frequently mentioned by Icelandic architectural historiography. Sverrir Runólfsson, *Æfiágrip Sverris Runólfssonar steinhöggvara* (Reykjavík: Prentsmiðjan Gutenberg, 1909); Guðmundur Hannesson, *Húsagerð á Íslandi*, pp. 231–34; Kjartan Bergmann Guðjónsson, "Sverrir steinhöggvari," *Tíminn* 2, no. 22 (June 9, 1963): p. 518; Guðný Gerður Gunnarsdóttir and Hjörleifur Stefánsson, *Kvosin*, pp. 284–85; Lýður Björnsson, *Steypa lögð og steinsmið rís*, p. 54; Hörður Ágústsson, *Íslensk byggingararfleifð I*, pp. 292–98; Seelow, *Die moderne Architektur in Island*, p. 54.

57   "[…] fór hann til Borgundarhólms að læra að brenna kalk, sement og múrstein (tíguIstein)." Sverrir Runólfsson, *Æfiágrip*, p. 7.

58   This peculiarity is due to the island's location: Bornholm is situated between the Fennoscandian Shield and the continental sedimentary basin. Helge Gry, *Geology of Bornholm* (Copenhagen: Theodor Sorgenfrei, 1960), pp. 3–4.

59   Johann Georg Forchhammer, *Danmarks geognostiske Forhold* (Copenhagen: Schultz, 1835).

60   The Schors cement plant was opened in Limensgade in 1741, and it produced an early version of cement out of argillaceous limestone. Torben Seir Hansen, "Bornholm Cement. A Danish Example of Roman Cement," Seminar Lecture (2008), http://www.romanportland.net/files/doc/seminar2008/torben_seir_seminar2008s.pdf, accessed June 6, 2023.

61   By 1855, already six plants were active. Gunnar M. Idorn, *Concrete Progress: From Antiquity to the Third Millennium* (London: Thomas Telford, 1997), p. 24.

62   On Roman (or natural) cement, see: María José Varas, Monica Alvarez de Buergo, and Rafael Fort, "Natural Cement as the Precursor of Portland Cement: Methodology for Its Identification," *Cement and Concrete Research* 35 (2005): pp. 2055–65; David Hughes, Simon Swann, and Alan Gardner, "Roman Cement. Part One: Its Origins and Properties," *Journal of Architectural Conservation* 13, no. (2007): pp. 21–36; Cédric Avenier, "Ciment naturel, la matière des moulages d'architecture au XIXe siècle," in *Édifice & Artifice. Histories constructives*, edited by Robert Carvais, André Guillerme, Valérie Nègre, and Joël Sakarovitch (Paris: Picard, 2012), pp. 577–86.

63   The walls of the church Østermariekirke, now in ruins, were made of granite ashlars, the vaults of limestone ashlars. The church Aa kirke, instead, was mainly made of sandstone and limestone ashlars. See: R. G. Bromley, "Field Meeting: Bornholm, Denmark, August 28 to September 4, 2000," *Proceedings of the Geologists' Association* 111, Part 1 (2002): pp. 80 and 84.

64   Sverrir Runólfsson, *Æfiágrip*, pp. 7–8.

65   Sverrir Runólfsson was the designer and builder of the church at Þingeyrar. The prison in Reykjavik was instead designed by Danish architect C. Klentz, although its construction technique was directly influenced by Sverrir Runólfsson, who had just rebuilt the nearby Skólavarða tower in 1868. Hjörleifur Stefánsson, *Hegningarhúsið við Skólavörðustíg* (Reykjavík: Árbæjarsafn, 1984), pp. 44–51.

66   Icelandic sources usually refer to these stones as *hraun*, a general term for lava and other volcanic products. The church was made in basalt ashlars quarried on the western side of Hóp Lake and carried to the building site on the frozen waters during winter. Þór Magnússon, "Þingeyrakirkja. Byggingarlist kirkjunnar," in *Kirkjur Íslands Vol. 8* (Reykjavík: Hið íslenska bókmenntafélag, 2006), pp. 270–72; Þorsteinn Gunnarsson, "Steinhlaðnar kirkjur á Íslandi," in *Kirkjur Íslands Vol. 31* (Reykjavík: Hið íslenska bókmenntafélag, 2018), pp. 52–58. The walls of the prison are made of coarse lavic ashlars, and only the quoins were geometrically cut.

67   Páll V. G. Kolka, "Þingeyrakirkja," *Lesbók Morgunblaðsins* 32, no. 45 (December 24, 1957): p. 687.

68   One short article, signed by Sverrir Runólfsson and published in 1878, refers to his knowledge both of lime and cement. Sverrir Runólfsson, "Kalk og sement," *Ísafold* 5, no. 19 (August 5, 1878): p. 76.

69   Þór Magnússon, "Þingeyrakirkja. Byggingarlist kirkjunnar," p. 271.

70   *Smiðjumór* is also a synonym for *mergill*, a mixture of limestone and clay. It may thus be considered marl, although it did not undergo any burning process.

71   "Tilraunir og uppástungur ýmsra manna um bæjabyggingar," *Bóndi* 1, no. 3 (1851): p. 42.

72   The building is protected by the Cultural Heritage Agency of Iceland and was restored in the nineteen-nineties by the National Museum of Iceland. "Sómastaðir við Reyðarfjörð," *Morgunblaðið* (April 5, 2004): p. 28.

73   See Table V with the amount of imported lime in 1865–1901 in Lýður Björnsson, *Steypa lögð og steinsmið rís*, p. 53.

74   Á. Ó. [Árni Óla], "Kalknám í Esjunni og kalkbrennsla í Reykjavík," *Lesbók Morgunblaðsins* 24, no. 39 (October 23, 1949): pp. 461–64; Lýður Björnsson, *Steypa lögð og steinsmið rís*, pp. 53–64; Guðjón Friðriksson, *Saga Reykjavíkur. Bærinn vaknar (1870–1940). Vol. 1* (Reykjavík: Iðunn, 1991), pp. 33–34.

75   This date was suggested both by Árni Óla and Lýður Björnsson while analyzing the report titled "En Kalkbrænderie i Island" [A Lime Kiln in Iceland]. The document is undated and is archived at the National Library of Iceland. Lbs, Handritasafn, JS 133 Fol., Örk 6. The date seems likely, as Jón Hjaltalín moved back to Iceland in 1851 after studying in Denmark and Germany. See: "Merkir Íslendingar. Jón Hjaltalín," *Morgunblaðið* 100, no. 98 (April 27, 2012): p. 39.

76   Limestone resources mainly derived from the area of Mógilsá, on the southern slope of Mount Esja. Á. Ó. [Árni Óla], "Kalknám í Esjunni og kalkbrennsla í Reykjavík," p. 462.

77   The street was then called Kalkofnsvegur, the lime kiln's street. Guðjón Friðriksson, *Saga Reykjavíkur. Bærinn vaknar (1870–1940). Vol. 1*, p. 34.

78 Lýður Björnsson, *Steypa lögð og steinsmíð rís*, p. 59; Á. Ó. [Árni Óla], "Kalknám í Esjunni og kalkbrennsla í Reykjavík," p. 462.

79 Sigurjón Baldur Hafsteinsson, "Icelandic Putridity," p. 68.

80 "Hið versta krabbamein fyrir Ísland". Jón Hjaltalín, "Um híbýli manna," *Heilbrigðistíðindi* 2, no. 11–12 (November/December 1872): p. 32. See also: Jón Hjaltalín, "Kalkbrennsla," *Heilbrigðistíðindi* 3, no. 7–8 (July 1873): p. 61; Jón Hjaltalín, "Um steinlím og ýmislegt, er þar að lýtur," *Þjóðólfur* 29, no. 1 (November 17, 1876): p. 3.

81 Jón Hjaltalín, "Um steinlím og ýmislegt, er þar að lýtur," p. 4.

82 Jón Hjaltalín, "Um híbýli manna," *Heilbrigðistíðindi* 2, no. 7–8 (July 1872): pp. 49–50; Jón Hjaltalín, "Kalkbrennsla," pp. 60–61; Jón Hjaltalín, "Um byggingar, kalkbrennslu og steinsmíði," *Heilbrigðistíðindi* 4, no. 1 (January 1879): pp. 5–6.

83 On the history and the properties of Iceland spar, see: Sveinn Þórðarson, "Saga silfurbergsins," *Náttúrufræðingurinn* 15, no. 2 (1945): pp. 96–107; Leó Kristjánsson, "Úr sögu íslenska silfurbergsins," *Náttúrufræðingurinn* 76, no. 1–2 (2008): pp. 37–48; Leó Kristjánsson, *Iceland Spar and Its Influence on the Development of Science and Technology in the Period 1780–1930: Notes and References* (Reykjavík: Institute of Earth Sciences, University of Iceland, 2015).

84 "Frumvarp til laga um forboð gegn útflutningi á öllum kalksteinum, silfurbergi og cementsteinum, samt beinum, út úr Íslandi," Alþingi, Alþingistíðindi, *Umræður* (1875), pp. 296–310.

85 "Frumvarp til laga um forboð gegn útflutningi á öllum kalksteinum, silfurbergi og cementsteinum, samt beinum, út úr Íslandi," Alþingi, Alþingistíðindi, *Umræður* (1875), p. 298.

86 The emigration of Icelanders towards North America, especially Canada, started around the eighteen-seventies and decreased slowly until the mid-nineteen-tens. Most *Vestur-Íslendingar* [Western Icelanders], as Icelandic emigrants were called, moved to the province of Manitoba. See: Gunnar Karlsson, *The History of Iceland*, pp. 234–38; Gunnar Karlsson, "Vesturheimsferðir," in *Saga Íslands X*, edited by Sigurður Líndal and Pétur Hrafn Árnason, pp. 20–33.

87 Lýður Björnsson, *Steypa lögð og steinsmíð rís*, pp. 59–60.

88 "Þetta var fyrsta steypuhúsið hér á landi og líklega á Norðurlöndum". Guðmundur Hannesson, *Húsagerð á Íslandi*, p. 242.

89 No biographical information is available on Sigurður Hansson.

90 Guðmundur Hannesson, *Húsagerð á Íslandi*, pp. 242–44; Lýður Björnsson, *Steypa lögð og steinsmíð rís*, pp. 61–64.

91 Guðmundur Hannesson, *Húsagerð á Íslandi*, p. 243.

92 The building is approximately 10x7 meters. Lýður Björnsson, *Steypa lögð og steinsmíð rís*, p. 63.

93 John Cederberg, "De første bygninger og bygværker af beton og jernbeton i Danmark," *Fabrik og Bolig* 2 (1999): p. 8.

94 Cederberg, "De første bygninger og bygværker af beton og jernbeton i Danmark," p. 11.

95 Lauri Putkonen, "The Early Years of Concrete Construction in Finland," in *Tehdään betonista: Concrete in Finnish Architecture*, edited by the Association of the Concrete Industry of Finland (Helsinki: Garamond, 1989), p. 9.

96 Georg Wästlund, "Betongteknikens historiska utveckling," *Beton-Teknik* no. 1 (1946): pp. 1–22.

97 Per Jahren and Tongbo Sui, *History of Concrete: A Very Old and Modern Material* (Singapore: World Scientific Publishing, 2017), pp. 50–56, 113–29, 130–43; in the same volume there is a short account on the first uses of concrete in the Nordic countries, pp. 167–72.

98 "Innlendar fréttir," *Þjóðólfur* 35 no. 3 (January 20, 1883): p. 7.

99 Helga Stemann, *F. Meldahl og hans Venner* (Copenhagen: H. Hagerups Forlag, 1926–32); Tobias Faber, *Dansk Arkitektur* (Copenhagen: Arkitektens Forlag, 1977), pp. 129–31.

100 Thanks to an increasing availability of print sources and engravings, from Joseph Furrtenbach's *Architectura civilis* (1628) to Pierre Clochar's *Palais, maisons et vues d'Italie* (1809), Mario Bevilacqua describes how Palazzo Pitti in Florence had become a widely-known model for nineteenth-century European architecture. This reference might have also affected Meldahl's project in Reykjavík. Mario Bevilacqua, "Prima di Grandjean: rilievi e incisioni di architettura a Firenze tra Cinquecento e Settecento," in *Tra Firenze e Rio. Auguste Grandjean de Montigny (1776–1850) e la riscoperta dell'architettura del Rinascimento toscano*, edited by Mario Bevilacqua (Firenze: Didapress, 2019), p. 34.

101 Guðmundur Hannesson, *Húsagerð á Íslandi*, pp. 234–37; Bergsteinn Jónsson, *Bygging Alþingishússins 1880–1881* (Reykjavík: Bókaútgáfa menningarsjóðs og þjóðvinafélagsins, 1972); Guðný Gerður Gunnarsdóttir, and Hjörleifur Stefánsson, *Kvosin*, pp. 214–26; Hörður Ágústsson, *Íslensk byggingararfleifð I*, pp. 299–308; Seelow, *Die moderne Architektur in Island*, p. 55.

102 Throughout his career, Bald worked extensively in Iceland and the Faroe Islands, and so did his son Valdemar (1872–1921). Ida Haugsted, "Tømrerog bygmester Bald & Søn på Island og Færøerne," *Architectura* 36 (2014): pp. 26–53.

103 "Jeg kýs íslenzkan mann til þess að byggja íslenzkt alþingishús." Alþingi, Alþingistíðindi, *Umræður* (1879), p. 467.

104 Anna D. Ágústsdóttir and Guðni Valberg, *Reykjavík sem ekki varð* (Reykjavík: Crymogea, 2014), pp. 14–27.

105 Guðmundur Hannesson, *Húsagerð á Íslandi*, p. 236.

106   The exact number of Icelandic masons working at the parliament house is unknown. Hörður Ágústsson listed the names of a few of them and traced their later works all around the country. Hörður Ágústsson, *Íslensk byggingararfleifð I*, p. 307.

107   "Íslendingarnir, sem höfðu lært að kljúfa grjót og höggva, fengu nú góð áhöld í sínar hendur og gátu farið að byggja sjálfir hús úr steini. Fjöldi manna fékk nú atvinnu að vetrinum við að kljúfa grjót og flytja það. Þetta eitt hefur sennilega margborgað allan byggingarkostnað þinghússins." Guðmundur Hannesson, *Húsagerð á Íslandi*, p. 236.

108   "[…] hinn bezti iðnaðarskóli." "Þinghúsið," *Þjóðólfur* 32, no. 29 (November 17, 1880): p. 114.

109   "Alþingishúsið," *Þjóðólfur* 33, no. 3 (January 29, 1881): p. 9.

110   "Jeg er viss um, að hægt hefði verið að fá innlendan mann til þess starfa fyrir minna kaup." Alþingi, Alþingistíðindi, *Umræður* (1881), p. 164.

111   Alþingi, Alþingistíðindi, *Umræður* (1881), p. 190.

112   Guðmundur Hannesson, *Húsagerð á Íslandi*, p. 237; Hörður Ágústsson, *Íslensk byggingararfleifð I*, p. 307.

113   Helgi Helgason, "Um steinsteypu," *Fróði* 4, no. 113 (1883): pp. 265–67; Georg Ahrens, "Um sementsteypu," *Þjóðólfur* 37, no. 3 (January 17, 1885): pp. 9–10.

114   On Helgi Helgason, see: Páll Eggert Ólason, ed., *Íslenzkar æviskrár frá landnámstímum til ársloka 1940, Vol. 2* (Reykjavík: Hið Íslenska bókmenntafélag, 1949): p. 337.

115   The author mentioned, in particular, the settlement of Victoriastadt in Berlin and the cities of Gotha and Hamburg. Georg Ahrens, "Um sementsteypu," pp. 9–10. On German experiments regarding above-ground constructions, see: Salvatore Aprea, *German Concrete. The Science of Cement from Trass to Portland, 1819-1877* (Lausanne: EPFL Press, 2016), pp. 212–23.

116   Guðmundur Hannesson, *Húsagerð á Íslandi*, p. 246; Lýður Björnsson, *Steypa lögð og steinsmíð rís*, p. 49.

117   Guðmundur Hannesson, *Húsagerð á Íslandi*, p. 249.

118   Guðmundur Hannesson, *Húsagerð á Íslandi*, p. 248.

119   "Hér voru þá íslenzkur sveitabóndi og steinsmiður að gera tilraunir eftir sínu höfði og *uppgötvuðu sementssteypu*!". Guðmundur Hannesson, *Húsagerð á Íslandi*, p. 247. For a more detailed analysis, see: Sofia Nannini, "From Reception to Invention: The Arrival of Concrete to Iceland and the Rhetoric of Guðmundur Hannesson," *Arts* 7, no. 68 (2018): pp. 1–13; Nannini, *Icelandic Farmhouses*, pp. 38–40.

120   "[…] vieler kleiner, aufeinanderfolgender oder auch zeitlich paralleler Erfindungen". Alexander Kierdorf and Hubert K. Hilsdorf, "Zur Geschichte des Bauens mit Beton," in *Was der Architekt vom Stahlbeton Wissen Sollte: Ein Leitfaden für Denkmalpfleger und Architekten*, edited by Uta Hassler (Zürich: gta Verlag), p. 11.

121   Adrian Forty, *Concrete and Culture. A Material History* (London: Reaktion Books, 2012), p. 15.

Chapter 2

Steinsteypuöldin: Building the Age of Concrete (1899–1915)

SOME THOUGHTS ON WHAT THE ICELANDERS MUST DO IF THEY WANT TO TAP THE NATURAL RESOURCES OF THEIR BELOVED COUNTRY TO THE GREATEST EXTENT POSSIBLE. FIRST OF ALL, THEY HAVE TO REFRAIN FROM EMIGRATING: ICELAND IS LACKING HANDS; CULTIVATE THEIR FIELDS, WHICH THEY ARE NEGLECTING, BETTER THAN THEY ARE CURRENTLY DOING BY DRAINING THEM; BUILD ROADS; BUILD SHELTERS FOR THE SHEEP; TRADE FOR COMPRESSED HAY, WHICH WILL FEED THE COWS AND HORSES DURING THE WINTER, THE FISH WHICH FREQUENT THE COASTS IN GREAT SHOALS, AND WHICH THE ICELANDERS HAVE JUST STARTED FISHING; THEY HAVE TO CHANGE THEIR NATIONAL EDUCATION SYSTEM AND, INSTEAD OF CONTEMPLATING THE ANCIENT SAGAS LIKE NAVEL-GAZING FAKIRS, STUDY THE APPLIED SCIENCES. WOULD YOU BELIEVE THAT THERE IS NOT A SINGLE ENGINEER IN THE WHOLE ISLAND! THAT PHYSICS, CHEMISTRY, ETC., ARE ABSOLUTELY IGNORED, AND THAT, IN ORDER TO LAY OUT A SIMPLE ROAD, AS I HAVE SEEN, THEY HAVE TO BRING IN SURVEYORS FROM THE CONTINENT AT GREAT EXPENSE!

Henry Labonne, *L'Islande et l'archipel des Færoeer*, 1888[1]

THERE IS NO LONGER ANY DOUBT THAT THE COUNTRY'S BUILDING TRADITIONS ARE CHANGING. THE AGE OF TIMBER CONSTRUCTION, WHICH HAS BEEN ONGOING FOR A WHILE, IS ABOUT TO END, WHILE THE AGE OF CONCRETE IS RISING.

Jón Þorláksson, "Hvernig reynast steinsteypuhúsin?," 1911[2]

In 1886–87, French natural scientist and explorer Henry Labonne (1855–1944) sailed to Iceland and the Faroe Islands on a scientific mission promoted by the French Ministry of Education.[3] Labonne described Iceland's nature and culture, and he harshly criticized its society, which he perceived as poorly developed. Labonne's patronizing travel report echoed the voices of many other European visitors who, as Oslund puts it, "tended to portray the North Atlantic as a static place, where technology did not advance beyond 'primitive' conditions and the natives continued to struggle with the same problems over the course of centuries".[4] According to Labonne, Iceland's economic and material backwardness could be fixed by the opening of its society towards the applied sciences and, particularly, the engineering field.

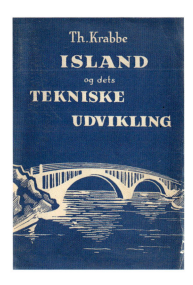

Almost sixty years later, in 1946, the Danish–Icelandic civil engineer Thorvald Krabbe (1876–1953) published a book titled *Island og dets tekniske udvikling gennem tiderne* [Iceland and Its Technical Development Over Time]. He claimed that whoever had visited Iceland at the turn of the century would have seen a "completely different country" when returning in the nineteen-forties. Its natural landmarks were still the same: the snow-capped dome of the Snæfellsjökull in the Faxaflói bay, Mount Esja—"the intimate friend" of all the inhabitants of Reykjavík—and "the silence of the lava fields". Below the grandness of nature, however, one would have encountered endless telephone wires, growing suburbs, racing cars, wide roads, and noisy harbors. All those infrastructures were the modern body of a "new Iceland", and it was this "new Iceland" that Krabbe's book dealt with.[5] Fig. 1

Fig. 1
Thorvald Krabbe, *Island og dets tekniske udvikling gennem tiderne* (Copenhagen: Danks-islandsk samfund, 1946). Book cover.

How was Iceland transformed from "the most deprived point of the globe"[6] into "quite another country"?[7] Who promoted, planned, and physically executed this abrupt change? The answers to these questions have to be found in the lives and works of the first Icelandic engineers, active in the first decades of the twentieth century. Emerging later than in the other Nordic countries,[8] the history of Icelandic engineering started as the scattered history of a few individuals, who graduated from the Polytechnic School of Denmark between 1891 and 1903.[9] When moving back to the island, they were entrusted with a great number of tasks, both public and private, therefore moving between a formal technical profession and political commitments.[10]

As described by Labonne, in the late eighteen-eighties there were no Icelandic engineers. Iceland was often a destination for foreign technicians who graduated from the Polytechnic School of Denmark or from the Trondheim Technical College and were generally active in the construction of lighthouses, harbors, and bridges.[11] In 1892, an anonymous Icelandic student in Copenhagen claimed that the country was lacking local experts to manage the streets and buildings of Reykjavík. Thus that expert "of course has to be a foreigner, because we still don't have an Icelandic engineer in our country".[12] The island's road network was in a critical state, and inviting experts from abroad resulted in very high yearly expenses. Mixing economic motivations with nationalistic attitudes, since the early eighteen-eighties some voices had been calling for public scholarships for Icelandic students to allow them to study engineering abroad.[13]

Ten years later, after several attempts through grants offered by the Icelandic parliament to engineering students,[14] Sigurður Thoroddsen (1863–1955) graduated in Copenhagen and became Iceland's first engineer.[15] He spent one year in Norway, specializing in road and bridge construction, and once back in Iceland, he was entrusted with many projects concerning the planning and building of a much-needed road network for the country. Sigurður Thoroddsen played a prominent role in the spread of technical knowledge in Iceland, yet his activities were mainly devoted to infrastructural projects such as several steel suspension bridges. State engineer between 1893 and 1905, he later became a teacher at the Junior College of Reykjavík.[16] Together with the improvement of roads across mountain ridges and through lava fields, and the building of bridges over its powerful rivers, Iceland's greatest challenge was its housing conditions. The first efforts in this direction were made by Sigurður Thoroddsen's first, and lesser known, colleague.

A SURVEY ON BUILDING TECHNIQUES

A very short life and the fact of being second did not contribute to the fame of Sigurður Pétursson (1870–1900), the second Icelander ever to graduate as an engineer.[17] Despite his brief career, Sigurður Pétursson carried out the first state-sponsored research on building techniques. After completing his studies at the Polytechnic School of Denmark in 1899, he was awarded a national grant to conduct "research on the building materials of Iceland and provide guidelines for construction".[18] This research program was requested by Búnaðarfélag Íslands, the Agricultural Society of Iceland,[19] and promoted by the *landhöfðingi,* the governor general.[20] Sigurður Pétursson worked on this task between winter and summer 1900, through fieldwork in Iceland and abroad. He visited the Paris World Exhibition and traveled to Denmark and Norway in order to research the production of bricks and lime.[21]

The greatest contribution to Sigurður Pétursson's research was fieldwork investigation on the state of Icelandic construction, with a particular attention to the most commonly used materials and their behavior in the Icelandic climate. The engineer conducted a survey all over the country by sending a printed form with ten questions to many rural districts.[22] The ten questions provided by Sigurður Pétursson to each delegate of the district board concerned a variety of issues on construction techniques and Icelandic building traditions.

The engineer was seeking to find out what were the most common building materials in each district and whether there had been recent experiments with new methods. He was also interested in the traditional construction techniques that survived the passage of time; in the durability of turf buildings; in the presence of humidity and the techniques adopted to limit its spread; in the fuels employed for heating; in the names of those who were considered experts in building matters. Nine sets of answers were written by the delegates of each district, whereas one was signed by Jakob Hálfdanarson (1836–1919), farmer at Grímsstaðir near Lake Mývatn and founder of the Þingeyinga Cooperative.[23]

The answers to the survey showed that the most common building materials were turf, gravel, and driftwood. The turf farms did not usually last more than forty or fifty years, depending on the quality of the materials and on natural events such as earthquakes or strong winds.[24] A few districts had seen an increase in timber houses, the main novelties of which were the outer cladding made of corrugated iron and the presence of a stone and lime cellar below the main floor.

In some cases, stone buildings were mentioned. These stone constructions represented an anomaly in the almost complete monopoly of turf farms. However, according to the inhabitants, they did not provide suitable living conditions. Sandstone was considered too weak and it was prone to swelling over time, with the result that the walls fell apart.[25] A basalt and tuff house apparently "did not prove well for residential purposes", as it was too cold during winter and too warm during summer.[26] From these reports, it is also possible to trace some of the first applications of concrete in rural Iceland, which was often employed for the construction of chimneys. Some representatives mentioned a mixture of gravel, sand, and cement in order to build chimneys, especially for the newly built houses with a timber structure and a lime-rendered stone cellar, as the body of the chimney rested on the floor of the cellar itself.[27] Only one representative mentioned the presence of a concrete house in the district.[28] At the same time, Jakob Hálfdanarson provided a very interesting detail: in 1875, a prison had been built in Þingeyjarsýsla, most likely in the village of Akureyri, following the recent regulations that ordered the construction of prisons all around the country.[29] Danish master mason Bald was entrusted with the design and construction of these prisons, and Jakob Hálfdanarson reported that:

> A new material and method was employed by a Danish master mason, Bald, which involved casting the whole wall between pillars and a framework—both the outer and the inner walls.[30]

It is easy to find direct connections between the building method described by Jakob Hálfdanarson and how master mason Bald coordinated the works on the parliament house in Reykjavík between 1880 and 1881. This may confirm the hypothesis that the first Icelandic experiments on concrete were carried out as part of Bald's projects.

In the survey, a particular focus was on the humidity of turf houses: damp walls were very common in turf construction.[31] Most delegates seemed to be aware of the links between humidity and diseases.[32] A district representative claimed that dampness within the farm could be reduced by not keeping cattle below the living area—a quite common practice in the countryside.[33] The troubles caused by humidity could not be fully solved without addressing the heating of the rooms. The use of stoves, and consequently thorough heating of the living quarters, was still very uncommon, thus the ordinary farm was generally very cold. Living spaces were usually heated by burning dried manure, the most commonly available source of fuel in the countryside. The answers to Sigurður Pétursson's ninth question—whether there were and who were the building experts in each district—highlighted the almost complete lack of master masons pursuing a career in the building industry.[34]

Sigurður Pétursson passed away too early to write an official report about his research: he died in October 1900 at the age of thirty.[35] Most of the replies to the survey were written months after his death. Since his task was of national importance, new names were soon brought up as possible substitutes to continue his job. One of them was Knud Zimsen (1875–1953), who, despite his promising expertise, appeared to be much more interested in and preoccupied with his entrepreneurial adventures, as the following paragraph will show.[36] Another emerging figure was very interested in Sigurður Pétursson's research and legacy— the future architect Rögnvaldur Ólafsson (1874–1917). Fig. 2

In fall 1900, he was still a student at the Reykjavík Seminary but had already showed a keen interest in architecture a few years earlier when he asked for advice from Guðmundur Finnbogason (1873–1944), at that time philosophy student in the Danish capital.[37] Rögnvaldur

Ólafsson was seeking information about the architectural program at the Academy of Fine Arts in Copenhagen. A few weeks after Sigurður Pétursson's death, Rögnvaldur Ólafsson wrote another letter to Guðmundur Finnbogason: not only did he stress his interest in architecture and his willingness to ask for a scholarship in order to study in

Fig. 2
Portrait of Rögnvaldur Ólafsson.

Copenhagen, but he also mentioned the death of Sigurður Pétursson with these words:

> You say that the engineer Sigurður Pétursson has died, and this is a great loss. There is nobody now who can continue his work on the issue concerning the improvement of housing conditions. This may turn out to be good for me: "the death of somebody is the life of another."[38]

Eventually, Sigurður Pétursson's task was entrusted neither to Knud Zimsen nor to Rögnvaldur Ólafsson but to another key protagonist of the Icelandic concrete *saga*: engineer Jón Þorláksson (1877–1935).

"CEMENT WAS A MAGIC CURE": CONCRETE CAST STONES AND AALBORG PORTLAND CEMENT

Knud Zimsen was the son of a Danish merchant whose family had moved to Iceland in 1855. He grew up in Hafnarfjörður, south-west of Reykjavík. Thanks to his family's prosperous background, he received a good education: he spoke Icelandic and Danish and was taught English and German.[39] Fig. 3

Between 1894 and 1897, he studied at the Polytechnic School of Denmark, together with fellows who would later become notable Danish engineers: Ivar Jantzen (1875–1961), Poul Sörensen (1873–1964), and Rudolf Christiani (1877–1960).[40] After graduating, Knud Zimsen worked for some years in the office of the Copenhagen city engineer, before sailing back to Iceland in 1902. Knud Zimsen later wrote that his country was fast approaching its "first age of progress", and it had to "nourish its engineers". Aware that Sigurður Pétursson had recently died, he felt that he "had to help Iceland's first engineer [Sigurður Thorodssen] improve the country's technical skills".[41] This age of progress matched with the political changes that were structurally transforming Iceland's governmental system. By 1902, the Home Rule Party had the majority at the Alþingi; in 1904, the *landshöfðingi* office was abolished, and Iceland entered the years of its home rule. This implied the establishment of the Ministry of Iceland as the country's political representative in the Danish Cabinet.[42] Mixing technology and business, Knud Zimsen had many entrepreneurial ambitions to advance his country and started several business ventures. His commercial activity and influence on Reykjavík's growing infrastructure led him to obtain several administrative roles: he was city engineer between 1904 and 1907, member of the city council between 1908 and 1914, and mayor of Reykjavík between 1914 and 1932. In the first decade of the century, Knud Zimsen worked on several urban projects, such as sewerage systems, supply of asphalt, street lighting, and services like the *þvottalaugar*, the washing pools in the area of Laugarnes, on the eastern outskirts. As one of Knud Zimsen's autobiographies is titled, Reykjavík was transforming itself "from a village to a city", and the harbingers of this change were its engineers.[43] Knud Zimsen was a member of The Danish Society of Engineers,[44] and the pride he showed for his still elitist profession could be seen in his telegraphic address: almost the one and only, *ingeniör*.[45] The fact that Knud Zimsen used the Danish term for engineer, instead of the Icelandic term *verkfræðingur*, should not come as a surprise: the Danish language was a recognizable sign of higher education and, more importantly, a link to Northern Europe's scientific debate.[46] His contribution to the Icelandic building practice was mostly materialized in two entrepreneurial activities: the establishment of the Mjölnir building company and the decade-long import trade of Portland cement from the Aalborg Portland-Cement-Fabrik in Denmark.

Among the treasures of the Icelandic language, there is the common saying *á mölinni*—"in a town"—, whose literal meaning could be translated as "on the gravel". The saying has been popular since the last

Fig. 3
Portrait of Knud Zimsen.

decades of the nineteenth century.⁴⁷ As the word *möl* means "gravel", this may be directly linked to the material employed for road construction, which made the city of Reykjavík resemble a huge gravel pile in the first decades of the twentieth century. In December 1903, Knud Zimsen established the Mjölnir construction company. Its members acquired the rights to excavate stones and produce gravel in the area of the Rauðará river, in the eastern part of the city. As observed by the director of the *Reykjavík* newspaper, *mjölnir* means "something that grinds".⁴⁸ However, the word also bears a mythological memory: in Norse mythology, *Mjölnir* was the hammer used by Thor. The modern version of Thor's *Mjölnir* were the firm's grinding machines, which Knud Zimsen bought from Europe. By the time of its opening, the company was a novelty for the Icelandic built environment, starting with its headquarters: one of Mjölnir's buildings boasted a shed roof for better natural lighting.⁴⁹ Fig. 4

The company not only produced gravel for road constructions, but it also specialized in the production of concrete cast stones. Iceland already had a history of cast stones in lime conglomerate, first used by the stonemason Sigurður Hansson in Garðar in the late eighteen-seventies. In Knud Zimsen's mind, the production of concrete cast stones could put an end to Iceland's centuries-long dependency on bricks imported from Denmark, which were expensive and not particularly

Fig. 4
Headquarters of the Mjölnir firm,
Reykjavík, ca. 1903–08.

suitable for the island's extreme climate.[50] When he founded Mjölnir, lime and concrete cast stones had become particularly popular in Sweden and Norway.[51] Knud Zimsen might have seen articles and advertisements of foreign products in the journal of the Danish Society of Engineers, as attested by one of his letters to a German formwork producer.[52] Cast stones were also mentioned in one of the volumes of the German *Handbuch der Architektur* series (1900), which was available in the National Library of Iceland at that time.[53] Some descriptions of elaborate kinds of hollow concrete blocks were also published in the pages of *Beton und Eisen* in 1906.[54] The production of Mjölnir met with both approval and criticism. Some newspapers claimed that the firm embodied a great progress and that the use of concrete would help eliminate the expensive trade of timber from Norway.[55] Others wrote that Mjölnir was a "most needed enterprise" and all public buildings should from then onwards be built only in concrete.[56] Yet, a few master masons were skeptical, claiming that the use of local dolerite would have been more suitable for the Icelandic environment.[57]

Knud Zimsen had a "blind faith" in this enterprise, hoping that it would become his "main occupation" in the years to come.[58] He continuously mentioned the firm in his letters and promoted his products to some of the most important figures in Iceland. In May 1904, he wrote to Tryggvi Gunnarsson (1835–1917), director of the National Bank, offering a purchase of cast stones.[59] Later in December 1905, he wrote to Thor Jensen (1863–1947), a prominent businessman and trading partner in Reykjavík, giving him information about the economy and the structure of the firm.[60] This network of commercial relations highlights the engineer's knowledge of society's most influential characters, particularly those who could have sway over the building industry.

In spite of his high hopes, Knud Zimsen's expectations had to match a quite different reality: as he acknowledged decades later, "sales went bad", and "people had no confidence in this building material", as they thought that "the houses would wobble and become cold".[61] In order to show the inhabitants of Reykjavík that concrete cast stones were solid and safe, Knud Zimsen engaged in a very ambitious form of advertising: he built himself a house made entirely of cast stones, located in the very city center. The house was built between 1905 and 1906, it was "all made from Mjölnir's stones", and named Gimli.[62] Although Knud Zimsen did not explain the choice of name, it is easy to find another mythological connection: in Norse mythology and as described by Snorri Sturluson in his *Prose Edda*, *Gimli* is a beautiful and bright shelter placed in the third heaven of the Norse cosmology, inhabited by those who survive the destruction of *Ragnarök*. With its almost three-story high tower and plastered white walls, Gimli dominated the urban core of Reykjavík. It differed from all the other residential dwellings, its monumentality rather resembling administrative buildings such as the ministry offices.

Gimli was designed and built as a surprising advertising machine in Reykjavík's urban landscape. 15-inch stones were used in the basement, 12-inch for the house, and 10-inch for its extension.[63] The house boasted a crenellated tower, which gave the building the appearance of a small urban castle. Its roof was all in concrete, and some authors even suggested that the engineer experimented with the first reinforced concrete floor slabs in the whole country.[64] In the kitchen and on the stairs, the engineer had the floors covered by a layer of *terrazzo*. Regardless of the perfect location for such an advertisement and the promises for a bright and safe dwelling as the one described in Snorri's *Edda*, Gimli did not bring the hoped-for luck to Mjölnir. The company scraped along by making concrete fences for some years and eventually closed down in 1910. Fig. 5

What Knud Zimsen considered to be the main cause of Mjölnir's failure was the rise of Steinar, another company that shortly produced concrete cast stones in the same years, as the next paragraph will

show.[65] However, other reasons can also explain the decline of this business. First, timber was still the first choice for the country's trading and ruling class: in 1907, for example, the rich merchant Thor Jensen chose timber to build his neoclassical villa with carved Ionic columns and colorful decorations on the shores of the Tjörnin Pond.[66] Second, people proved to be skeptical about concrete because of the cold and

Fig. 5
Knud Zimsen, Gimli, Reykjavík (1905–06).

damp buildings it produced, and the structures were considered vulnerable to earthquakes and weather damage. Third, these solid and heavy stones must have been quite difficult to transport to construction sites far from the city. In 1908, the *Reykjavík* newspaper published an article discussing a true American novelty: Thomas Edison's concrete houses. The article had been translated from English and written by an Icelander who had emigrated to Winnipeg. As the author claimed, a house completely built of cast concrete had survived the Great San Francisco Earthquake of 1906, thus proving to be safer than masonry or timber housing. According to the authors, all Mjölnir could do was grinding stones into gravel, and the remaining efforts had to be directed towards buying cement from abroad—or, even better, producing it directly in Iceland.[67]

Cement was at the core of cast stone production and of Knud Zimsen's research interests.[68] He proved to be one of the country's most far-sighted tradesmen when, in January 1903, he established a commercial connection with the Aalborg Portland-Cement-Fabrik in Denmark, opening an import trade of cement to Iceland which resulted in an almost decade-long monopoly controlled by the engineer. In his memoirs, he wrote about a widespread "thirst for cement":

> Cement! – Cement! There is a deep and heavy sound in this word, a word that all people know and understand. They know that, in this expression, behind this very word stand all the greatest and most reliable structures of the world.[69]

The imported quantity of cement had already grown since the last decades of the nineteenth century: between 1876 and 1903, it had increased from 54 to 5,051 barrels a year.[70] Between 1896 and 1898, the majority of cement was imported from Denmark; a smaller quantity from the UK, Norway, Sweden, and other countries.[71] Until 1903, cement was directly sold by merchants in Reykjavík, who were importing very small quantities from the Continent. As Knud Zimsen put it in his memories:

> Had I not come home to work for the improvement of the infrastructures in Iceland? And what could one do without cement? Had I not got to see how some inhabitants of Reykjavík tried to use all their available means in order to acquire some barrels or even only some buckets of this gray powder?[72]

Understanding that the inhabitants of Reykjavík "wanted to buy cement, a lot of cement, if that had not been sold at an exorbitant price",[73] Knud

Zimsen established a copious correspondence with the Aalborg factory, of which he became Iceland's only buyer and reseller, in order to guarantee a solid flow of good quality, affordable cement into the country.[74] Fig. 6

As Knud Zimsen claimed, the cost of one barrel of cement in Iceland was around 13–16kr before 1903.[75] Strategically buying in bulk, the engineer's first order to Aalborg was of 500–1,000 barrels of cement, acquired at 5kr per barrel and delivered by summer 1903.[76] Once in Iceland, the cement was sold only in certain stores selected by Knud Zimsen, especially Thor Jensen's store Godthaab—his "biggest client"[77]—and the one owned by Knud's brother, Jes Zimsen (1877–1938). Buying cement from the Continent obviously had its difficulties and drawbacks: the deliveries sometimes went wrong, as the cement barrels were under the constant threat of damages during shipping.[78] Nevertheless, his bulk strategy paid off: the import of larger quantities and the continuous shipping via specific cargo boats led to a decrease in the overall cost of cement on the island and, consequently, to an increase of its use throughout the country. He also stated that the cost of Aalborg cement was at times even lower in Iceland than in Denmark.[79]

Not only did Knud Zimsen resell the cement to some specific stores in Reykjavík, but he also put together a network of clients all around the country. He sold his product to clients in Hafnarfjörður, Westman Islands, Akureyri, Ísafjörður, Dýrafjörður, and other locations, either at his selling price—around 8.20kr in 1903—, or he had the cement shipped directly from Copenhagen to each harbor at around 5.35kr per barrel.[80] Knud Zimsen was particularly keen on the cement quality. As early as in the summer of 1903, he asked the Aalborg plant whether they could provide him with the results of stress tests on their cement.[81] In his instructions, he also made specific references to the kind of cement to buy: he would mention the "L" cement several times, meaning that he only ordered the variety marked with the Aalborg Portland logo, a lion holding a Danish

Fig. 6
Knud Zimsen, Advertisement for Aalborg Portland Cement. *Bæjarskrá Reykjavíkur* (1909): p. 95.

shield. Knud Zimsen soon became the factory's insider in Icelandic cement commerce, providing information on the quality, the acceptance of the product, and its competitors. In June 1903, he reported that Aalborg Portland's cement was well received by the inhabitants of Reykjavík.[82] Knud Zimsen's letters do not only refer to his buying and selling, but also to the amount of cement supplied by Aalborg Portland's competitors and their economic strategies on the island.

Aalborg Portland's first competitors were its neighboring factories, Norden and Danmark. Exactly when the engineer was securing his monopoly of Aalborg Portland in Iceland, the Danish plant was fighting a price war against the factories located in the same town.[83] In November 1904, Knud Zimsen informed Aalborg Portland of the possibility that Norden would open a trading connection to Iceland, cleverly using this information to have the price lowered on his partner's side. Amid an economic battle that extended far beyond Iceland's small boundaries, Knud Zimsen seemed to be quite confident of his trading skills, confidently stating to the Danish firm:

> For the past two years, I have been dealing in cement, I have conquered, so to speak, the whole market here with many connections, personal influence, a good product, and favorable prices. And I would have all the advantages on my side in a potential price war, if I were to come up with a cheaper offer in my hands.[84]

The struggle between the two plants soon ended. The majority of Norden's shares was acquired by Aalborg Portland in 1904; at the same time, Knud Zimsen claimed that Norden's cement had never really been appreciated in Iceland, as it was not compatible with the Icelandic climate and hardened too slowly.[85] Some competitors to Knud Zimsen's Danish cement came from other countries. In June 1909, he reported to Aalborg Portland on the quantity of cement imported into Iceland in the previous years. In 1906, Iceland imported 16,605 barrels of cement from Denmark, and 408 from other countries; in 1907, 15,190 and 3,976 barrels respectively had been imported from Denmark and abroad. Since 1903, the quantity of cement in Iceland had at least tripled. Among the "other countries" from which cement was bought, Knud Zimsen mentioned England and Belgium, sold by the Scottish firm Copland & Berrie.[86] Apparently, the popularity of Aalborg Portland cement was being jeopardized by other companies wanting to sell their own products. In July 1909, Knud Zimsen reported that a shipment of Belgian cement had arrived, yet it was labeled under the name of "Löve-cement".[87] In a strong business connection with his Danish partner, he even proposed to Aalborg Portland that he might buy a small amount of that Belgian cement and send it to them, for the Danish plant to test it.[88]

The engineer's letters and memories rarely referred to the buildings that his cement importation enabled. In connection with the widespread availability of cement that his trade made possible, the use of this material increased astonishingly, and the engineer's commerce had a massive influence on the development of modern Iceland. When Knud Zimsen's monopoly came to an end—in 1914, he became mayor of Reykjavík and handed over his license to other traders—, cement had indeed turned into the:

> … magic cure, that had changed many theories of civil engineering. With it in one's hands, it was possible to create things that the smartest engineers had never even dared to dream of before this important powder appeared on the scenes.[89]

By 1913, after ten years of restless trades and countless letters, Knud Zimsen had transformed cement from an exclusive good to an ordinary commodity, ready to be employed in all aspects of the Icelandic building industry, which would shape its architectural language.

THE ICELANDIC WAR: THE BATTLE AGAINST COLD AND HUMIDITY

The heir to Sigurður Pétursson's research on building was engineer Jón Þorláksson, son of farmers from Vesturhópshólar in northern Iceland. Following a trajectory similar to that of Knud Zimsen's, Jón Þorláksson was trained as an engineer at the Polytechnic School of Denmark and worked as such for a couple of decades, before pursuing a career in politics. He was elected to the Alþingi in 1921 and was appointed Prime Minister in 1926. In 1929, he became the first secretary of the Independence Party, and from 1932 until his death in 1935, he was Mayor of Reykjavík.[90] Fig. 7

In 1903, the parliament entrusted the recently graduated engineer with a one-year grant to research the production and application of building materials in the country. The project was coordinated by Jón Þorláksson together with the Agricultural Society of Iceland. The grant officially started in October 1903, and by the end of the month, Jón Þorláksson traveled to Scotland, residing there for a month. He later traveled to Denmark, Sweden, and Norway.[91] Between January and March 1904, the engineer lived in Copenhagen and Berlin, researching

clay and brick production. Although it is not possible to determine precisely which plants he visited, Jón Þorláksson may in all likelihood have stopped by Denmark's largest brickworks—Cathrinesminde Teglværk near Flensburg—and several brick factories active in the Brandenburg area. Not far from there, the city of Stettin, now Szczecin, was home to Germany's first cement plant, built in 1855. In May, the engineer returned to Iceland, engaging in a five-month relentless voyage around the island.[92] From Seyðisfjörður to Akureyri, from Sauðárkrókur to Akranes, Jón Þorláksson visited villages and farmsteads and met with the local population, who was encouraged to send him letters in order to ask questions and receive specific answers.[93] Thanks to a continuous dissemination of his work, his voyage left an important mark on the Icelandic society and its building traditions. Jón Þorláksson engaged in an intense communication task anchored in *Búnaðarrít*, the journal of the Agricultural Society, which published two detailed articles by the engineer between 1903 and 1904. Figs. 8–9

    The first essay, entitled "Nýtt byggingarlag" [A New Building Method], provided a down-to-earth explanation of what concrete is, how to use it best, and how to avoid cold and damp dwellings.[94] The text described the inner structure of cement, and consequently of concrete; the author suggested which kinds of sand and aggregates to use and highlighted the perils of salt within the structures. His aim was to make this "new

Fig. 7
Portrait of Jón Þorláksson.

Nýtt byggingarlag.
Steyptir steinar, tvöfaldir veggir.

Steinsteypa er samansett úr sandi, möl, smágrjóti, vatni og einhverju bindiefni, sem getur verið sement, kalk eða hvorttveggja til samans, auk fleiri efna. Gæði steypunnar og eiginlegleikar eru undir því komin, að öll efni í hana séu góð, að hæfilega mikið sé brúkað af hverju og rétt farið að við tilbúning hennar frá upphafi til enda.

Bindiefnið er hjá oss venjulega sement, oftast portlands-sement. Það er búið til úr kalki og leir. Hér um bil 60%, er kalk, en alt að 40%, leir; þessum efnum er blandað vandlega saman, og úr blöndunni eru búnir til steinar, svipaðir og tigulsteinar; þeir eru síðan þurkaðir og brendir í stórum ofnum við svo mikinn hita, að steinarnir eru um það bil að bráðna. Síðan eru þeir teknir út og malaðir mjög fínt; þetta mél er sement.

Í Danmörku, Þýzkalandi og fleiri löndum eru settar fastar reglur um það, hvernig selja skuli sement, og er með því trygður hagur bæði seljanda og kaupanda; enn fremur er ákveðið, hvaða eiginlegleika það eigi að hafa, og eru allsstaðar til rannsóknastofnanir, þar sem kaupendur geta fengið sementið prófað, til þess að vita hvort það fullnægir þeim skilyrðum, sem sett eru. Þetta er mjög þýðingarmikið, því sement getur verið ákaflega mismunandi að gæðum, án þess að það verði á því séð í fljótu bragði.

Sementið er selt í heiltunnum eða hálftunnum, heiltunna vegur 360 pd. brúttó, en innihaldið 340 pd.; hálf-

Kuldinn og rakinn.
Orsakir þeirra og ráðin við þeim.
Eftir
Jón Þorláksson.

Kuldinn og rakinn eru tveir gestir, sem ekki sjaldan gera vart við sig í híbýlum manna hér á landi og það er víst óhætt að segja, að þeir séu hverjum manni hvumleiðir og að menn vilja flest til vinna að losna við þá; en þeir eru sendisveinar okkar óblíðu náttúru, fylgja þeim lögum sem hún hefir sett þeim, koma og fara eftir hennar boði og banni og gegna engum öðrum fyrirskipunum, bænum eða boðum. Eina ráðið til að hafa hemil á þessum vogestum er því að rannsaka þau lögmál, sem náttúran hefir sett þeim, og þegar vér erum búnir að brjóta þau til mergjar og kynna oss þau til fulls, þá verðum vér að beita þessum lögum réttilega og gera hina óboðnu gesti með því útlæga úr húsum vorum; það er með öðrum orðum, að vér verðum að komast eftir *eðli* og *orsökum* kuldans og rakans, því það er eini áreiðanleni vegurinn til að finna *ráðin* við þeim. Þetta er annars algild regla í baráttu mannsins við náttúruna. Meðan vér þekkjum ekki orsakir viðburðanna, stöndum vér ráðalausir og getum ekki afstýrt því sem skaðlegt er og ilt, eða framleitt það sem hagkvæmt er og gott, en þekkingin á orsökunum gefur oss það vald í hendur, sem er fyrsta skilyrðið til að geta drotnað yfir náttúrunni og gert sér hana undirgefna, beint öflum hennar og hreyfingum inn á þær brautir, sem oss eru hagkvæmar, en frá hinum, sem eru oss skaðlegar. Náttúrunni verður ekki stjórnað, nema eftir órjúfanlegum lögum hennar sjálfrar, og því er ómögulegt fyrir neinn að stjórna henni, nema hann þekki þessi lög.

building method" accessible to anyone. This goal mirrors the words of Adrian Forty: "Concrete offered a chance to bypass the traditional trades altogether, and to break their monopoly over construction, by making it possible to build without any need for them at all".[95]

Because there were still no national regulations on concrete construction, Jón Þorláksson made reference to the mixing ratios adopted in Germany, probably referring to what he learned while traveling the same year. The engineer highlighted two characteristics of concrete to be aware of: its density and its ability to conduct heat. If more density was due to a higher percentage of cement, resulting in waterproof walls, it also meant higher costs and structures that were more prone to conduct heat to the outside. On the contrary, a weaker concrete was cheaper and less prone to heat loss, but dangerously apt to absorb water.[96]

Jón Þorláksson described the two methods to build a concrete house: with cast-in-place walls or using cast stones. As for the first approach, he suggested the use of two timber or iron formworks, around 1 ½ ell in height (ca. 90cm) and connected by iron binders. Interestingly, he also suggested placing iron bars within the walls if one wanted to continue casting the inner walls in the following days—thus mentioning reinforced concrete for the first time in the Icelandic debate. However, the engineer claimed that casting the walls in place had several drawbacks in the Icelandic context: it took too much time to prepare the formwork, it was too expensive, and it was limited to the very short timeframe of late springtime and summer—when concrete could dry properly. He also added that all these disadvantages were particularly severe when the workers were unskilled, as was the case especially in the countryside.[97] Furthermore, a cast-in-place wall would need to be extremely thick in order to retain enough heat inside the rooms and prevent the formation of moisture on interior surfaces, which in turn resulted in higher costs. The engineer's suggestion for building concrete walls that were able to resist the cold and humidity was the construction of double walls, enclosing a cavity inside where the air could act as a shield against colder temperatures. This prompted him to suggest the use of cast stones, which implied the construction of double walls with two rows of 4 ½-inch thick cast stones and an equivalent 4 ½-inch wide cavity in between. To have the two walls support the weight together, and also to make the house more resistant to earthquakes, the engineer recommended the use of cross stones connecting the two layers of the wall. Double walls could also be a heritage of traditional turf buildings, whose vertical structures were usually composed of a double layer of turf blocks enclosing a rubble core. Jón

Þorláksson also mentioned the production method of these stones: cast in timber frames, covered with an iron layer inside and on its corners. The stones were to be left still for approximately ten days before they were ready. In case of window sills and architraves, they could also be reinforced with iron bars. When building the walls, a layer of cement mortar had to be applied between each stone.

Jón Þorláksson listed a few advantages of concrete cast stones in the Icelandic context. First, they would make walls able to stand "for eternity" and withstand the common earthquakes. Second, they would be much cheaper than cast-in-place walls or structures in natural stone ashlars. Sand and gravel could be gathered during the winter, and the stones could be made during wintertime, maybe in a cattle shed or a stable. Regarding the shipping of cement, the engineer recommended that cement would be bought in small amounts, year by year, in order to avoid the damages caused by humidity and water while stored. Third, Jón Þorláksson also highlighted the "nicer look" of cast stone walls, if compared to cast-in-place buildings. He suggested the use of different kinds of sand in the stones, producing differently colored elements to place around windows, doors, or corners. Although only a hint, this was the start of a decade-long search for a decoration of the concrete surface that struggled to reconcile the material need for adequate housing and aesthetic demands on architecture.[98] The suggested use of concrete cast stones matched the opening of Jón Þorláksson's firm Steinar, which produced concrete cast stones for housing and pipes as a competitor of Knud Zimsen's Mjölnir. As reported by the *Þjóðólfur* newspaper, Jón Þorláksson had acquired the patent to produce cast stones from the Dane Peter Jørgensen (1852–1933) from Schleswig-Holstein, who had been filing patents on the production of concrete stones, especially for roofs, since the late nineteenth century.[99] In 1907, Jón Þorláksson also founded the Pípuverksmiðjan company, which produced sewers made of cement and sand to replace the usual clay sewers sourced from Denmark.[100]

Jón Þorláksson's second essay in the *Búnaðarrít* journal was titled "Kuldinn og rakinn" [Cold and Humidity].[101] Besides providing a general scientific explanation of these phenomena, the article was also a call for action addressed to the readers and to the whole of Icelandic society. Since the time of its settlement, Iceland had always stayed out of European wars or conflicts. According to the author, however, a constant battle had been fought silently since the first ship landed on the Icelandic shores—the daily war against the natural elements.[102] In this "battle against nature", "the delivery boys" of Iceland's "harsh nature" were the cold and the dampness, like actors following the plot of a play, or subjects of a terrible king. In order to fight these unwelcome guests, the engineer stressed the importance of studying the laws of nature, meaning the laws of science and scientific research: only by knowing how a physical phenomenon occurs and behaves, one could hope to mitigate it. Research and science: these words mirrored the author's positivistic attitude towards the study of natural phenomena.

In August 1906, Jón Þorláksson visited the county of Þingeyjarsýsla and the rural area of Mývatnssveit, where he met Jakob Hálfdanarson, who had already taken part in Sigurður Pétursson's survey on building techniques.[103] They spoke about concrete construction, and the engineer gave Jakob Hálfdanarson what was believed to be the correct recipe for building both concrete walls and roads. The composition provided by the engineer was 1 : 5 : 10 (cement : sand : gravel), changing to 1 : 3 : 5 in case of underwater construction. Because cement was still quite an exclusive resource at the beginning of the century, the most common mixing ratios were still scarce in the use of the binding agent and characterized by an extensive use of sand and gravel.[104]

Visits of the traveling engineer were usually welcomed like that of a prophet, bearer of knowledge and hopes for a better living—many newspaper accounts stated that people had "faith" in his task and knowledge.[105] However, Jón Þorláksson encountered obstacles similar to those faced by his colleague Knud Zimsen. He strived for the general acceptance of his profession within the country, especially regarding the construction of farmhouses in rural areas: the presence of engineers was still quite uncommon in the countryside. The importance of the engineer's mission is especially highlighted by a letter written in 1904 and sent to the Ministry of Iceland.[106] Possibly because of the young age of the Icelandic engineering profession, people still did not regularly turn to engineers when it came to the construction or refurbishment of houses. Jón Þorláksson's plea to the Ministry of Iceland for better involvement of engineers did not only underscore the struggle for recognition of their profession and building expertise, but also the difficulty of spreading information beyond the boundaries of the trading centers. The engineer's involvement in the improvement of rural construction was particularly evident in the following years, as he collaborated with physician Guðmundur Hannesson in a 1911 survey on concrete farmhouses built in the countryside.[107]

Jón Þorláksson also complained about the poor educational offer in the natural sciences. He addressed this very issue in a letter to philosophy graduate Guðmundur Finnbogason in 1904, concerning the educational changes of the Junior College of Iceland. Due to the lack of adequate courses in mathematics and physics, an Icelandic student seeking a degree at the Polytechnic School of Copenhagen was forced to take extra classes. Therefore, the educational path towards an engineering degree was harder and consequently longer, adding an extra year to the regular four and a half years. On top of that, Jón Þorláksson also mentioned the need to learn French before entering the Polytechnic School. The improvement of the high school's educational curricula would benefit the Icelandic students enrolling in technical faculties, and also the whole Icelandic society. By so doing, young engineering graduates could have had more time for practice and experience abroad, before returning to Iceland and engaging in what he defined a "complicated job".[108]

Jón Þorláksson's teaching mission was not limited to newspapers or personal relations. In October 1904, as member of Iðnaðarmannafélagið [The Craftsman Association], Jón Þorláksson prompted the foundation of the first technical school of Iceland, Iðnskólinn, located in Reykjavík.[109] The school was supported by a 4,000kr yearly grant from the parliament.[110] With the engineer as its director, the school offered evening courses in drawing, calculation, Icelandic and Danish languages, but also day classes in construction techniques, math, physics, technical drawing, and English.[111] The school's aim was to offer courses to those who wanted to become skilled professionals in construction issues, such as carpenters and stonemasons. It also served to render the students competent in the languages they would need to know to benefit from the pool of building information available abroad, specifically in Denmark. With this educational offer, Jón Þorláksson wanted to fill the gap of the missing "building experts" highlighted by Sigurður Pétursson in his survey. In its first winter, the school already had fifty students, mainly carpenters.[112] By 1906, the classes were transferred to the newly built main building on the banks of the Tjörnin Pond. In 1908, the school had grown to sixty students, with their number continuing to increase year by year. [Fig. 10]

It is hard to imagine the difficulties of starting an educational program focusing on technical matters in early twentieth-century Iceland. One of the most challenging tasks was to expose the Icelandic students to topics that had never been taught in Iceland before, creating a new vocabulary and adapting these topics to the Icelandic environment and language. One of these subjects was material technology. To help his students with his teaching of construction matters, in 1909, Jón Þorláksson published a short handbook titled *Burðarþolfræði: Ágrip* [Material Technology: An Outline].[113] [Fig. 11]

Between 1887 and 1908, only a few books concerning architecture and construction matters had been acquired by the National Library.

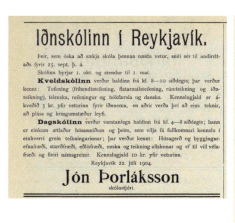
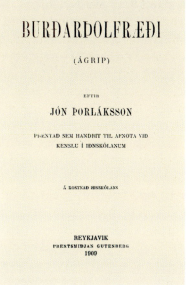

Some of these texts covered the history of architecture and architectural styles, such as Franz Kugler's *Geschichte der Baukunst* (1856–59) or Eduard Sacken's *Katechismus der Baustile* (1894).[114] The collection also included some technical publications, especially *Haandbog i husbygningskunst* (1891) by Norwegian engineer Edvard Kolderup (1847–1911), which included a detailed overview of several building techniques with practical advice, and some volumes of the well-known German series *Handbuch der Architektur*.[115] Jón Þorláksson's scientific knowledge was surely not limited to the holdings of the local library, because during his years at the Polytechnic School of Denmark, he had become acquainted with numerous Danish studies, especially on structural engineering and construction. The university in Copenhagen had been shaped by professors and scholars, including prominent mathematician Julius Pedersen (1839–1910), author of *Statik* (1881), and pioneering engineer Asger Skovgaard Ostenfeld (1866–1931), author of *Teknisk Statik* (1900) and several books on steel and reinforced concrete structures.[116]

Jón Þorláksson was therefore moving between two opposite poles of knowledge: that of experience and practical advice, and that of abstract theories and precise calculations. However, a complete separation of these skills and their related corresponding individuals—the master masons on one side, the scientific engineers on the other—was not suitable for the small Icelandic context. Jón Þorláksson acknowledged that the future Icelandic builders he was educating had to be able to work without engineers—because the engineers were still very few and

Fig. 10
Jón Þorláksson, Advertisement for Iðnskólinn. *Þjóðólfur* 56, no. 33 (July 29, 1904): p. 132.

Fig. 11
Jón Þorláksson, *Burðarþolfræði: Ágrip* (Reykjavík: Iðnskólinn, 1909). Book cover.

too busy for the many tasks they were assigned. According to him, a master mason would have to be independent and fully capable of calculating the height of a beam or determining its flexural strength. By publishing *Burðarþolfræði*, Jón Þorláksson engaged in a very interesting endeavor, which was very different from the other publications available in the collection of the National Library at that time. His text did not include axonometric sections of walls, nor instructions on how to use concrete or lime. He might have thought that such information would have been provided in the field, through the experience gained at the building sites. At the same time, he did not indulge in detailed explanations of the laws of structural analysis, avoiding the sophistication of a mathematical argument. The handbook had to be very practical: in less than fifty pages, the engineer explained how to understand an element's load-bearing capacity. Elasticity, stress, bending moment, moment of inertia, factor of safety: Jón Þorláksson introduced the Icelandic audience to a whole universe of physical definitions and theories. His attitude was pragmatic and direct: the important message to be conveyed was how to find the desired height for a beam in a roof, or the desired thickness for a concrete plinth. However, the Icelandic language was also lacking the vocabulary to describe the new world of structural analysis. Alongside definitions and calculations, Jón Þorláksson offered a translation of each term which he might have learned during his studies at the Polytechnic School of Denmark. He followed the local habit of translating loan words using Norse etymologies, which had been a popular practice since the late eighteenth century. From then onwards, the Icelandic language could boast the translation of concepts like moment of inertia, factor of safety, bending moment, and so on.[117]

In the last ten pages of the handbook, some tables with useful factors and values were printed, for example, the moments of inertia for square or round sections. He also added measures and values for particular steel beams (I-, C-, and T-sections), most likely according to the German standards.[118] The most interesting table is that dedicated to building materials and their strength resistance—such as strain concentration factor, tensile, compressive, and flexural strength. Having to adapt to the Icelandic construction tradition and environment, the engineer did not limit his list to common continental materials such as steel, certain kinds of timber (oak, pine), glass, or concrete, but he also included local materials such as granite, dolerite, basalt, and even hardened soil, i.e. turf. In another table, which listed the weight per square meter of several construction systems such as timber slabs, he also included the weight of a turf roof and the medium load of snow and wind on the structures. Two final tables helped the students translate a Danish or an English unit of measure to meters.

Despite the limited audience that this handbook might have had, Jón Þorláksson's publication was epoch-making. For the first time, structural analysis and material technology were available to the local public, written in Icelandic, and even adaptable to the specific Icelandic conditions. Not only had Icelanders been importing foreign building materials for decades, but they had also been buying foreign construction handbooks, thus reading in different languages and always trying to accommodate such readings to their own specific environment. Thanks to his polytechnic education, Jón Þorláksson changed this habit, moving these topics closer to the local needs and starting to change Icelandic construction from within. It was indeed an accomplishment of technical, cultural, and sociolinguistic value. While the engineer was establishing a new form of education for Icelandic builders, it was his very polytechnic background that was key to Iceland's opening up to reinforced concrete construction.

REINFORCED CONCRETE MOVES NORTH

So far, Icelandic concrete history had been a history of lime, amateurishly cast stones, and a harsh trade of cement on the turbulent waves of the Atlantic. When in 1903 Jón Þorláksson suggested the use of iron bars in the casting of concrete walls, reinforcement in concrete had most likely never been employed in the country and rarely been discussed. Since the eighteen-fifties, reinforced concrete had entered the spotlight of worldwide attention thanks to the pioneering experiments by Joseph-Louis Lambot (1814–1887) and François Coignet (1814–1888). Its recognition expanded through a series of patents filed by Joseph Monier (1823–1906) between 1868 and the 1880s.[119] However, these novelties remained largely unknown in the Icelandic context until the turn of the century. On the one hand, Iceland's surprising openness to the acceptance and employment of concrete was embodied by the construction of the houses at Garðar and Sveinatunga. At the same time, however, the growing use of concrete, first in the countryside and then in Reykjavík, did not necessarily involve the use of reinforcement bars. This was clearly due to the difficulty in purchasing and importing iron bars in sufficient quantities, on top of the basic need for timber formwork and cement. While cement made its praised entrance into Iceland in the form of plaster and as a key ingredient for cast stones, Europe was experiencing its hectic era of reinforced concrete patents and methods for calculating new, daring structures. In this dynamic period, the patents that mostly influenced the European construction in reinforced concrete were those filed by French entrepreneur François Hennebique (1842–1921) in 1892 and 1898,[120] and the German version of Monier's patent, published in 1887 by German engineer Gustav Adolf Wayss (1851–1917) in a very successful pamphlet.[121] On top of Hennebique's and Monier's patents, dozens of patents were filed in Europe and the United States. By 1903, as documented by German engineer and reinforced concrete pioneer Emil Mörsch (1872–1950), each week a new method was added to the countless number of those already active.[122]

At the beginning of the twentieth century, the understanding of the behavior of reinforced concrete was breaching the boundaries of private patents and companies, thanks to the publication of internationally distributed handbooks such as *Le béton armé et ses applications* by Paul Cristophe (1902) and *Der Betoneisenbau: seine Anwendung und Theorie* by Emil Mörsch (1903).[123] At the same time, new international journals were being printed, with the aim of collecting as many opinions and experiences on this building method as possible. In the German-speaking world, and generally in Nordic Europe, the most influential journal was *Beton und Eisen*, published since 1902 in Vienna by Austrian engineer Fritz von Emperger (1862–1942).[124] Despite the fortunate and quick success of some of these patents—in particular the worldwide monopoly of Hennebique's complex network of agents and concessionaires—, their continental fame came to an end when each country started framing the use of reinforced concrete within its national regulations. First in Switzerland and the German Empire (1904), then in France (1906), Italy (1907), and the UK (1911), reinforced concrete slowly became a matter of national policies.[125] Once privately pioneered innovations ruled by patents, reinforced concrete building techniques slowly became regulated by national committees.[126]

Icelandic building history embraced the European reinforced concrete patents—especially Hennebique's—only at the end of the patent era, when some European countries had already drafted their own regulations. Two episodes show the employment of the Hennebique patent in Iceland: one was the bridge over the Fnjóská river, designed and built by the Danish firm Christiani and Nielsen (1906–08), and second were the floor slabs of the new Iðunn wool factory, rebuilt in Reykjavík after a fire destroyed its original headquarters (1907). However delayed, the surge of reinforced concrete patents in the country was a clear consequence of the working presence of its engineers, their international connections with continental building firms, and their knowledge of scientific literature on construction topics. Behind them was the great expertise on reinforced concrete that had developed in Denmark since the last decade of the nineteenth century.[127]

The construction of the bridge over the Fnjóská river in northern Iceland was only one piece in the monumental task of developing the country's road network, particularly embodied by the construction of *hringvegur*: the national road connecting the whole island in one, continuous ring.[128] The daunting project of building and maintaining the country's road system had been a key priority of the Icelandic parliament since the last decades of the nineteenth century, and by the beginning of the twentieth century, an efficient transportation network was thought to be at the core of the country's future development. In 1887, the parliament issued a law which divided the roads into different categories, with different characteristics.[129] In 1893, a new law was issued, with updated guidelines and a general plan regarding areas of the country in need of new road connections.[130] By that time, the planning of the road construction was assigned to engineer Sigurður Thoroddsen, who was substituted in 1905 by Jón Þorláksson.[131] The building of Iceland's road network was a true national and collective enterprise, which went hand in hand with Jón Þorláksson's research on building materials: adequate roads meant adequate transportation, thus easier distribution of construction supplies around the country. If Iceland was in need of roads, its roads needed bridges over the copious and powerful rivers that divided the valleys. The presence of dynamic glacial rivers had always interfered with the movement of people and goods, especially during the summer months, when waterways carry the highest volume. The construction and maintenance of the country's bridges was a source of pride and a promise for a better and quicker economic development. It probably represented the biggest chapter in the history of the struggle between the Icelandic society and the natural elements.[132] Figs. 12–13

Steel bridges became the first option for contributing to the country's network. The first steel suspension bridge was that over the Ölfusá river at Selfoss (1891), its final design was signed by engineers Vauchan & Dymond from Newcastle. In 1894, the same engineers built the bridge over the Þjórsá river. Following these examples, Sigurður Thoroddsen worked on a good number of steel suspension bridges around the country.[133] Fig. 14

Beginning in 1905, Jón Þorláksson simultaneously started to research building materials and work on the road network. Therefore, it is not surprising that he supervised the construction of the first concrete bridge in 1907. The bridge over the Bláskeggsá river was only 7.2 meters long, with stone abutments and a vaulted concrete arch. If this small

90

Fig. 12
Fording Hvítá near Bláfell, ca. 1900.

Fig. 13
Jökulsá á Brú. Kláfur, or wire rope bridge,
ca. 1900.

Fig. 14
Ölfursárbrú, ca. 1900.

bridge was connected to Jón Þorláksson's first experiments with concrete and his research on local building materials, then the bridge over the Fnjóská river became the built proof of the engineer's ongoing relations with Denmark and the Danish reinforced concrete engineering school. Fig. 15

A bridge connecting the east and the west bank of the Fnjóská river, near a forest known as Skógar, had been a pressing need for years, and a number of possibilities had been debated since the late nineteenth century. This bridge was pivotal to allow a direct link between the village of Akureyri and Lake Mývatn, both populated farming areas in northern Iceland. Eventually, this project became Iceland's first reinforced concrete bridge, designed by the Danish firm Christiani & Nielsen.[134] The bridge, completed in 1908, was followed by many reinforced concrete bridges built all over the island.[135] This small but elegant piece of infrastructural engineering was described in detail in the local newspapers, and the bridge has also been published internationally several times.[136] One year after completion, the structure was featured in the *Beton und*

Fig. 15
Bridge over the Bláskeggsá river.

Eisen journal, and the article did not conceal the difficulties experienced by the Danish workers during construction. A late river flood in June 1908 destroyed part of the timber formwork, causing some delay in construction.[137] Fig. 16

In 1933, a picture of the bridge was included by British architectural critic Philip Morton Shand (1888–1960) in the British journal *The Concrete Way*.[138] This "very elegant" bridge was mentioned in later publications by the Danish firm as one of their first completed projects.[139] The construction of the bridge was of key importance not only in terms of Iceland's infrastructural challenges but also in the wider picture of the transformation of its building tradition.[140] Fig. 17

As Jón Þorláksson took control over the planning of the road and bridge network, he strongly insisted to the Ministry of Iceland that the bridge had to be made of reinforced concrete, and he suggested his Danish colleagues Christiani and Nielsen. The engineer stressed this opinion even against his own evaluation regarding the final price: according to his documentation, he attested that a suspended steel bridge would have cost 30,000kr, as opposed to at least 33,000kr for a reinforced concrete one.[141] A few sentences written by Jón Þorláksson to the Ministry of Iceland are striking for their clarity, and they explain why the Icelandic government had to build such an avant-garde bridge in a remote area of the country. He claimed that the chosen spot for the bridge offered enough aggregates for making concrete. By so doing, Jón Þorláksson highlighted the strong link between natural resources and man-made construction, which he had been researching for years. Despite admitting that a reinforced concrete structure would have been more expensive, he added that the only way of having cheaper reinforced concrete bridges around the island was to train the local builders on how to build them. This knowledge necessarily had to come from abroad, and specifically from Denmark.[142]

Fig. 16
The bridge under construction, ca. 1906.

The engineer's suggestions to the Icelandic government did play a pivotal role. After a call for tenders, launched in Denmark and published in the *Ingeniøren* journal, in January 1908 the task was assigned to the firm Christiani & Nielsen.[143] Jón Þorláksson had received their project one year earlier, and those drawings attest that the firm was still proudly boasting its status as Hennebique concessionaire. Fig. 18

Yet, by 1908, the name of Christiani & Nielsen no longer appeared in the pages of *Le Beton Armé*—Hennebique's monthly journal—, thus the construction was not mentioned as a Hennebique product. Although it was not possible to determine who the Danish workers employed at the construction site were, one name emerges from the narration of a local clergyman, reported in an Icelandic newspaper decades later.[144] The director of the works was engineer Knud Reffstrup, employed by Christiani & Nielsen—of whom, however, no archival records can be found, with the exception of a photograph of the bridge on which the workers' names were noted. In 1908, in a remote corner of the Icelandic landscape, over a powerful river and between wild mountains, the up-to-date European technology of reinforced concrete was embraced for the first time in the history of the country. The building of the bridge was a turning point for Icelandic construction and emerged at the crossroads where Icelandic infrastructural needs met with European engineering tradition. The bridge over the Fnjóská river served as a stage where Icelandic engineers could share their expertise originating from the Continent. Fig. 19

In 1903, after years of research and a national grant, engineer Knud Zimsen had established a wool factory named Iðunn, located on the eastern outskirts of Reykjavík and close to the sea.[145] In 1906, the company headquarters burned down.[146] Soon after the fire, local newspapers wrote about a forthcoming building in concrete.[147] The factory had to be rebuilt quickly, and with a guarantee of better resistance to fire. Reinforced concrete patents had already conquered Europe with their gospel of fireproof qualities and enduring resistance to earthquakes: the reconstruction of Iðunn was also the perfect opportunity to demonstrate these properties to the Icelandic audience.

The new factory was built on the same spot as the old one, in what is today's Skúlagata 42. Wool production stopped in 1914, and the building was transformed into a paint and varnish factory. The structure was destroyed in 1989, and absence of the original structural drawings makes it difficult to analyze and evaluate the actual contribution of the Hennebique patent. A few photographs attest the presence of what could have been a Hennebique system of pillars, beams, and ribbed slabs.[148] Fig. 20

Fig. 17
Christiani & Nielsen, Bridge over the
Fnjóská river, Skógar (1906–08).

Fig. 18
Christiani & Nielsen, Bro over Fnjóska ved Skógar [Bridge over the Fnjóská river, Skógar], 1907.

Fig. 19
Bridge over the Fnjóská river, postcard, ca. 1908–09. The third figure from the left is Knud Reffstrup, director of the works.

Furthermore, the news of the reconstruction of Iðunn spread through Icelandic newspapers. A short article published in June 1907 mentioned a "novelty in architecture", claiming that the new factory was going to be rebuilt in reinforced concrete using the "Hennebique method". The article asserted the fireproof qualities and the resistance to earthquakes of such structures. Moreover, the text stated that "the construction will be handled by Danish experts", and this was a chance for the Icelanders involved in the process "to learn from them and bring this knowledge into the country". Eventually, it claimed that the "moving spirit" of this method was engineer Thorvald Krabbe.[149]

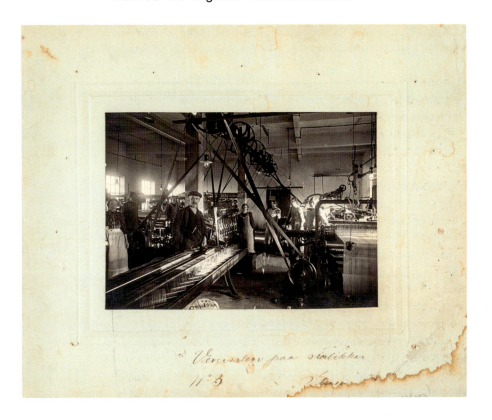

By summer 1907, Danish-Icelandic engineer Krabbe, graduated from the Polytechnic School of Denmark, had already moved to Reykjavík and was active as state engineer.[150] During his career, Krabbe traveled extensively around the country, taking an astounding number of photographs depicting the very "technical development" which he would later describe in his book in 1946.[151] His tasks were mainly related to infrastructures: he supervised the construction of several harbors, lighthouses, electricity stations, and he also spent years working on a

Fig. 20
Iðunn wool factory, ca. 1906–15.

proposal for a railway connection between Reykjavík and Selfoss.[152] His connections to Danish reinforced concrete construction might have stemmed from his use of concrete in building piers and breakwaters for Icelandic harbors. In those years, in fact, Krabbe's letters attest that he was working on the harbors of Ísafjörður, Akureyri, and the Westman Islands, among others. Moreover, Krabbe was also consulted by Iceland's Ministry Office regarding the issues of earthquakes and structural improvements. Interestingly, in February 1909, he mentioned a request made by the Ministry of Iceland for him to comment on the news of the tragic earthquake that had struck southern Italy on December 28, 1908.[153] Echoing in the news across the Continent, the 1908 earthquake was a truly tragic and exceptional event that sparked a continental debate on construction matters and led to a number of improvements on reinforced concrete methods, particularly regarding the Hennebique patent.[154]

What may truly attest to Krabbe's role as the "moving spirit" behind the use of the Hennebique method at Iðunn are two letters written by the engineer. The first, dated November 10, 1906 and sent to an atelier in Copenhagen, mentions a drawing to be reproduced in two copies, then sent to Christiani & Nielsen and to master mason Carl Schiøtz—both Hennebique concessionaires in Denmark.[155] It is therefore likely that Krabbe provided his project for the reconstruction of the wool factory and then asked the Hennebique firms to produce the authorized version of the structural design.[156] The second letter is dated April 17, 1907, when the "Danish experts" were probably already working on the reconstruction of the factory in Reykjavík. Krabbe wrote to the commission in charge of the construction of the National Library in Reykjavík and, on behalf of the Iðunn factory, suggested that they hire two "workers" who had already been employed by Iðunn to build the library's reinforced concrete slabs. These workers should not be paid more than the regular wage for a master mason in Reykjavík; Krabbe attested that for their work at Iðunn they had been paid 500kr.[157] If the former letter confirms some direct connections between Krabbe and Hennebique concessionaires in Denmark, the latter highlights an interesting fact: the Hennebique patent was used, or at least proposed, for the construction of the National Library and Museum in Reykjavík, as will be seen further in this chapter. It is also important to consider that in the same year, 1907, the use of reinforced concrete was first taught in a series of lectures at the Polytechnic School of Denmark by Danish engineer Edouard Suenson. The developments of the technique in Denmark were soon mirrored in its first applications in the remote Icelandic context.[158]

In the case of the bridge over the Fnjóská river, the drawings prove that Christiani & Nielsen were operating as concessionaires of the Hennebique patent. The same cannot be said, however, for the rebuilding of the wool factory, as the original drawings are missing.[159] Although it is impossible to be entirely sure of an official use of the Hennebique patent in the factory, in July 1907, *Le Beton Armé* mentioned a project for a "plancher de filature", under the direction of the concessionaire C. Schiøtz in the "bureau de Copenhague". Perhaps it was the Iðunn factory, for the first time pulling Iceland closer to the center of the European building technology. Perhaps, however, the project was never considered by the Hennebique offices, as it was far too humble compared to what the enterprise had been designing on the Continent. However, no matter how small the building was, it represented a step towards the country's "technical development" praised and photographed by Thorvald Krabbe during his travels around the country.

By the early nineteen-tens, the increasing popularity of cement and concrete was manifest among Icelandic engineers and builders. In 1911, Jón Þorláksson reported that, during the previous year, Reykjavík had seen more new houses built in concrete than in timber. Less than ten years after graduating as an engineer, he stated that Icelandic history was entering a new era: *steinsteypuöldin*, the age of concrete.[160]

THE FOUNDATION OF THE ICELANDIC ENGINEERS' SOCIETY

Over the course of a decade, the number of engineers active in Iceland had rapidly increased. Iceland's youngest profession was represented by a good number of members, who needed a platform to discuss their work. Following the example of the Dansk Ingeniørforening, in 1912 twelve engineers and one architect founded Verkfræðingafélag Íslands [The Icelandic Engineers' Society], with Jón Þorláksson as its first president.[161] The first members of the Society were a mixed group of individuals, representing the different specializations of the profession. Among its members were Sigurður Thoroddsen, Knud Zimsen, Jón Þorláksson, and Thorvald Krabbe, together with other civil engineers, but the list also included one chemical engineer, one mechanical engineer, and two experts in telegraph communication. One of the founding members was Rögnvaldur Ólafsson, who had trained as an architect at Det Tekniske Selskabs Skole in Copenhagen. He did not graduate due to health problems, but by 1912 he had already designed several buildings all over Iceland. His presence among the members of the Engineers' Society is a proof of the strong connections between each expert in the construction field. Rögnvaldur Ólafsson's importance in the Icelandic "concrete age" was a consequence of his personal relations with Icelandic engineers, who regarded the architect as one of them. Just like the engineers, Rögnvaldur Ólafsson played a pivotal role in the modernization of the country, which was the Society's foremost goal. As claimed by the Society's charter, the main aim was to "strengthen the partnership between engineering experts in Iceland".[162] Following this ambition, in 1919 the Society also accepted the young architecture graduate and future state architect Guðjón Samúelsson as a member.[163]

Thanks to the diverse education of its affiliates, the open-minded approach of the Icelandic Engineers' Society was manifest in the pages of its journal. The engineers first published a short yearly report before launching the first issue of *Tímarit Verkfræðingafélags Íslands* [Journal of the Engineers' Society of Iceland] in 1916, which became the main platform for debating Iceland's infrastructural needs.[164] Fig. 21

The journal was edited similarly to the *Ingeniøren*, from which it was clearly influenced. The background of the Icelandic engineers was their Danish Polytechnic education, and the majority of the Icelandic Society's members were also affiliated with the Danish Society. The Icelandic journal published reports from the Society's meetings, lectures held by prominent members or foreign engineers, articles, book reviews, and continuous updates about the infrastructural progress in Iceland. The journal had also an international stance, publishing articles

Fig. 21
Tímarit Verkfræðingafélags Íslands 1 (1916).
Cover of the first issue.

in Icelandic and Danish, often providing translations in English, French, and German, thus opening the local debate to the world. As reported in the journal's first issue, the Icelandic Society was in contact with several engineering and architecture societies in various countries, such as Denmark, Norway, Sweden, Finland, Germany, and Austria. This open-minded internationality is the same characteristic that emerged from Knud Zimsen's and Thorvald Krabbe's letters, written in several languages and sent from Iceland to Europe and the United States. Another example of the engineers' international approach can be found in the texts collected at the National Library, such as Frank B. Gilbreth's *Concrete System* (1908). According to the loan tag still present in the copy of the book collected at the National Library of Iceland, the book was borrowed by Jón Þorláksson in 1915.[165] This cosmopolitan approach was surely at the professional core of a country that longed for faster connections and better trade.

From the beginning, the journal published many articles dedicated to cement, reinforced concrete, and concrete aggregates, highlighting the growing importance of this matter in the country. The journal encouraged a scientific dialogue regarding building materials, which seemed to outdistance vernacular building traditions. Already in its first meetings, the Society invited a few Danish engineers to give some lectures on the use of reinforced concrete for underwater construction, in relation to the project for the harbor of Reykjavík—one of the city's biggest infrastructural projects at the beginning of the century.[166]

In 1916, the Society published the "Standard Specification for the Sale and Testing of Portland Cement", written by the Society's Cement Commission, at the suggestion of Knud Zimsen.[167] The short text, available in Icelandic, Danish, German, and English, was divided into five articles that defined the properties of cement to be sold and employed for building in Iceland. This standard specification highlighted the growing gap between the engineers' normative attitude towards architecture and construction and the local building tradition which was still vernacular at its core.[168] The same issue also emerged from an article titled "Icelandic Aggregates", whose aim was to present the results of a few tests run on Icelandic sand and gravel samples.[169] The tests were conducted in Copenhagen by engineer Niels Christensen Monberg (1856–1930), with samples collected on the Skólavörðuholt hill in Reykjavík and in the Westman Islands. This short text marked the beginning of a four-decades long series of trials, tests, and research on Icelandic natural resources towards the fully independent production of concrete. If cement was initially just a matter of regulations and testing, the journal quickly became the stage for the most heated debate of the Icelandic concrete *saga*: the building of Iceland's first cement plant.

The pages of the journal's first issues show a small group of experts and technicians who had been educated abroad, had been exposed to an international network of studies and research, and were optimistic about the fact that their knowledge could create a better future for their country. Technical expertise quickly turned into political power: some members would become prominent political figures, such as Knud Zimsen and Jón Þorláksson. Already by 1916, Icelandic engineers thought themselves as ahead of the times and far better connected to the Continent than many of their fellow citizens. Their careers were often discussed with an enthusiastic attitude, painting their figures with a certain degree of heroism. Over the years, the Society's journal published an obituary for every deceased member, remembering their activities and milestones. One word was repeatedly used in many obituaries: *brautryðjandi*, literally a "trailblazer", a pioneer.[170]

PUBLIC BUILDINGS IN THE HOME RULE YEARS

The first decade of the twentieth century was a turning point for Icelandic architecture, merging late nineteenth-century influences, recent industrial progress, and a growing political autonomy. It was the moment when the last public buildings designed and supervised by Danish professionals were built in Reykjavík. At the same time, with the establishment of home rule, Iceland's distancing from Denmark's direct political control matched with the creation of a new position: the consultant for public buildings. The country's first architecture student, Rögnvaldur Ólafsson, was appointed to this role in 1906.[171] As a result, the emergence of both architectural and engineering professions allowed the construction of buildings that were locally designed and built by Icelandic experts.

Between 1899 and 1909, three major public buildings were completed in Reykjavík: two banks—Landsbanki (1896–99) and Íslandsbanki (1904–06)—and the National Museum and Library, commonly known as Safnahúsið (1906–09). They were the heritage of Iceland's dependency from Danish architects, master masons, and building knowledge in general. At the same time, these buildings characterized the end of an era and marked some very important steps in the process of creating an Icelandic working class within the construction industry. These structures are often referred to as Iceland's last "Danish" buildings. As a matter of fact, it is only recent historiography that has emphasized the nationality of the architects active in these projects.[172] Since the construction of the early stone buildings in the late eighteenth century, these designs were usually signed by architects who had never visited the country.[173] Despite some contrasts in the reception of Danish materials for the construction of the cathedral in Reykjavík, the nationality of a project was less an issue of debate in the local newspapers than it is today a label for historians. The national boundaries of architecture had become slightly blurred already since the construction of the Icelandic parliament house. Although the project was a creation of Danish architect Meldahl, overseen by Danish master mason Bald, the building site was made possible by local builders and, as seen in Chapter 1, it became a practical school for the Icelanders active in the construction field. Almost twenty years after the inauguration of the parliament house, by the late eighteen-nineties Iceland was becoming more and more autonomous on technical matters. By looking at the construction of the two banks and of the national library, it is possible to detect the increasing role of Icelandic manpower in the building phase, and also the greater importance of Icelandic construction experts in the public debate. Although designed and supervised by Danish technicians, each of the three buildings marked one step forward in the development of the Icelandic construction industry and its decisional autonomy.

Between 1899 and 1906, two banks were built in the heart of Reykjavík's city center as headquarters of Iceland's oldest bank institutions: Landsbanki [The national bank] (1896–99) and the private bank Íslandsbanki (1904–06).[174] Figs. 22–23

Both buildings rose on the same street, Austurstræti, not far from the parliament house and the cathedral. Their close proximity constituted a financial core in the small city center. Although the two were independent institutions, both architectural projects were signed by the same Danish architect, Christian Lauritz Thuren (1846–1926). Thuren's work was largely influenced by a historicist and eclectic education.[175] The bank institutes in Reykjavík were designed according to a widespread "convenient eclecticism"—as Sergio Pace defines it—that suited most of nineteenth-century European banks.[176] In particular, the most common reference was that of the Florentine rusticated palazzo, considered the highest symbol of a bank's reliability and solidity.[177] Both buildings represented a true catalog of technical solutions that were almost novelties in Iceland at the turn of the century.

The construction of the National Bank was overseen by Frederik Bald's son Valdemar (1872–1921).[178] The Bald family had established a building firm active both in Iceland and in the Faroe Islands, specializing in public buildings such as schools, lighthouses, hospitals, prisons, and

Fig. 22
Postcard of Reykjavik, ca. 1900. View of Austurstræti with Landsbanki.

Fig. 23
Íslandsbanki, ca. 1905–20.

banks.[179] The walls were mainly composed of dolerite ashlars, which only emerged as rusticated quoins, while the rest of the facade was covered with a thick layer of plaster with carvings that imitated the stone pattern. As an absolute novelty in the Icelandic context, the floor slabs were made in steel girders covered by a layer of concrete, and a central heating system was installed.[180] The final outcome was a sober and elegant building. If European banks were characterized by architectural understatement and austerity, which was supposed to reflect the ethical qualities of banking institutions, the building of the National Bank generated much awe among the inhabitants of Reykjavík. When the works came to an end, the building was welcomed as one of the "beauties in the city" and praised as one of the "finest and best buildings in the country".[181] Fig. 24

The original project for Íslandsbanki, dated January 1905, comprised an elegant, two-story building with a double entrance. Both entrances were marked by Doric columns supporting pediments, and the facade was all covered with roughly rusticated stone ashlars. Quite interestingly, the building's execution turned out to be quite different than expected, and this was mainly because of local decision-making that interfered

Fig. 24
Landsbanki under construction.

with Thuren's preliminary proposal. First, it was perhaps considered too big and too expensive: by February 1905, Thuren sent a smaller version of the original project, only one story high.[182] The architect did not directly supervise the construction, which was overseen by a Danish master mason. Thuren's drawings show steel girders on the ground and first floors and timber beams for the top floor and the roof. At first, local newspapers reported that the foundations were to be in concrete and the upper walls in dolerite.[183] The construction was entrusted to a local building firm named Völundur, founded in 1904 and specialized in timber construction.[184] The firm eventually opted for a double-wall structure, with an outer layer in rough dolerite ashlars and an inner layer in concrete cast stone, produced by Jón Þorláksson's building company Steinar—the first large-scale application of Icelandic cast stones. Fig. 25

Ironically, the last building designed by a Danish architect was the country's most representative institution, possibly even more important than the house of parliament—the National Library and Museum. Throughout the political journey towards independence, the Icelandic language played a great role in asserting the cultural autonomy of the country in relation to Denmark. A particular source of pride was Norse history and the literature of the sagas, thus it is easy to imagine the value ascribed to Iceland's archival and librarian collections.

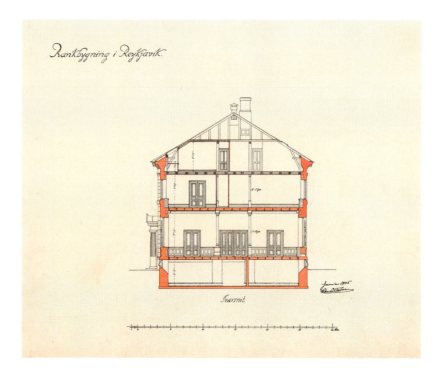

Fig. 25
Christian Lauritz Thuren, Project for Íslandsbanki. Cross section.

The National Library and Museum in Reykjavík was built after most Scandinavian national museums, which had acquired particular importance in Nordic capital cities since the last decades of the nineteenth century.[185] Despite the changes in the collections that have occurred during the twentieth century, the building is still an icon of Icelandic culture.[186]

Until the turn of the century, the Icelandic library and its archeological and natural collections had been housed in various, unpractical places around Reykjavík, such as the attic of the parliament, the cathedral, and the headquarters of Íslandsbanki. A suitable location for the collections was needed, and the building process was supported by the recently established Ministry for Iceland. From the beginning, the National Library was not only a matter of architecture and construction. As Guðmundur Hálfdanarson puts it:

> The library was not only a building but also a sort of statement of the Icelanders in relation to the recently acquired home rule government; Icelanders were a cultural people among cultural peoples, fully able to erect their own buildings.[187]

Although the final outcome was a Danish architectural product, there were moments in which local decision-making took the lead and contributed to some substantial changes in the architecture and materials. First of all, the library's earliest design was not sketched in Copenhagen but in Reykjavík. As a newly nominated consultant for public buildings, Rögnvaldur Ólafsson reported to the Alþingi his ideas regarding the architecture of the library.[188] Although in the end the parliament refused his proposal, Rögnvaldur Ólafsson's design became a model for the development of the project.[189] Eventually, the project was signed by Danish architect Johannes Magdahl Nielsen (1862–1941), assistant to Jørgen Holm (1835–1916) in the construction of the Royal Library at Slotsholmen in Copenhagen.[190] Figs. 26–27

Nielsen never visited Reykjavík, and evidence of his contribution is more or less limited to a few pencil drawings and letters kept at the National Archives.[191] However, the construction was supervised by his delegate Frederik Kiørboe (1878–1952), who moved to Iceland to work on the building site, also overseeing other construction projects in the meantime, including the school at Landakot and the Reykjanes Lighthouse, together with engineer Thorvald Krabbe.[192]

The final project envisaged a three-story building with a prominent gabled entrance and a large reading room facing the rear facade. Originally, the structure would have been in dolerite ashlars with a copper roof. This is where Icelandic autonomy emerged: the choice of the building materials was eventually all in the hands of the Völundur firm, that had won a call for tenders for the project in 1906. The firm opted for a solution that echoed Íslandsbanki: the double walls had a 40 cm thick outer layer of dolerite blocks and a 12 cm inner layer of Steinar concrete cast stones.[193] Clearly, the firm's decision was economical: concrete and concrete stones were much cheaper than cut stones.[194] It is also likely that because Völundur was specialized in timber construction, concrete could provide extra work in making formwork. Furthermore, the roofing was eventually made in iron, as a cheaper alternative to copper. Iceland's growing technical independence was not only visible in the contractor's choices of building materials but also in connection to local engineering knowledge. As seen previously, most probably the Hennebique patent—employed for the slabs of the library's reading room—was suggested by engineer Krabbe after it had been used in the reconstruction of the wool factory.[195] When inaugurated, the library was described as "the finest and best concrete building of this country".[196] Fig. 28

At the library building site, for the first time, the entire construction was in the hands of Icelandic builders. This awareness among contemporary observers quickly became part of the national rhetoric about the building: as soon as the library was inaugurated, the librarian boasted that "everything inside has been made in Iceland".[197] Although this was not entirely true, the majority of the architectural elements were local products.[198] For example, two granite columns located in the reading room were quarried in the vicinity of Reykjavík and carved by Icelandic stonemasons. Two characteristics increased the "Icelandicness" of the building, although they do not pertain to the realm of construction. First, the library is located on the historically and mythically significant Arnarhóll Hill. Second, perhaps to underline that it was a symbol of national culture, the building commission decided to decorate the facades with the names of eight famous Icelandic writers and intellectuals, from Snorri Sturluson (1179–1241) to Hallgrímur Pétursson (1614–74). The names were included in the drawings signed by Nielsen.[199]

The project was also featured in the Danish journal *Architekten*, with special attention to its construction and technological features, in an article signed by Kiørboe.[200] The construction of the library was indeed a turning point for Icelandic architectural history and a mirror of the establishment of home rule. The increasing presence of Icelandic contractors, and specifically their freedom in decision-making, reflected the country's recent industrial changes. Eventually, that very same development was the motor behind Iceland's goal of a full political

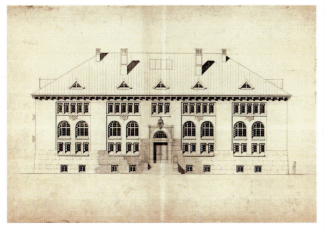

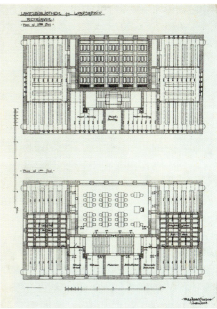

Fig. 26
Johannes Magdahl Nielsen, National Library of Iceland. Elevation.

Fig. 27
Johannes Magdahl Nielsen, National Library of Iceland. Plan of first and second floors.

Fig. 28
The National Library under construction. Photograph by Vigfús Sigurðsson, ca. 1906–07.

independence in the decades to come.[201] As if condensed into a single architectural piece, all the elements of the puzzle—culture, industry, politics—merged in the construction of the National Library. Fig. 29

The last building to be designed and supervised by a Danish architect was the elegant and central National Library. Instead, Iceland's first locally designed public building was much less classy and much more peripheral: a sanatorium in Vífilsstaðir, in Garðabær, south of Reykjavík. The strongest promoter of the sanatorium was Guðmundur Björnsson (1864–1937), physician and director of public health between 1906 and 1931. He complained about the country's lack of facilities for the cure of tuberculosis, as its uncontrollable spread also affected Iceland. In 1909, Guðmundur Björnsson claimed that all countries had already built sanatoriums to cure the disease, "even the Faroese people, the smallest nation … . We Icelanders are the only ones left behind".[202] It might not be a coincidence that Iceland's first all-concrete public building was a tuberculosis sanatorium. As Beatriz Colomina suggests, early twentieth-century architects largely experimented on sanatorium buildings, which became "the testing ground of new materials and techniques of construction and often involved experimental collaborations between architects, engineers, and doctors."[203] Switzerland is a striking example:

Fig. 29
The National Library of Iceland.
Photograph by Vigfús Sigurðsson,
ca. 1920–30.

the country's first building in reinforced concrete was the Schatzalp Sanatorium in Davos, built in 1907 under the structural supervision of engineer Robert Maillart (1872–1940).[204]

The sanatorium project in Vífilsstaðir was appointed to Rögnvaldur Ólafsson in 1908. By that time, the architect had suggested some renovation works on the cathedral in Reykjavík in 1904, and he had enlarged the nearby Free Church in 1905.[205] In particular, Rögnvaldur Ólafsson's church design became an experimental field for shifting from timber to concrete structures all over the country: he designed and built the first concrete church of Iceland, Bíldudalskirkja (1905–06), that was later on followed by a number of other churches.[206]

For Rögnvaldur Ólafsson, designing a sanatorium was a very special task: he was himself affected by tuberculosis and had resided for some months at the Boserup sanatorium near Roskilde.[207] As Björn Björnsson suggests, the Danish sanatorium directly influenced Rögnvaldur Ólafsson's project in terms of planimetric layout and overall design.[208] The original layout consisted of a longitudinal structure intersected by three transversal wings. The building had three stories above ground and a basement level. Unlike many sanatorium buildings of the time, the sanatorium at Vífilsstaðir was not equipped with balconies, perhaps due to the strong winds. Heliotherapy was thus practiced in a covered portico on the ground floor, connected to the main building, where patients could lie in the open air facing south.[209] The decoration was kept at a minimum: the facade was only accentuated by horizontal

CHAPTER 2 111

STEINSTEYPUÖLDIN

Fig. 30
The Sanatorium at Vífilsstaðir. Photograph by Magnús Ólafsson, ca. 1912–20.

bas-relief bands. However, this should not be seen as an early sign of functionalism: Rögnvaldur Ólafsson's contemporary projects were much more eclectic. The reason behind the sanatorium's sober appearance can be found in its function as a healing center, and it may also be linked to the great number of engineers involved on the building site, bearers of a more technical and less ornamental approach to architecture. Fig. 30

The construction proceeded very quickly: between 1909 and 1910, the building reunited all of Iceland's architecture and engineering professionals. From the pioneers of reinforced concrete and cast stones—Knud Zimsen, Thorvald Krabbe, Jón Þorláksson—to the workers of the Völundur firm, Rögnvaldur Ólafsson directed the works by grouping together the country's leading technicians.[210] The result was "the first all-Icelandic large building"[211] and Rögnvaldur Ólafsson's "main work".[212] The sanatorium was the first large-scale architectural outcome of Iceland's "age of concrete", with concrete outer walls and reinforced concrete slabs on the first, second, and third floors.[213] Steinar concrete cast stones were used for air ducts. Knud Zimsen officially supervised the design of the sanatorium's heating system, and he also played an important role in selling Aalborg cement to Rögnvaldur Ólafsson and the sanatorium's building committee. Throughout 1909, Knud Zimsen made several offers to the architect regarding the price of cement and consequently organized a number of deliveries to the building site.[214] Knud Zimsen saw the sanatorium project as an opportunity to strengthen his business connections to the Aalborg plant: from his perspective, the sanatorium was mainly seen as a "large delivery" of cement, and he mentioned the building to his Danish partners.[215] Knud Zimsen's role was also important for the procurement of other building materials: he sold corrugated iron to Rögnvaldur Ólafsson,[216] concrete pipes to Jón Þorláksson,[217] and, most importantly, "Monier iron"—that is, reinforcement bars—to Thorvald Krabbe,[218] who was in charge of the structural calculations of reinforced concrete slabs.[219] Once again, after the Iðunn wool factory and the National Library, Krabbe turned out to be the link between Iceland's building sites and a scientific approach to concrete.[220] The building did not boast a fully reinforced concrete skeleton: iron bars were only placed within the floor slabs and the stairs. Figs. 31-32

No evidence of Krabbe's structural calculations has been found, but in 1916 the engineer and the architect worked together again on a much smaller construction project—a cowshed close to the sanatorium. Rögnvaldur Ólafsson envisaged a reinforced concrete structure, for which the engineer provided all the calculations, and in this case, reinforcement bars were also used in the vertical pillars.[221] In a context where animal husbandry was a pivotal contribution to human life, the

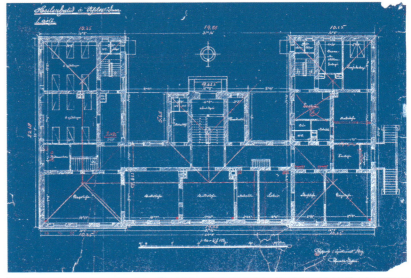

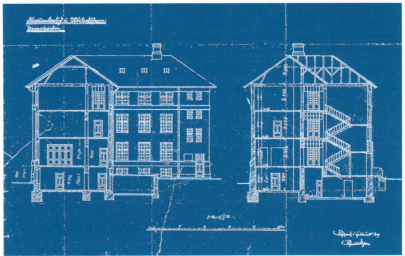

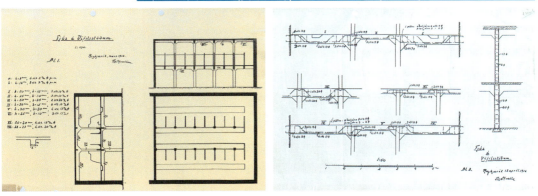

CHAPTER 2

STEINSTEYPUÖLDIN

Fig. 31
Rögnvaldur Ólafsson, Project for the sanatorium at Vífilsstaðir. Plan of first floor.

Fig. 32
Rögnvaldur Ólafsson, Project for the sanatorium at Vífilsstaðir. Cross sections.

Fig. 33
Thorvald Krabbe, Project for a cowshed at Vífilsstaðir. Structural drawings, March 1916.

Fig. 34
Thorvald Krabbe, Project for a cowshed at Vífilsstaðir. Structural drawings, April 1916.

application of durable reinforced concrete in an ordinary cowshed is not surprising and this technology had profound effects on the local farming practices. Figs. 33-34

When the sanatorium was inaugurated, it was welcomed as the "safest" construction of the country, "located on a rock and itself a whole rock"—a building that could last a thousand years.[222] It was, in short, the symbol of a new, technically independent Iceland: a country that could autonomously build its own architecture. Concrete and everything that revolved around it played a huge part during the building process and in the rhetoric that surrounded the project. The transition from the natural stone of the National Library to the concrete of the sanatorium mirrored the increasing autonomy of Iceland, and this departure from a building material may be seen as a "liberation from the Danish building technique and architecture".[223] This is consistent with the early-twentieth-century rhetoric of an independent Iceland that would also be autonomous in the supply of building materials. However, what occurred during the Icelandic home rule years should not be seen as a "liberation", neither politically nor materially speaking. When it comes to architecture and construction, although Iceland finally formed its own élite of professionals, these experts were largely indebted to and

Fig. 35
The remains of the portico today.
Photograph by author, 2019.

saturated with Danish and Continental scientific building knowledge. What probably occurred was not a sharp break between two cultures but a slow appropriation of technical tools to be used in a different context. [Fig. 35]

Rögnvaldur Ólafsson's career as Iceland's first architect of public buildings commenced only after his sanatorium project. From 1910 until his untimely death in 1917, he designed and built residential houses in the city center of Reykjavík, all three agricultural schools of the country, and also Reykjavík's post office.[224] His last project is thought to be the aforementioned cowshed at Vífilsstaðir. In 1916, Rögnvaldur Ólafsson lived in the sanatorium as a patient, where he died the following year. A memorial plaque dedicated to him now adorns the walls of the nursing home at Vífilsstaðir.

CONCRETE AND FIRE REGULATIONS

> We are in Hyperborea. That shore is Iceland, and this city is its capital: Reykjavík. ... It is built entirely of timber, except for four public buildings: the cathedral, the parliament house (Althing), the bank, and the prison.[225]
>
> Pierre Piobb, "Une Capitale en bois: Reykjavík," 1902

When foreign travelers arrived in Reykjavík at the turn of the century, they would walk through a tiny village, made up of low timber houses surrounding an unsheltered harbor, and turf farms hidden among the surrounding grass fields. Since the times of the settlement and until the first decades of the nineteenth century, Icelandic settlements had not developed as villages or cities: on the contrary, the island was largely populated by scattered turf farms, present in almost all its regions, with the exception of the central, barren highlands. Until today, one of the Icelandic terms for city, *bær*, also means "farm".

In 1786, the settlement of Reykjavík, together with five other coastal outposts around the country, was granted the status of *kaupstaður* [trading center] by royal decree. This happened in the year that followed the abolition of the Danish-Icelandic trade monopoly: at first, Reykjavík was only a trading spot for Danish and Icelandic merchants, but it slowly acquired social and political functions.[226] The first attempt towards a building regulation for the village is to be found in the so-called *opið bréf* [open letter] issued on May 29, 1839, which established a building commission for Reykjavík.[227] In 1894, some additional clauses were issued: among them, one represented the beginning of a forthcoming revolution in the island's almost one-thousand-year old construction habits: while still accepted on the outskirts of Reykjavík, turf houses were banned from the city center.[228] In order to have a compulsory building code, however, the city had to wait for the turn of the century. At that time, Reykjavík was still a small settlement compared to European standards, but it had already expanded considerably in comparison to other Icelandic trading centers. Moreover, Reykjavík had been gaining considerable political and cultural importance. Above all, it was the location of the restored Icelandic parliament and of the junior college. Fig. 36

This increasingly growing city—both in size and in population—required guidelines for its development. At first, the regulations did not refer to a general planning of the city: the first planning commission for Reykjavík was established only in the nineteen-twenties.[229] The building regulations for Reykjavík were limited to the obtaining of a building permit, to where, when, and if to build a house, and—most importantly—they also served as guidelines for landowners on how to build.[230] It is no coincidence that the building code was written with the help of Knud Zimsen—who later became one of the strongest advocates of concrete construction—soon after his return to Iceland from his educational years in Copenhagen. By 1903, only a handful of concrete buildings had been constructed in the small city: the first being a stable in Barónsstígur (1897–98), followed by the houses at Bankastræti 4 and Ingólfsstræti 21 (1903). Fig. 37 Knud Zimsen responded to the growing demand of concrete

Fig. 36
View of Reykjavík, ca. 1890–1900.

Fig. 37
Building at Bankastræti 4, Reykjavík (1903).

STEINSTEYPUÖLDIN

by opening commercial trade with Aalborg Portland, while simultaneously establishing some basic rules regarding the use of concrete for architectural purposes in his building code.

It should not come as a surprise that the building code of 1903 assigned quite a large role to cement and concrete as building materials and also devoted a lot of attention to explanations regarding construction techniques.[231] As claimed in a local newspaper, the building code had "three aims": reaching proper hygienic conditions, avoiding the risk of fires, building stronger and durable housing.[232] The building code predated Iceland's home rule: it was published on September 7, 1903, signed by Iceland's governor-general Magnús Stephensen, and it was divided into thirty-three articles.[233] The first fifteen articles pertained to the duties of the city's building commission and the relationship between new construction and the city—such as the street width, the distance of a new house from the street and from other buildings, and its height. In particular, timber houses were limited to a height of 14 álnir (ca. 9 m, being one Danish alin—an ell—ca. 0.63 m), while stone and concrete houses could be as high as 25 álnir (ca. 16 m). In general, the height of houses was not allowed to exceed the street width.[234]

The following articles referred to construction topics, such as foundations, materials, and building techniques. For all buildings of two or more stories, foundations had to be made of stone or gravel, bound with lime or cement. In order to avoid damp within the walls, a layer of tar or cement was mandatory, and it had to be located right above the ground floor.[235] A precise mixing ratio for load-bearing concrete walls was specified, as concrete could not be weaker than 1 : 5 : 10 (cement : sand : gravel); and it was also stated that it was forbidden to cast concrete structures if the temperature was 2°C or below.[236] The code very briefly mentioned the possibility of reinforced concrete walls, although reinforcement bars were not largely in use at that time. The code's relatively high degree of precision regarding concrete construction techniques aimed at one single scope, as stated by Knud Zimsen in one of his autobiographies:

> I set out very strong rules regarding the construction of stone/concrete houses, as I believed that with such material it was possible to build for the future, and a great effort was made in order to have houses of the best quality.[237]

For Knud Zimsen, building for the future meant building lasting houses. This might be the reason why one of the final clauses of the code became a turning point for Icelandic history: turf houses were entirely banned, both in the city center and on its outskirts.[238] The ban on turf houses in the city had no instant effects, and for decades turf farms coexisted next to concrete and timber buildings. The transition from traditional to globalized building practices had deep social consequences, as it radically changed the living conditions of most inhabitants. This "vanishing world"[239] was poetically narrated by Halldór Laxness in his novel *The Fish Can Sing*, set in one of Reykjavík's last turf farms.[240] In the novel, the farm at Brekkukot is a house "which was to be razed to the ground tomorrow".[241] Referring to the growth of Reykjavík, Laxness ironically described the living conditions offered by urban life. As the population was prompted to leave the countryside to settle in the city, families often ended up living in unhealthy concrete basements:

> 'I want to buy this cottage,' said Gúðmúnsen in all seriousness. 'They will soon be building palaces in Iceland. What do you say, Björn? I shall let you have a first-class basement up in Laugavegur. And gold in your hand like dirt, to last you the rest of your life.'[242]

The majority of the 1903 code's articles were devoted to carpentry. Nevertheless, timber construction had two main drawbacks: it was expensive and it was under the constant threat of fire. This risk was at the center of the building code's attention, and it was the reason why Reykjavík first developed as a town of low houses surrounded by small plots of land. Houses had to be isolated by means of unbuilt areas with dimensions comparable to those of the house,[243] or—in case of constructions closer than 5 álnir (ca. 3 m)—divided by a fireproof wall, usually built in stone or concrete.[244]

In October 1906, a fire destroyed some timber houses in the village of Akureyri, and soon after, the local newspaper stated that "the construction of timber houses has to stop", so that the reconstructed buildings would only be "of cement and sand".[245] Some years later, in 1912, this wish was echoed by the newly founded Engineers' Society. Rögnvaldur Ólafsson gave a lecture on the need to update the 1903 building code. Timber construction had to be more strictly limited, especially in the city center, and greater details had to be provided on the use of concrete and its reinforcement. As a builder, Rögnvaldur Ólafsson was very interested in technical issues, such as the resistance of concrete structures against earthquakes and fires. Also, as an architect and urban planning enthusiast, he also understood that the materials with which they were building Reykjavík would change the appearance and organization of the city:

An alteration which seems to me absolutely necessary is an improved arrangement of the town. On the whole it should be more densely populated. It may seem going the wrong way to make population denser, when there in other countries is a strong movement rising, tending towards its scattering. I mean the Garden Cities. ... As far as I can see, the wide expanse of this town renders it very difficult to keep it decently clean, to take care of the make and the repair of streets and pavements and to procure lighting, sewerage and other things ... . In my opinion, some parts of the town must be built more densely, and then it will be necessary to build from a material more fire-resisting and more durable than wood is known to be.[246]

In short, houses of concrete meant more density—less unbuilt plots of land between each building, therefore a denser urban fabric that could finally give Reykjavík the look of a city. Rögnvaldur Ólafsson's plea for a revision of the code was not received as expected, and more detailed rules on reinforced concrete were not included until the new building code for Reykjavík issued in 1945. The architect was especially worried about the large presence of timber houses in the city center of Reykjavík and suggested imposing a restriction on them. Three years later, his words sounded almost prophetic.

During the night of April 25, 1915, a tragic fire burst in Reykjavík: the event destroyed most of the houses in Kvosin, the area corresponding to the city center, between the pond and the harbor.[247] Fig. 38

A few weeks after the fire, the local newspaper *Morgunblaðið* ran a front-page article with the headline "Steinbær", indicating a wish for the Reykjavík of the future to become a "city of stone".[248] *Steinbær* was not only a wish but a mandatory rule that changed the current building code: in the future, with a few exceptions, all houses of Reykjavík would have to be built of fireproof materials such as stone or concrete. This break in local building traditions is similar to the events that occurred in 1904 in Ålesund, Norway, after a fire had destroyed most of its city center.[249] Rögnvaldur Ólafsson's proposal of abandoning timber houses did not seem absurd anymore. Less than two months after the Great Fire, an additional clause was added to the code: "From now on, all new houses in Reykjavík will have to be built of stone or concrete, or other reliable and fireproof materials". The only exception was for isolated buildings standing at least 3.15 m away from a neighboring plot and 2 m from the street boundary.[250] After a decade of experiments and tryouts, Reykjavík was truly entering its age of concrete, and so were all the other villages in the country: from Borgarnes (1914) to Ísafjörður (1943), all Icelandic urban settlements slowly adopted a building code, generally modeled on

CHAPTER 2 121

STEINSTEYPUÖLDIN

Fig. 38
The fire of Reykjavík, April 1915.

that of Reykjavík. Prompted by a fire, the revision of the building code marked the heyday of Icelandic concrete architecture both in urban and rural contexts.

STEINSTEYPUKLASSÍK: ICELANDIC CONCRETE CLASSICISM

The Great Fire of Reykjavík in 1915 gave a new direction to the building traditions of the city and all Icelandic settlements. Until then, concrete had been rarely used for urban residences or commercial buildings: the majority of recent dwellings were in timber and had been built according to the guidelines of the 1903 building code.[251] However, the decade-long efforts of Iceland's first engineers to promote the use of concrete and the import of cement had already begun to show architectural results, such as the sanatorium in Vífilsstaðir and the growing number of concrete farms in the countryside.[252] This process soon took over timber structures in the city as well. In 1912, there were only 19 concrete houses in Reykjavík; after the fire of 1915, all new houses of the capital were either built or rebuilt in concrete.[253]

Since the early nineteen-tens, a new way of building emerged in the expanding suburbs of the capital, later known as *steinsteypuklassík*— concrete classicism—, a term first coined by architectural historian and artist Hörður Ágústsson.[254] Concrete classicism was not the product of a single architect nor a well-established trend, rather it was a common approach shared by the first Icelandic architects who were looking for certain architectural features to represent the wealthiest families and trading companies in the city. Merging eclectic decorations, Danish neo-baroque historicism, and simplified classical elements, the outcomes of "concrete classicism" were very popular until the early nineteen-thirties.[255] Icelandic *steinsteypuklassík* owes its nature to Danish historicist and eclectic architecture, built in concrete for practical reasons, and therefore it had nothing in common either with what has been defined as Nordic classicism, nor with the rigorous search of a concrete classical architecture by reinforced concrete enthusiasts such as Auguste Perret (1874–1954).[256] However, *steinsteypuklassík* was a direct result of the Icelandic concrete age: the first generation of trained Icelandic architects followed the suggestions of their engineering colleagues and adopted concrete as their preferred building technology, while giving shape to the demands of the increasing number of urban residents. Among them were Einar Erlendsson (1883–1968), assistant to Rögnvaldur Ólafsson between 1905 and 1917, Finnur Thorlacius (1883–1974), and Jens Eyjólfsson (1879–1959).[257] Figs. 39–40

CHAPTER 2

STEINSTEYPUÖLDIN

Fig. 39
Rögnvaldur Ólafsson,
House at Skólabrú 2, Reykjavík (1912).

Fig. 40
Einar Erlendsson,
House at Þingholtsstræti 29A,
former City Library, Reykjavík (1916).

From a structural point of view, concrete was used in the same way as in the rural areas—in single or double walls, rarely and lightly reinforced, at times with cast concrete stones.[258] The plasticity of concrete made it easier for architects and masons to produce architectural details faster and at lower prices, which resulted in a rather sophisticated application of cement plaster for decoration and abstract versions of columns, cornices, and crenellations. The latter might have become popular since the construction of the Gimli House by Knud Zimsen in 1905–06.[259] *Steinsteypuklassík* experiments might have also been influenced by key European buildings. One example is Gamla Bíó, a movie theatre designed by Einar Erlendsson (1883–1968) and built in Reykjavík's city center in 1925–26. The structure is in cast concrete, yet the overall balance of the facade, with a tripartite rusticated entrance and a massive pediment resting on four simplified composite lesenes, bears strong resemblance to eminent neoclassical models of city theaters, stemming from the La Scala theatre in Milan.[260] Fig. 41

The material results of *steinsteypuklassík* represented a testing ground for Icelandic builders on the artistic and decorative uses of concrete. Furthermore, they could be interpreted as a translation—into concrete—of the previous timber dwellings which had been popular in Reykjavík until the 1915 fire. "Concrete classicism" firmly established the concrete age in Reykjavík, and it made way for further uses of the material as a means of reproducing a mythical medieval past or translating vernacular architecture and natural landscape.[261]

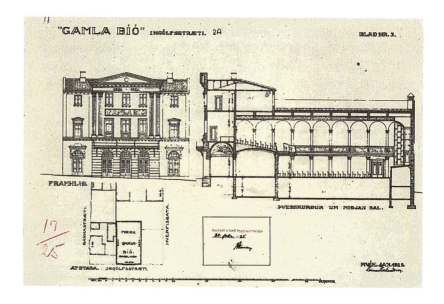

Fig. 41
Einar Erlendsson, Project for the
Gamla Bíó movie theatre, Reykjavík,
January 1925.

Fig. 42
Einar Erlendsson, Gamla Bíó movie theatre, Reykjavík (1925–26).

STEINSTEYPUÖLDIN

ENDNOTES

1   "Quelques réflexions sur ce qu'ont à faire les Islandais, s'ils veulent développer autant qu'il est possible les ressources naturelles de leur chère patrie. Ils doivent tout d'abord renoncer à l'émigration: l'Islande manque de bras; cultiver mieux qu'ils ne le font leurs prairies, qu'ils négligent, et les drainer; construire des routes; abriter les moutons; échanger contre du foin comprimé, qui nourrira vaches ou poneys durant l'hiver, le poisson qui fréquente les côtes en bancs incroyables et qu'ils commencent à savoir pêcher; ils doivent changer tout leur système d'éducation national et, au lieu de s'absorber dans la contemplation des antiques sagas, comme de fakirs qui se regardent le nombril, étudier les sciences appliquées. Croirait-on qu'il n'y a pas un seul ingénieur dans tout l'île! que physique, chimie, etc., sont absolument ignorées, et que, pour tracer un simple chemin, ils ont recours, comme je l'ai vu, à des géomètres qu'ils font venir à grands frais du continent!". Henry Labonne, *L'Islande et l'archipel des Færoeer*, (Paris: Libraire Hachette, 1888), pp. 298–99.

2   "Það er nú ekki lengur neinum efa undirorpið, að húsgerðarlagið í landinu er að breytast. Timburhúsaöld sú, sem hér hefir gengið yfir um hríð, er að enda, en steinsteypuöldin upp runnin". Jón Þorláksson, "Hvernig reynast steinsteypuhúsin?," p. 207.

3   Henry Mamy, "L'Islande," *Le Génie Civil: revue générale des industries françaises et étrangères* 10, no. 19 (March 12, 1887): pp. 301–03.

4   Oslund, *Iceland Imagined*, pp. 83–84.

5   Thorvald H. Krabbe, *Island og dets tekniske udvikling gennem tiderne* (Copenhagen: Danks-islandsk samfund, 1946), pp. 10–11.

6   "[…] le point le plus déshérité du globe". Labonne, *L'Islande et l'archipel des Færoeer*, p. xvii.

7   "[…] et ganske andet Land". Krabbe, *Island og dets tekniske udvikling gennem tiderne*, p. 10.

8   Sweden established the first engineering schools between 1827 and 1829, with the opening of the Royal Institute of Technology in Stockholm and the Chalmers University of Technology in Gothenburg. See: Sven Olving, "Education of Graduate Engineers in Sweden," *European Journal of Engineering Education* 2, no. 1 (1977): p. 110. The first Norwegian engineering school was the Kongsberg School of Mines (1757), which was moved to the University of Christiania (now Oslo) in 1811. In 1870 and 1875, new courses were opened in Trondheim and Bergen respectively. See: Trygve Karlsen, "Engineering Education in Norway," *European Journal of Engineering Education* 2, no. 1 (1977): p. 105. In Finland, the first technical schools were founded in 1849. In 1872, the Technical School of Helsinki was transformed into a Polytechnic School. See: Pasi Tulkki, "The Birth of Engineer Education in Finland," *European Journal of Engineering Education* 24, no. 1 (1999): p. 87.

9   Den Polytekniske Læreanstalt, now the Technical University of Demark (DTU), was founded in 1829. See: J. T. Lundbye, *Den polytekniske Læreanstalt 1829–1929* (Copenhagen: Gad, 1929). The school was later moved to Kongens Lyngby, north of Copenhagen. On the foundation of the school, see also: Michael F. Wagner, "Danish Polytechnical Education Between Handicraft and Science," in *European Historiography of Technology. Proceedings from the TISC-Conference in Roskilde*, edited by Dan Ch. Christensen (Odense: Odense University Press, 1993), pp. 146–63.

10   Sveinn Þórðarson, *Frumherjar í verkfræði á Íslandi* (Reykjavík: Verkfræðingafélag Íslands, 2002). See also: Guðmundur Magnússon, *Tækni fleygir fram. Tæknifræði á Íslandi og saga Tæknifræðingafélags Íslands* (Reykjavík: Iðnsaga Íslendinga og hið íslenska bókmenntafélag, 2010), pp. 26–34.

11   Icelandic newspapers mentioned: Ib Windfeld–Hansen (1845–1926), Alexander Rothe (?–1914), Udo von Ripperda (1859–1949), and also several unspecified "Norwegian engineers". See: "Brúagjörð yfir Þjórsá og Ölfusá," *Vikverji* 1, no. 20 (1873): pp. 77–78; "Landstjórn," *Fréttir frá Íslandi* 7, no. 1 (1878): p. 5; "Ölfursárbrúin," *Ísafold* 18, no. 47 (1891): p. 187.

12   "Auðvitað yrði það að vera útlendingur, því engan íslenzkan verkfræðing eigum við enn á landi voru." "Götur og byggingar o. fl. í Reykjavík," *Reykvíkingur* 2, no. 4 (1892): pp. 14–15.

13   A promoter for the improvement of Icelandic technical knowledge was Sigvatur Árnason (1823–1911), member of parliament several times since the eighteen-sixties. In the pages of the *Þjóðólfur* newspaper, he stressed the importance of a modern road network to improve communication and exchanges, along with the education of experts in this matter. Sighvatur Árnason, "Um samgöngur og vegagjörðir," *Þjóðólfur* 35, no. 25 (1883): p. 75.

14   In 1883, a carpenter, Gísli Guðmundsson, was granted a scholarship to study engineering in Copenhagen. In 1887, another scholarship was issued to allow him to continue his studies in Trondheim, under the supervision of Norwegian engineer Nils Olaf Hovdenak (1854–1942). However, as early as 1887, the parliament committee discontinued the grant, and there are no further records of Gísli Guðmundsson's academic accomplishments. Records of these early scholarships can be found in: "Alþing II," *Þjóðólfur* 39, no. 29 (July 8, 1887): p. 114; Alþingi, Alþingistíðindi, Þingskjöl (1887): pp. 42–43. See also: Sveinn Þórðarson, *Frumherjar í verkfræði á Íslandi*, pp. 15–16.

15   "Íslenzkur verkfræðingur," *Ísafold* 20, no. 39 (1893): p. 155.

16   Sveinn Þórðarson, *Frumherjar í verkfræði á Íslandi*, pp. 19–27. See also the obituary by Geir G. Zoëga, "Sigurður Thoroddsen, fyrrverandi landsverkfræðingur og yfirkennari," *Tímarit Verkfræðingafélags Íslands* 40, no. 6 (December 1955): pp. 89–90.

17   Sveinn Þórðarson, *Frumherjar í verkfræði á Íslandi*, pp. 29–34.

18   "… til rannsóknar á byggingarefnum landsins og leiðbeiningar í húsabyggingum". See: Sigurður Pétursson, "Um vegi og brýr á aðalleiðinni frá Reykjavík austur í Holt," *Ísafold* 27, no. 18 (April 4, 1900): p. 69. The funding of this research was debated in the Icelandic parliament in 1899. See: "Umræður í efri deild og sameinuðu þingi," Alþingi, Alþingistíðindi, Þingskjöl (1899): p. 390.

19   The earliest agricultural society was Suðuramtsins húss- og bústjórnarfélags, which published a journal between 1839 and 1846. The society later merged in the Búnaðarfélag Suðuramtsins, and the *Búnaðarrit* journal was founded in 1887. The Icelandic Agricultural Society was eventually founded in 1899.

20   The *landhöfðingi* was the official representative of the Kingdom of Denmark in Iceland. The position was established in 1872 as the highest government official on the island. It was eventually replaced in 1904 by Stjórnarráð Íslands, the Ministry of Iceland. Magnús Stephensen (1863–1917) was in charge between 1886 and 1904, and he was the governor general who signed the research on building materials.

21   "Mannalát," *Þjóðviljinn* 14, no. 38 (October 30, 1900): p. 151. He researched limestone from Mount Esja, north of Reykjavík, and clay from Laxárvogur í Kjós, in Hvalfjörður. "Kalkstein," *Fjallkonan* 17, no. 33 (August 25, 1900): p. 4; Þ. B., "Sigurður Pjetursson og byggingarannsóknirnar," *Búnaðarrit* 15, no. 1 (1901): p. 10.

22   For the scope of this research, I analyzed the answers provided by the rural districts of the Þingeyjarsýsla county in north-east Iceland, an important trading and agricultural region. Lbs, Handritasafn, 767 Fol., Örk 8. The districts to which the forms were sent to and answered by were: Sauðaneshreppur; Svalbarðshreppur; Axarfjarðarhreppur; Kelduhverfi; Fjallahreppur; Mývatnssveit; Reykdælahreppur; Aðaldælahreppur; Grýtubakkahreppur. This survey and its importance on a national scale was recently discussed in Hjörleifur Stefánsson's book *Hvílíkt torf – Tóm steypa! Úr torfhúsum í steypuhús* (Reykjavík: Háskólaútgáfan, 2020). I would like to thank Óskar Örn Arnórsson for pointing me to this source.

23   The Kaupfélag Þingeyinga was founded in 1882. See: Andrés Kristjánsson, *Aldarsaga Kaupfélags Þingeyinga* (Húsavík: Kaupfélag Þingeyinga, 1982); Pétur Sumarliðason and Einar Laxness, eds., *Sjálfsævisaga: bernskúar Kaupfélags Þingeyinga: úr fórum Jakobs Hálfdanarsonar* (Reykjavík: Ísafold, 1982). Jakob Hálfdanarson provided an extremely detailed answer to the engineer's questions, composing a handwritten document of 78 pages. Lbs, Handritasafn, 4 NF. Jakob Hálfdanarson (1836–1919). *Bréfa- og handritasafn 1865–1940*, Askja 18, Örk 6. "Um húsabyggingar". The document was digitized and is available at: https://issuu.com/heradsskjalasafnthingeyinga/docs/um_h__sabyggingar, accessed May 5, 2023.

24   The lowest estimates set the maximum lifespan of a turf farm at 30–35 years; the most positive estimate, on the other hand, was 70–90 years. Most answers claimed that 40–50 years was the ordinary lifespan for turf farms.

25   "Sandsteinn þessi er þó lélegt byggingarefni því hann blæs upp með tímanum að utanverðu í veggjum". [However, this sandstone is a weak building material because it tends to expand towards the exterior part of the walls"]. Lbs, Handritasafn, 767 Fol., Örk 8, Answer by the Kelduhverfi district.

26   "Hús þetta hefir ekki reynst vel til íbúðar". Lbs, Handritasafn, 767 Fol., Örk 8, Answer by the Reykdælahreppur district (Benedikt Jónsson).

27   Chimneys could also be built with bricks—*tígulsteinn*—, but they had to be imported from the Continent. In addition, the presence of heating systems in the farmhouses was relatively recent. Lbs, Handritasafn, 767 Fol., Örk 8, Answer by the Reykdælahreppur district (Benedikt Jónsson).

28   "Undanfarið 10 ára skeið hafa hér í hreppi verið byggð 10 timburhús og 1 steinsteypuhús (í Nesi)." [In the previous ten years, ten timber houses and one concrete house have been built in the municipality]. Lbs, Handritasafn, 767 Fol., Örk 8, Answer by the Grýtubakkahreppur district (Árni Jóhansson).

29   "Byggt og búið í gamla daga," *Tíminn* 63, no. 151 (July 7, 1979): p. 8. The regulation had been accepted with much criticism. "Fangelsi," *Víkverji* 2, no. 1 (June 16, 1874): pp. 117–18.

30   "Þá var af dönskum byggingameistara, Bald, viðhaft nýtt efni og aðferð, sem sé að steypa upp alla veggina milli stöpla og bindinga í grindina—bæði útveggi alla og milli veggi." Lbs, Handritasafn, 4 NF. Jakob Hálfdanarson (1836–1919). *Bréfa- og handritasafn 1865–1940*, Askja 18, Örk 6. "Um húsabyggingar," 10. The construction of the prison is also mentioned in: "Póstskipið," *Víkverji* 2, no. 1 (June 16, 1874): p. 118.

31   "Raki er hér allmikill í flestum eða öllum húsum sem er eðlileg afleiðing þess að þau eru svo mikið gjörð af torfi … ." [There is a lot of humidity in some or almost all houses, which is a natural consequence as they are mainly made of turf …]. Lbs, Handritasafn, 767 Fol., Örk 8, Answer by the Svalbartshreppur district (Hjörfur Þorklesson).

32   "Almennt álíta menn að rakinn hafi ill áhrif að heilsu manna". [In general, many think that humidity has a negative influence on people's health]. Lbs, Handritasafn, 767 Fol., Örk 8, Answer by the Sauðaneshreppur district. "… að hann sé háskalegur fyrir heilsufarið yfir höfuð, og fyrir útbreiðslu næmra sjúkdóma, sem fremur virðast verða illkynyaðir … í rökum en þurrum húsum, þykjast menn einkum hafa veitt þessu eftirtekst um taugaveiki og um difterítis." [… that it is generally dangerous for health, for the propagation of contagious diseases, which may become lethal … in damp rather than in dry houses; it is assumed that people had paid attention to typhoid fever and diphtheria]. Lbs 767 Fol., Örk 8, Answer by the Reykdælahreppur district (Benedikt Jónsson).

33   "Á 3 bæjum í sveitinni eru kýr ekki hafðar undir baðstofulofti og ber það mest á raka." [In three farms in the area, there are no cows under the living area, and that fights humidity well]. Lbs, Handritasafn, 767 Fol., Örk 8, Answer by the Kelduhverfi district.

34   The answers to this question are all quite similar. "Hér enginn sérstakur maður sem menn snúi sér til með húsabyggingar" [There isn't a particular man to whom people turn to regarding construction matters]. Lbs, Handritasafn, 767 Fol., Örk 8, Answer by the Sauðaneshreppur district.

35   News of his death was also spread in Denmark in the pages of the *Ingeniøren* journal: "Dødsfald," *Ingeniøren* 9, no. 42 (October 27, 1900): p. 338. The short career of the engineer was also mentioned in J. J. Voigt, *Statistike Oplysninger angaaende den polytekniske Læreanstalts Kandidater samt Fortegnelse over dens Direktører og Lærere (1829–1902)* (Copenhagen: Schultz, 1903), p. 224.

36   "Húsabótarannsóknirnar," *Ísafold* 27, no. 65 (October 20, 1900): p. 259.

37   Björn Björnsson, *Fyrsti arkitektinn. Rögnvaldur Águst Ólafsson og verk hans* (Reykjavík: Hið íslenska bókmenntafélag, 2016): p. 8. Guðmundur Finnbogason later became one of the most important intellectuals in the country. Rögnvaldur Ólafsson's letters to Guðmundur Finnbogason are archived in the Lbs, Handritasafn, 12 NF. Guðmundur Finnbogason. Skjalasafn. *Bréfasafn. Bréf til Guðmundar Finnbogasonar*. Askja 21. They have been partially reprinted in Finnbogi Guðmundsson, ed. "Þrjú bréf Rögnvalds Ág. Ólafssonar til Guðmundar Finnbogasonar," *Árbók Landsbókasafn Íslands* 10 (1984): pp. 53–60.

38   "Þú fréttir nú lát Sigurðar Péturssonar ingeniörs, og var skaði að honum. Er nú enginn til að takast starfa hans á hendur í húsabótamálinu. Vera má, að það gæti greitt fyrir mér – 'eins dauði er annars líf'". Lbs, Handritasafn, 12 NF. Guðmundur Finnbogason. Skjalasafn. *Bréfasafn. Bréf til Guðmundar Finnbogasonar*. Askja 21. Letter from Rögnvaldur Ólafsson to Guðmundur Finnbogason, Reykjavík, October 25, 1900.

39   Lúðvík Kristjánsson, ed., *Við fjörð og vík. Brot úr endurminningum Knud Zimsens fyrrverandi borgarstjóra* (Reykjavík: Helgafell, 1948).

40   Jantzen became head of the mint at the Bank of Denmark between 1918 and 1946 and worked in the microeconomics field; Sörensen specialized in hydraulic engineering and was director of the Copenhagen groundwater service between 1922 and 1943; Christiani was the co-founder of the world-renowned building firm Christiani & Nielsen, established in 1904.

41   Lúðvík Kristjánsson, ed., *Við fjörð og vík*, p. 95.

42   The *heimastjórn* [home rule] officially started on February 1, 1904, when Hannes Hafstein (1861–1922) was appointed Minister of Iceland in the Danish Cabinet. He was the first Icelander ever to be appointed to this position. In 1903, the parliament agreed that the Minister of Iceland should write and speak Icelandic and reside in Reykjavík, therefore implying that he had to be an Icelander. See: Gunnar Karlsson, *The History of Iceland*, pp. 267–72; Helgi Skúli Kjartansson, *Ísland á 20. öld* (Reykjavík: Sögufélag, 2002), pp. 20–26; Gunnar Karlsson, "Atvinnubylting og rýkismyndun 1874–1918," in *Saga Íslands X*, edited by Sigurður Líndal and Pétur Hrafn Árnason, pp. 263–68.

43   Lúðvík Kristjánsson, ed., *Úr bæ í borg: nokkrar endurminningar Knud Zimsens fyrrverandi borgarstjóra um þróun Reykjavíkur* (Reykjavík: Helgafell, 1952). See also: Sveinn Þorðarson, *Frumherjar í verkfræði á Íslandi*, pp. 39–41.

44   BR, Einkaskjalasafn nr. 25 (E25 KZ), Askja 1, Bréfabók 1903–1905, 458. February 15, 1907.

45   Knud Zimsen started using the telegraph in 1908: he had been promoting the opening of a telephone line to Reykjavik since 1904. Lúðvík Kristjánsson, ed., *Við fjörð og vík*, pp. 139–46.

46   On the role of the Danish language in Iceland, see: Auður Hauksdóttir, "Language and the Development of National Identity: Icelanders' Attitudes to Danish in Turbulent Times," pp. 93–94.

47   Jón G. Friðjónsson, *Mergur málsins. Íslensk orðatiltæki: uppruni, saga og notkun* (Reykjavík: Mál og menning, 2006), p. 450.

48   "Mjölnir," *Reykjavík* 5, no. 12 (1904): p. 45.

49   Seelow, *Die moderne Architektur in Island*, pp. 74–75.

50   Mjölnir produced several kinds of stones, with different dimensions, all cast in timber formwork and with a mixing ratio of 1 : 4 : 7 (cement : sand : gravel). Stones were most probably solid and not hollow. Compared to the price of one cast stone, timber formwork was exceptionally expensive: one formwork costed 3kr, and one medium stone costed 1.30kr. Guðmundur Hannesson, *Húsagerð á Íslandi*, p. 251; "Mjölnir," *Reykjavík* 5, no. 12 (1904): p. 45.

51   Lime cast stones were first produced in Sweden by Ragnhildsborgs kalksandstensfabrik in 1902. In 1916, the Norwegian newspaper *Bergens Tidende* claimed that a Norwegian engineer had researched Swedish concrete cast stones in order to start the production in Norway. "Billigere bygninger," *Bergens Tidende* 49, no. 107 (1916): p. 5.

52   BR, E25 KZ, Askja 1, Bréfabók 1903–1905, 433. September 30, 1906.

53   Erwin Marx, *Wände und Wandöffnungen* (Stuttgart: Arnold Bergsträsser Verlagsbuchhandlung, 1900), pp. 122–24.

54   Albrecht, "Der Betonhohlstein, ein neues Baumaterial," *Beton und Eisen* 5, no. 7 (1906): pp. 166–68.

55   "Verksmiðjan 'Mjölnir'," *Þjóðólfur* 56, no. 3 (January 15, 1904): p. 9.

56   "Mjölnir", *Reykjavík* 5, no. 12 (March 18, 1904): p. 45.

57   Páll Ólafsson, "Um grástein og steypustein," *Reykjavík* 5, no. 15 (April 8, 1904): p. 59. See also the newspaper director's answer to the article, *Reykjavík* 5, no. 17 (April 21, 1904): pp. 66–67. Some experts researched the possibility of producing masonry from Icelandic clay resources. Preben Lange, "Tigulsteinsgerð og móhnoð," *Reykjavík* 5, no. 8 (1904): p. 30, and *Reykjavík* 5, no. 15 (April 8, 1904): p. 58.

58   "[…] því ég hafði svo mikla tröllatrú á þessu fyrirtæki, að ég helt mig geta haft við það aðalatvinnu í framtíðinni". Lúðvík Kristjánsson, ed., *Við fjörð og vík*, p. 120.

59   The letter includes a sketch of a concrete stone by Knud Zimsen. BR, E25 KZ, Askja 1, Bréfabók 1903–1905, 60. May 27, 1904.

60   BR, E25 KZ, Askja 1, Bréfabók 1903–1905, 440. December 9, 1905.

61   "En salan á steininum gekk illa, menn höfðu ekki trú á þessu efni til húsagerðar. Var því einkum fundið það til foráttu, að húsin myndu slaga og verða köld." Lúðvik Kristjánsson, ed., Við fjörð og vík, p. 121.

62   "Húsið Gimli var allt hlaðið úr Mjölnissteini". Lúðvik Kristjánsson, ed., Við fjörð og vík, p. 122.

63   1 inch—þumlungur—is equivalent to approximately 2.4 cm.

64   Guðmundur Hannesson, Húsagerð á Íslandi, p. 252; Lýður Björnsson, Steypa lögð og steinsmíð rís, p. 73.

65   Lúðvik Kristjánsson, ed., Við fjörð og vík, p. 124.

66   Seelow, Die moderne Architektur in Island, pp. 91–92.

67   A. J. Johnson, "Framtíðar húsagjörð. Er hún ekki framkvæmanleg á Íslandi?," Reykjavík 9, no. 27 (1908): pp. 105–06.

68   In 1903, Knud Zimsen conducted research on the production of Trass-sement, which he named veikt sement [weak cement], from clay sources in a gravel bed south of Reykjavík, but the study did not produce any results. Lúðvik Kristjánsson, ed., Við fjörð og vík, p. 85.

69   "Sement! – Sement! Það er djúpstæður og þungur hljómur í þessu orði, sem allar menningarþjóðir þekkja og skilja. Þær vita, að í tjáningu þess, að á baksviði við það sjálft standa mestu og traustustu mannvirki heimsins." Lúðvik Kristjánsson, ed., Við fjörð og vík, p. 128.

70   The gross weight of one barrel was approximately 360pd [pund, meaning pounds]. Lýður Björnsson, Steypa lögð og steinsmíð rís, p. 49.

71   Lbs, Íslandssafn, Stjórnartíðindi fyrir Ísland, C-deild (1882–1907), Aðfluttar vörur.

72   "Var ég ekki kominn heim til þess að starfa að umbótum í mannvirkjagerð á Íslandi? Og hvað var hægt að gera í þeim efnum án sements? Hafði ég ekki kynnzt því, hvernig sumir Reykvíkingar reyndu að hafa úti allar klær til þess að eignast nokkrar tunnur eða jafnvel aðeins nokkrar fötur af þessu grámyglulega dufti?" Lúðvik Kristjánsson, ed., Við fjörð og vík, p. 128.

73   "… að þeir vildu kaupa sement, mikið sement, ef það væri ekki selt við okurverði." Lúðvik Kristjánsson, ed., Við fjörð og vík, p. 127.

74   Founded in 1889, Aalborg Portland-Cement-Fabrik was already one of the most active cement factories in Denmark, perhaps even in all of Northern Europe. Behind the opening of the plant was the Danish company F. L. Smidth & Co. By 1913, the city of Aalborg hosted five cement plants, which exploited Denmark's geological resources, naturally rich in limestone and clay. See: Henning Bender and Morten Pedersen, Aalborg og cementen (Aalborg: Aalborgbogen, 2006); Morten Pedersen, Cementen (Aarhus: Aarhus Universitetsforlag, 2019). On the early stages of Danish cement production, see: Alex Foss, "Nyere Metodere i Cementfabrikationen, særlig Aalborg Portland-Cementfabrik," Den Tekniske Forenings Tidsskrift 15 (1892): pp. 178–82.

75   Lúðvik Kristjánsson, ed., Við fjörð og vík, p. 129.

76   BR, E25 KZ, Askja 1, Bréfabók 1901–1903, 235. January 21, 1903.

77   "Forretningen Godthaab; h. Th. Jensen, der er min störste Kunde her […]". BR, E25 KZ, Askja 1, Bréfabók 1903–1905, 206. March 17, 1905.

78   BR, E25 KZ, Askja 1, Bréfabók 1901–1903, 253. March 20, 1903; BR, E25 KZ, Askja 1, Bréfabók 1903–1905, 225–26. March 26, 1905.

79   Lúðvik Kristjánsson, ed., Við fjörð og vík, p. 129.

80   BR, E25 KZ, Askja 1, Bréfabók 1903–1905, 18–19. February 23, 1904; 20. March 4, 1904; 49. April 29, 1904; 459. February 16, 1907. In order to plan the shipments to several parts of Iceland, Knud Zimsen hired an agent to keep the due correspondence with the plant. BR, E25 KZ, Askja 1, Bréfabók 1903–1905, 222. March 26, 1905.

81   BR, E25 KZ, Askja 1, Bréfabók 1901–1903, 369–70. July 24, 1903.

82   BR, E25 KZ, Askja 1, Bréfabók 1901–1903, 333–34. June 15, 1903.

83   F. L. Smidth-Koncernen, Cementbranchens konkurrenceforhold (Copenhagen: S. L. Møllers Bogtrykkeri, 1959), p. 14.

84   "I Löbet af de 2 Aar, jeg har forhandlet Cement, har jeg erobret saa at sige hele Markedet her ved gerde Forbindelser, personlig Indflydelsen, god Vare og billige Priser og jer har um alle Fordelene paa min Side i en eventuel Priskamp, naar jeg staar med et billigt Tilbud i Hænder". BR, E25 KZ, Askja 1, Bréfabók 1903–1905, 126–29. November 10, 1904.

85   Lúðvik Kristjánsson, ed., Við fjörð og vík, p. 130. See also: BR, E25 KZ, Askja 1, Bréfabók 1903–1905, 252. April 29, 1905.

86   BR, E25 KZ, Askja 2, Bréfabók 1909–1913, 157. June 26, 1909.

87   BR, E25 KZ, Askja 2, Bréfabók 1909–1913, 188–91. July 13, 1909. Löve in Danish means "lion", as was the logo of Aalborg Portland.

88   BR, E25 KZ, Askja 2, Bréfabók 1909–1913, 266–70. August 20, 1909.

89   "Sementið var töfralyf, sem hafði gerbreytt ýmsum kennisetningum mannvirkjafræðinnar. Með það í höndum var hægt að gera þá hluti, sem vísustu verkfræðingar höfðu ekki látið sig dreyma um að nokkurn tíma yrði framkvæmdir, áður en þetta mikilvæga duft kom til sögunnar". Lúðvik Kristjánsson, ed., Við fjörð og vík, p. 128.

90   Sjálfstæðisflokkurinn [The Independence Party] was founded in 1929. Jón Þorláksson's political career can be retraced through a rather laudatory biography written by political science professor Hannes Hólmsteinn Gissurarson, Jón Þorláksson. Forsætisráðherra (Kópavogur: Almenna Bókafélagið, 1992).

91   "Framhaldsreikningar yfir kostnað við rannsókn á byggingarefnum landsins og leiðbeining í húsagerð árið 1903" [Expenses regarding the research on building materials and construction guidelines, 1903], May 11, 1904. ÞÍ, Stjórnarráð Íslands II, Skrifstofa. Bréfasafn, Skrifstofa B/1, Örk 4 (1906).

92   "Reikningur fyrir ferðakostnaði, rannsóknum og áhaldakaupum við rannsókn á byggingarefnum landsins og leiðbeining í húsagerð, árið 1904" [Expenses for travels, research, and purchases regarding the research on building materials and construction guidelines]. January 18, 1905. ÞÍ, Stjórnarráð Íslands II, Skrifstofa. Bréfasafn, Skrifstofa B/1, Örk 4 (1906).

93   "Jon Þorláksson," *Norðurland* 2, no. 48 (1903): p. 191.

94   Jón Þorláksson, "Nýtt byggingarlag. Steyptir steinar, tvöfaldir veggir," *Búnaðarrit* 17, no. 1 (1903): pp. 277–302.

95   Forty, *Concrete and Culture*, p. 226.

96   Jón Þorláksson, "Nýtt byggingarlag," p. 287.

97   Jón Þorláksson, "Nýtt byggingarlag," p. 290.

98   Jón Þorláksson, "Nýtt byggingarlag," p. 301.

99   "Nýt hlutafélag," *Þjóðólfur* 57, no. 6 (February 3, 1905): p. 21. On Peter Jørgensen, see: Eberhard Schunck, Hans Jochen Oster, Rainer Barthel, and Kurt Kießl, *Dach Atlas* (München: Institut für internationale Architektur-Dokumentation, 2002), p. 13.

100   Hannes Hólmsteinn Gissurarson, *Jón Þorláksson*, pp. 151–52.

101   Jón Þorláksson, "Kuldinn og rakinn," *Búnaðarrit* 18, no. 1 (1904): pp. 99–131

102   The metaphor of an ongoing, hopeless war between the Icelandic population and the local climate would become a recurring theme in Halldór Laxness' *Independent People*.

103   Meeting the engineer must have felt a very important occasion. Jakob Hálfdanarson wrote a note about their encounter, which was introduced by the phrase "Til minnis" [to remember]. Lbs, Handritasafn, 4 NF. Askja 18, Örk 6.

104   Erwin Marx's *Wände und Wandöffnungen* suggested slightly stronger ratios up to 1 : 6 : 6 (cement : sand : gravel). For more examples, see: Erwin Marx, *Wände und Wandöffnungen*, pp. 115–16. A copy of this book was available in the National Library in Jón Þorláksson's time.

105   "Mesti húsbruni á Íslandi 1906," *Norðurland* 6, no. 8 (October 20, 1906): p. 27.

106   ÞÍ, Stjórnarráð Íslands II, Skrifstofa. Bréfasafn, Skrifstofa B/6, Örk 2 (1904). See the letter written on July 22, 1904.

107   Jón Þorláksson, "Hvernig reynast steinsteypuhúsin?". Guðmundur Hannesson later published an essay on rural buildings with a special focus on concrete construction: Guðmundur Hannesson, *Skipulag sveitabæja* (Reykjavík: Þorsteinn Gíslason, 1919). See also: Guðmundur Hannesson. "Hlý og rakalaus steinhús. Tillögur og leiðbeiningarm," *Búnaðarrit* 27, no.1 (1913): pp. 1–26. On the developments of Icelandic rural construction in concrete, see: Nannini, *Icelandic Farmhouses*.

108   Lbs, Handritasafn, 12 NF, Guðmundur Finnbogason. Skjalasafn, Bréfasafn, Askja 18.

109   The society had been active since 1867, and in 1904, Knud Zimsen was appointed president. Gísli Jónsson, *Saga Iðnaðarmannafélagsins í Reykjavík* (Reykjavík: Iðnaðarmannafélagið í Reykjavík, 1967).

110   "Iðnskóli Reykjavíkur," *Bæjarskrá Reykjavíkur* (1905): p. 140.

111   Jón Þorláksson, "Iðnskólinn í Reykjavík," *Þjóðólfur* 56, no. 33 (1904): p. 132. On the history of the Technical School, see: Jón Ólafur Ísberg, ed., *Iðnskóli í eina öld: Iðnskólinn in Reykjavík 1904–2004* (Reykjavík: Hólar, 2004).

112   "Iðnskólinn," *Reykjavík* 6, no. 15 (1905): p. 59.

113   Jón Þorláksson, *Burðarþolfræði: Ágrip* (Reykjavík: Iðnskólinn, 1909). The word merges the term *burðarþol* [weight resistance] with the suffix -*fræði* [studies]. Perhaps the Icelandic term *burðarþolfræði* is a direct translation from the German term *Tragwerkslehre*, which may have been used in the literature available to Jón Þorláksson in his study years in Copenhagen.

114   Franz Kugler, *Geschichte der Baukunst. Vol. 1–3* (Stuttgart: Verlag von Ebner & Seubert, 1856–59); Eduard Sacken, *Katechismus der Baustile* (Leipzig: J. J. Weber, 1894).

115   Edvard Kolderup, *Haandbog i husbygningskunst* (Kristiania: H. Ascheoug & Co. Forlag, 1891). The German series, edited by Josef Durm, Hermann Ende, Heinrich Wagner, and Eduard Schmitt, comprised more than a hundred of titles and was published between 1880 and 1943. On the specific volumes held by the National Library of Iceland, see: Lbs, Ritaukaskrá Landsbókasafnsins (1887–1943).

116   Julius Pedersen, *Statik* (Copenhagen: Høst, 1881); also translated in German as *Lehrbuch der Statik fester Körper* (Copenhagen: Høst, 1882). Asger Skovgaard Ostenfeld, *Teknisk Statik* (Copenhagen: Gjellerup, 1900); also translated in German as *Technische Statik. Vorlesungen über die Theorie der Tragkonstruktionen* (Leipzig: Druck und Verlag Von B. G. Teubner, 1904). Ostenfeld was one of the corresponding authors of the journal *Beton und Eisen*, founded by Fritz von Emperger in 1902. See: Karl-Eugen Kurrer, *Geschichte der Baustatik* (Berlin: Ernst, 2003), p. 363, and p. 484 for a short biographical note of Ostenfeld.

117   *Þverflatartregvægi, traustatala, beygjuátakið*. Since the late eighteenth century, the purity of the Icelandic language had been one of the cultural battles in the political struggle for independence from the Danish kingdom. Guðmundur Hálfdanarson, "Severing the Ties," pp. 239–41. See also: Guðmundur Hálfdanarson, and Ólafur Rastrick, "Culture and the Constitution of the Icelandic in the 19th and 20th Centuries," in *Power and Culture: Hegemony, Interaction and Dissent*, edited by Jonathan Osmond, and Ausma Cimdina (Pisa: Pisa University Press, 2006), pp. 87–102.

118 The measures and values of each beam provided by Jón Þorláksson are similar, at times even identical, to the German standards published by Friedrich Heinzerling and Otto Intze, *Deutsches Normalprofil-Buch für Walzeisen zu Bau- und Schiffbau-Zwecken* (Aachen: Verlag Von Jos. La Ruelle, 1897). The volume was reprinted in 1904, a copy of which is held at the DTU library today, which perhaps might have been avaiable to Jón Þorláksson in his years as a student.

119 For an overview on the first reinforced concrete patents, see: Cyrille Simonnet, *Le béton: historie d'un matériau: économie, technique, architecture* (Marseille: Parenthèses, 2005), pp. 39–55; Frank Newby, ed., *Early Reinforced Concrete* (Aldershot: Ashgate, 2001). On the influence of reinforced concrete on the development of structural engineering, see: Hans Straub, *Die Geschichte der Bauingenieurkunst* (Basel: Birkhäuser, 1975), pp. 254–66; Kurrer, *Geschichte der Baustatik*, pp. 336–73; Alexander Kierdorf and Hubert K. Hilsdorf, "Zur Geschichte des Bauens mit Beton," in *Was der Architekt vom Stahlbeton Wissen Sollte: Ein Leitfaden für Denkmalpfleger und Architekten*, edited by Uta Hassler (Zürich: gta Verlag, 2010), pp. 11–54.

120 Gwenaël Delhumeau, *L'invention du béton armé: Hennebique, 1890–1914* (Paris: Norma, 1999).

121 The pamphlet edited by Wayss, *Das System Monier in seiner Anwendung auf das gesamte Bauwesen* (Berlin: Seydel, 1887) soon became the "classic text" on reinforced concrete until the turn of the century, particularly thanks to the calculation theories developed by engineer Matthias Koenen (1849–1924). Kurrer, *Geschichte der Baustatik*, pp. 344–45.

122 Karl-Eugen Kurrer, "La dalle dans le système Monier," in *L'architrave, le plancher, la plate-forme: nouvelle historie de la construction*, edited by Roberto Gargiani (Lausanne: Presses polytechniques et universitaires romandes, 2012), p. 552.

123 Tullia Iori, *Il cemento armato in Italia. Dalle origini alla Seconda Guerra Mondiale* (Roma: Edilstampa, 2001), pp. 60–61. Emil Mörsch, *Der Eisenbetonbau: seine Theorie und Anwendung* (Neustadt: Wayss & Freytag, 1908).

124 Kurrer, *Geschichte der Baustatik*, pp. 358–66.

125 Stephanie Van de Voorde, Sabine Kuban, and David Yeomans, "Early Regulations and Guidelines on Reinforced Concrete in Europe (1900–1950). Towards an International Comparison," in *Building Histories. The Proceedings of the Fourth Conference of the Construction History Society*, edited by James Campbell et al. (Cambridge: The Construction History Society 2017), pp. 345–56. On the first Danish regulations regarding reinforced concrete, see: Ervin Poulsen, *Betonkrav og –praksis. Normen, forskrifter, dokumenter og faglitteratur 1888–1988 i uddrag til brug i skadesager vedr. betonkonstruktioner* (Hørsholm: Statens Byggeforskninsinstitut, 1989), pp. 28–29.

126 Sabine Kuban, "Konstruieren in einer regellosen Zeit. Eisenbetonbemessung zwischen Monier-Broschüre und den ersten behördlichen Vorschriften (1887–1904)," in *Alltag und Veränderung. Praktiken des Bauens und Konstruierens*, edited by Werner Lorenz et al. (Dresden: Thelem, 2017), pp. 205–20.

127 For a brief overview of the history of reinforced concrete in Denmark and its connection to Iceland, see: Sofia Nannini, "Hennebique Moves North: The First Applications of Reinforced Concrete in Iceland (1907–10)," in *Storia della costruzione. Percorsi politecnici*, edited by Edoardo Piccoli, Mauro Volpiano, and Valentina Burgassi (Torino: Politecnico di Torino, 2021), pp. 161–65. See also: Cederberg, "De første bygninger og bygværker af beton og jernbeton i Danmark"; Gunnar M. Idorn, *Concrete Progress: From Antiquity to the Third Millennium*, pp. 24–26.

128 The road was completed only in 1974 with the construction of the last sector in Skeiðarársandur, in southern Iceland. See: "Nú stækkar landið," *Morgunblaðið* 61, no. 121 (July 12, 1974): pp. 14–15.

129 "Alþingi," *Ísafold* 14, no. 40 (August 24, 1887): p. 158.

130 "Alþingi," *Ísafold* 20, no. 59 (August 30, 1893): p. 235.

131 For a brief overview of Iceland's road network and its construction, see: Krabbe, *Island og dets tekniske udvikling gennem tiderne*, pp. 13–34.

132 Sveinn Þórðarson, *Brýr að baki. Brýr á Íslandi í 1100 ár* (Reykjavík: Verkfræðingafélag Íslands, 2006); Krabbe, *Island og dets tekniske udvikling gennem tiderne*, pp. 35–66.

133 Sveinn Þórðarson, *Brýr að baki*, pp. 75–108.

134 The firm was founded in 1904 by civil engineer Rudolf Christiani and captain Aage Nielsen (1873–1945). Their first office was in Copenhagen; soon they opened branches in Aarhus (1906), Hamburg (1908), St. Petersburg (1910), attaining worldwide expansion with offices in South America, Africa, and Asia by the 1940s. Christen Ostenfeld, *Christiani & Nielsen: jernbetonens danske pionerer*; on the first decades of the firm's activities and projects, see: *Christiani & Nielsen. Twenty-Five Years of Civil Engineering. 1904–1929* (Copenhagen: Krohns Bogtrykkeri, 1929). In 1904, the firm became a concessionaire of the Hennebique patent: Nannini, "Hennebique Moves North," pp. 164–65.

135 Pétur H. Ármannsson, "Concrete's Furthest North," *Docomomo Journal: Bridges and Infrastructures* 45, no. 2 (2011): pp. 87–89.

136 The local press followed the construction of the bridge with great attention. See: "Fnjóskárbrúin," *Norðri* 3, no. 22 (June 2, 1908): p. 88; "Fnjóskárbrúin," *Norðri* 3, no. 26 (June 30, 1908): p. 103; "Fnjóskárbrúin hrunin!," *Austri* 18, no. 25 (July 9, 1908): p. 88; "Fnjóskárbrúin," *Óðinn* 5, no. 2 (May 1, 1909): p. 12.

137 Ludwig Hess, "Fnjóská-Brücke auf Island – Landungssteg im Hafen von Hundested," *Beton und Eisen* 8, no. 8 (1909): pp. 188–89.

138 Philip Morton Shand, "In Concrete. Third Series-IV," *The Concrete Way* 5, no. 4 (January 1933): p. 200.

139 Ostenfeld, *Christiani & Nielsen: jernbetonens danske pionerer,* pp. 71–72.

140 Sveinn Þórðarson, *Brýr að baki. Brýr á Íslandi í 1100 ár*, pp. 173–78.

141 ÞÍ, Stjórnarráð Íslands II, Skrifstofa. Bréfasafn, Skrifstofa B/63, Db. 2, nr. 698 (1909). Jón Þorláksson, "Áætlun um kostnað við brúargerð á Fnjóská hjá Vothamri" [Cost evaluation for the construction of a bridge over the Fnjóská river in the area of Vothamri], January 26, 1907.

142 ÞÍ, Stjórnarráð Íslands II, Skrifstofa. Bréfasafn, Skrifstofa B/63, Db. 2, nr. 698 (1909). Letter by Jón Þorláksson to the Cabinet of Iceland, January 26, 1907. The engineer's opinion was also included in the parliament debate. See: "Frumvarp til fjárlaga fyrir árin 1908 og 1909," Alþingi, Alþingistíðindi, *Alþingiskjöl* (1907): p. 45.

143 The call for tenders was published twice in *Ingeniøren*, on November 13 and 15, 1907. The contract was signed by Christiani & Nielsen in January 1908. See: ÞÍ, Stjórnarráð Íslands II, Skrifstofa. Bréfasafn, Skrifstofa B/63, Db. 2, nr. 698 (1909). Letter by the Copenhagen office to the Cabinet of Iceland, January 18, 1908.

144 Pétur Ingólfsson, "Bogabrúin á Fnjóská," *Lesbók Morgunblaðsins* (July 3, 1993): pp. 6–7.

145 Knud Zimsen, *Skýrsla um rannsóknir stjórnarinnar til undirbúnings klæðaverksmiðju á Íslandi* (Copenhagen: J. H. Schultz, 1901).

146 "Mikill húsbruni enn," *Ísafold* 33, no. 50 (August 4, 1906): p. 199. "Klæðaverksmiðjan 'Iðunn'," *Óðinn* 1, no. 1 (April 1, 1905): pp. 4–6.

147 "Klæðaverksmiðjan 'Iðunn'," *Þjóðólfur* 58, no. 49 (November 9, 1906): p. 188.

148 Lýður Björnsson, *Steypa lögð og steinsmíð rís*, p. 73.

149 "Félagið reisir nú á ný verksmiðjuna úr rústum og ríður á vaðið með það að nota nýja húsagerð úr járni og steinsteypu, eftir aðferð *Hennebiques*. … Fyrir smiðinni standa danskir sérfræðingar, vanir þessu byggingarlagi, en svo mun til ætlast að nokkurir Íslendingar, sem taka þátt í vinnunni, læri af þeim og flytji með því þessa þekkingu inn í landið. … Potturinn og pannan í þessari góðu nýung í húsagerð er Krabbe verkfræðingur er …". "Nýung í húsagerð," *Norðurlandi* 6, no. 48 (June 8, 1907): p. 168.

150 Thorvald Krabbe had both Icelandic and Danish origins. His father was a Danish physician and professor. His mother was Icelandic. Despite having worked for three decades in Iceland, apparently Krabbe never spoke good Icelandic, and he moved back to Denmark after his retirement. On Krabbe's work as engineer in Iceland, see: Sveinn Þórðarson, *Frumherjar í verkfræði á Íslandi*, pp. 71–80.

151 The photographs are digitized on the Sarpur database: ÞMÍ, Thorvald Krabbe 2 (TK2) collection.

152 Eventually, Iceland never built a railway network, with the exception of a small rail used during the construction of the Reykjavík harbor in 1917. Krabbe, *Island og dets tekniske udvikling*, pp. 66–71. For an overview of Iceland's railway proposals between 1894 and 1930, see: Þórður Atli Þórðarson, "Land án járnbrauta. Tilraunir Íslendinga til járnbrautvæðingar," Bachelor Thesis in History, University of Iceland, September 2011; Þorleifur Þorleifsson, "Járnbrautin í Reykjavík 1913–1928," *Saga* 11, no. 1 (1973): pp. 116–61. On Krabbe's work in the construction of lighthouses, see: Thorvald Krabbe, *A Few Remarks on Icelandic Lighthouse Practise* (Reykjavík: Iceland Lighthouse Service, 1932).

153 ÞÍ, Vita- og hafnarmálastofnun. Bréfasafn (VHS), B-BDA 1. Bréfabók landsverkfræðings 1906–1909, 932. February 27, 1909.

154 Ornella Fiandaca, *Le béton armé "système Hennebique" a Messina fra XIX e XX secolo: dalle sperimentazioni pre-terremoto del brevetto alle sue declinazioni antisismiche* (Ariccia: Aracne, 2014).

155 ÞÍ, VHS. B-BDA 1. Bréfabók landsverkfræðings 1906–1909, 102. November 10, 1906.

156 The name of the project is not mentioned in the letter, thus one may suggest that Krabbe was dealing with the drawings for the Fnjóská bridge. Although this is a plausible option, the active presence of Krabbe is, however, more certain regarding the reconstruction of Iðunn, while it was Jón Þorláksson who played a prominent role in the coordination of the works at the Fnjóská bridge. Therefore, the project for the factory might have been designed by Krabbe and proposed to both concessionaires before accepting the best deal.

157 ÞÍ, VHS. B-BDA 1. Bréfabók landsverkfræðings 1906–1909, 387. April 17, 1907.

158 Louise Karlskov Skyggebjerg, "E. Suenson og tidlig materialelære i Danmark," *Historisk Beton* lecture series, https://www.youtube.com/watch?v=WT-T8Rbf7U_g, 1:06:41, accessed May 11, 2023.

159 Despite evidence derived from local sources, the Hennebique archival fonds at La Cité de l'architecture et du patrimoine in Paris hold no documents of projects built in Iceland. However, Guðmundur Hannesson refers to the Hennebique patent when describing the Iðunn project. See: Guðmundur Hannesson, *Húsagerð á Íslandi*, p. 252.

160 Jón Þorláksson, "Hvernig reynast steinsteypuhúsin?," p. 207.

161 Jón Guðnason, *Verkfræðingafélag Íslands: 1912–1962* (Reykjavík: Verkfræðingafélag Íslands, 1962).

162 "Tilgangur fjelagsins er að efla fjelagslyndi meðal verkfróðra manna á Íslandi". "Lög fjelagsins," *Ársrit Verkfræðingafélags Íslands 1912/1913* 1 (1914): p. 3.

163 "Nýr fjelagsmaður," *Tímarit Verkfræðingafélags Íslands* 4, no. 3 (1919): p. 32.

164 Respectively: *Ársrit Verkfræðingafélag Íslands* (1912/1913–1914) and *Tímarit Verkfræðingafélags Íslands* (1916–).

165 Frank B. Gilbreth, *Concrete System* (New York: The Engineering News Publishing Company, 1908). See the copy in: Lbs, Íslandssafn.

166 In 1912 and 1913, both Danish engineer C. Bech and his colleague Chr. Petersen visited Reykjavík and discussed the issue. C. Bech, "Jærnbeton, særlig dets Anvendelse ved Vandbygningsarbejder," *Ársrit Verkfræðingafélags Íslands 1912/1913*, pp. 6–7; see also the list of the Society's activities: "Fundarhöld" [Meetings], *Ársrit Verkfræðingafélags Íslands 1912/1913*, p. 4. The first works related to the harbor in Reykjavík took place in 1912–17, then the harbor was continuously enlarged until the postwar years. See: Krabbe, *Island og dets tekniske Udvikling*, pp. 161–69. On the construction of the harbor in Reykjavík and other harbors in the Faxaflói bay, see: Guðjón Friðriksson, *Hér heilsast skipin: saga Faxaflóahafna* (Akranes: Uppheimar, 2013).

167 The establishment of a cement commission was proposed by Knud Zimsen, as reported in: "Önnur störf," *Ársrit Verkfræðingafélags Íslands 1912/1913*, p. 5.

168   "Reglur Verkfræðingafélags Íslands um sölu og prófun Portland-sements," *Tímarit Verkfræðingafélags Íslands* 1, no. 1 (1916): pp. 3–7.

169   Mayntz Petersen, "Íslenzkt steypuefni," *Tímarit Verkfræðingafélags Íslands* 1, no. 1 (1916): pp. 13–16.

170   See the following obituaries: Geir Zoëga, "Jón Þorláksson," *Tímarit Verkfræðingafélags Íslands* 20, no. 1 (1935): pp. 1–2; Steingrímur Jónsson, "Knud Zimsen," *Tímarit Verkfræðingafélags Íslands* 38, no. 4 (1953): pp. 95–96; Emil Jónsson, "Thorvald Krabbe," *Tímarit Verkfræðingafélags Íslands* 38, no. 5 (1953): pp. 111–12; Geir Zoëga, "Sigurður Thoroddsen," *Tímarit Verkfræðingafélags Íslands* 40, no. 6 (1955): pp. 89–90.

171   Björn G. Björnsson, *Fyrsti arkitektinn*, p. 18.

172   Guðný Gerður Gunnarsdóttir and Hjörleifur Stefánsson, *Kvosin*, p. 288; Hörður Ágústsson, *Íslensk byggingararfleifð I*, p. 307; Seelow, *Die moderne Architektur in Island*, pp. 56–57; Pétur H. Ármannsson, "'Veglegasta og vandaðasta steinhús þessa lands'. Safnahúsið frá sjónarhóli íslenskrar húsagerðarsögu," in *Safnahúsið 1909–2009: Þjóðmenningarhúsið*, edited by Eggert Þór Bernharðsson, (Reykjavík: Þjóðmenningarhúsið, 2009), pp. 20–25.

173   Seelow, *Die moderne Architektur in Island*, p. 50. The only exception to this rule was Winstrup, who traveled to Reykjavík before the restoration and expansion of the cathedral in 1846, as seen in Chapter 1.

174   The National Bank was founded in 1885 as the first banking institution of Iceland. Íslandsbanki followed in 1903 as a private institution. See: Pétur Hrafn Árnason and Sigurður Líndal, eds., *Saga Íslands X*, pp. 58–60.

175   Thuren had been a student of architect and Royal Academy of Arts teacher Johan Henrik Nebelong (1817–1871). Seelow, *Die moderne Architektur in Island*, p. 56.

176   Sergio Pace, *Un eclettismo conveniente. L'architettura delle banche in Europa e in Italia, 1788–1925* (Milano: FrancoAngeli, 1999), p. 17.

177   Pace, *Un eclettismo conveniente*, p. 68. As suggested by Seelow, Thuren might have been inspired by the building of Denmark's National Bank, designed in 1865–70 by Johan Daniel Herholdt (1818–1902), and also by Meldahl's Icelandic parliament. Both banks were expanded in the following decades. The National Bank was largely damaged by the Great Fire of 1915. In 1923, the building was restored by state architect Guðjón Samúelsson, who added an extra story and enlarged the plan. A further modernist extension was added by Gunnlaugur Halldórsson in 1934–38. See: Seelow, *Die moderne Architektur in Island*, pp. 340–41; Guðný Gerður Gunnarsdóttir, and Hjörleifur Stefánsson, *Kvosin*, p. 111. In contrast, Íslandsbanki was almost completely transformed in 1962, when four stories were added on top of the original building. See: Guðný Gerður Gunnarsdóttir and Hjörleifur Stefánsson, *Kvosin*, p. 127.

178   "Bankastjóri," *Ísafold* 25, no. 6 (February 2, 1898): p. 21.

179   Haugsted, "Tømrer- og bygmester Bald & Søn."

180   "Myndirnar," *Sunnanfari* 8, no. 3 (June 1, 1900): p. 22; Guðný Gerður Gunnarsdóttir and Hjörleifur Stefánsson, *Kvosin*, pp. 110–11; Seelow, *Die moderne Architektur in Island*, p. 56.

181   "Bankahúsið er til hinnar mestu prýði í bænum …". *Dagskrá* 3, no. 10 (September 24, 1898): p. 39. "Bankahús þetta er sjálfsagt hið vandaðasta og veglegasta hús á landinu". "Myndirnar," *Sunnanfari* 8, no. 3 (June 1, 1900): p. 22.

182   The drawing is reprinted in: Helga Maureen Gylfadóttir and Guðný Gerður Gunnarsdóttir, "Húsakönnun. Austurstræti – Pósthússtræti – Hafnarstræti – Lækjargata" (Reykjavík: Minjasafn Reykjavíkur, 2006), p. 8. The paper is available online at: https://husaskraning.minjastofnun.is/Husakonnun_38.pdf, accessed October 16, 2023.

183   "Bankahúsið nýja," *Ísafold* 32, no. 27 (May 13, 1905): p. 106.

184   "Völundur," *Óðinn* 2, no. 12 (March 1, 1907): p. 92; Leifur Sveinsson, "Þættir úr sögu Timburverzlunarinnar Völundar h.f.," *Morgunblaðið* (February 25, 1979): pp. 36–37.

185   For an overview of Scandinavian national museums built at the turn of the century, see: Barbara Miller Lane, *National Romanticism and Modern Architecture in Germany and the Scandinavian Countries* (Cambridge: Cambridge University Press, 2000), pp. 207–13.

186   Although the core of the Icelandic National Museum collections were moved to a new location in 1950 and a new National Library opened in 1994, the former National Library and Museum is still a symbol for Icelandic culture and a venue for events and exhibitions. In 2000, the original name, Safnahúsið (merging the words *að safna*, to collect, and *hús*, house) was changed into Þjóðmenningarhúsið [The House of National Culture]. The most important accounts on the architectural history of the building are: Finnbogi Guðmundsson, *Úr sögu Safnahússins við Hverfisgötu* (Reykjavík: Árbók Landsbókasafns, 1982); Hörður Ágústsson, *Íslensk byggingararfleifð I*, pp. 307–18; Eggert Þór Bernharðsson, ed., *Safnahúsið*.

187   "Húsið var því ekki aðeins bygging, heldur jafnframt eins konar stefnuyfirlýsing Íslendinga í tilefni nýfenginnar heimastjórnar; Íslendingar voru menningarþjóð með menningarþjóðum sem var fyllilega fær um að reisa sín hús upp á eigin spýtur." Guðmundur Hálfdanarson, "Safnahúsið – Varðkastali og forðabúr íslenskrar þjóðernistilfinningar?", in *Safnahúsið 1909–2009*, edited by Eggert Þór Bernharðsson, p. 51.

188   Pétur H. Ármannsson, "'Veglegasta og vandaðasta steinhús þessa lands'. Safnahúsið frá sjónarhóli íslenskrar húsagerðarsögu," p. 20.

189   On the project by Rögnvaldur Ólafsson, see: Anna D. Ágústsdóttir and Guðni Valberg, *Reykjavík sem ekki varð*, pp. 33–36. The original project is collected in: ÞÍ, Teikningasafn, C. VII. 1. a, b, c, d, e. Skúffa 8, Númer 5.

190   Pétur H. Ármannsson, "'Veglegasta og vandaðasta steinhús þessa lands'. Safnahúsið frá sjónarhóli íslenskrar húsagerðarsögu," pp. 21–23.

191   Johannes Magdahl Nielsen did engage in a correspondence with Icelandic librarians and curators, asking questions on the building's future users and capacity. Traces of this dialogue are in the National Archives of Iceland: ÞÍ, Stjórnarráð Íslands I, Skrifstofa. Bréfasafn, Skrifstofa B/18, Örk 14 (1908). See also: Pétur H. Ármannsson, "'Veglegasta og vandaðasta steinhús þessa lands'. Safnahúsið frá sjónarhóli íslenskrar húsagerðarsögu," in *Safnahúsið*, edited by Eggert Þór Bernharðsson, pp. 24–25.

192   Hörður Ágústsson, *Íslensk byggingararfleifð I*, p. 330.

193   Pétur H. Ármannsson, "'Veglegasta og vandaðasta steinhús þessa lands'. Safnahúsið frá sjónarhóli íslenskrar húsagerðarsögu," p. 30.

194   "Landsbókasafnið nýja," *Ísafold* 33, no. 46 (July 14, 1906): p. 182.

195   The description of the building attached to the construction files reported that the coffered ceiling over the reading room was built according to the Hennebique system. It is hard to confirm whether the adoption of the patent was suggested by Krabbe or by Kiørboe. A short article published in 1909 did refer to "Hennebique-gerðin", meaning that the Hennebique system was adopted for the slabs. See: ÞÍ, Stjórnarráð Íslands I, Skrifstofa. Bréfasafn, Skrifstofa B/18, Örk 14 (1908), "Landsbibliothek og Landsarkiv i Reykjavik. Beskrivelse af Bygningen," p. 4. See also the article: "Landsbókasafnið," *Lögrétta* 4, no. 16 (March 31, 1909): p. 61.

196   "Veglegasta og vandaðasta steinhús þessa lands". "Landsbókasafnið," *Lögrétta* 4, no. 16 (March 31, 1909): pp. 61–62.

197   "Mentasafnið," *Ísafold* 36, no. 24 (May 1, 1909): p. 93. Also reprinted in: "Fjögur söfn undir sama þaki. Á hraðferð um húsið árið 1909," in *Safnahúsið 1909–2009*, p. 14.

198   The main entrance, carved in granite, was imported from Denmark. Pétur H. Ármannsson, "'Veglegasta og vandaðasta steinhús þessa lands'. Safnahúsið frá sjónarhóli íslenskrar húsagerðarsögu," p. 31.

199   Þórunn Sigurðardóttir, "Nafnasveigur á Safnahúsi," in *Safnahúsið 1909–2009*, pp. 36–45.

200   Frederik Kiørboe, "Landsbibliotek i Reykjavik," *Architekten* 12, no. 16 (January 15, 1910): pp. 169–74. See also: Pétur H. Ármannsson, "'Veglegasta og vandaðasta steinhús þessa lands'. Safnahúsið frá sjónarhóli íslenskrar húsagerðarsögu," p. 32.

201   Guðmundur Hálfdanarson, "Severing the Ties," p. 247.

202   "Allar frændþjóðir okkar hafa reist heilsuhæli handa brjóstveikum mönnum, meira að segja Færeyingar fámennasta þjóðin — … Við Íslendingar erum einir eftir." Guðmundur Björnsson, "Ræða landlæknis,*"* *Ársrit Heilsuhælisfélagsins* 1 (1909): p. 24.

203   Beatriz Colomina, *X-Ray Architecture* (Zürich: Lars Müller Publishers, 2019), p. 74.

204   The Schatzalp Sanatorium was designed by Otto Pflegard (1869–1958) and Max Haefeli (1869–1941), together with Robert Maillart, between 1899 and 1900. See: Colomina, *X-Ray Architecture*, pp. 88–90.

205   Björn G. Björnsson, *Fyrsti arkitektinn*, pp. 22–25.

206   Seelow, *Die moderne Architektur in Island*, pp. 86–90; Björn G. Björnsson, *Fyrsti arkitektinn*, 132.

207   In the early twentieth century, being affected by tuberculosis was a rather common condition: the designers of sanatoria were often patients. See, for example, Josef Hoffmann (1870–1956), who frequently checked in at the Purkerdsorf sanatorium which he designed in 1903, and Alvar Aalto (1898–1976), who claimed to have been inspired by a period of illness at the hospital before designing his sanatorium in Paimio (1929–33). On the architecture of the sanatorium and its architects, see: Colomina, *X-Ray Architecture*, pp. 61–116. On the construction of sanatoria in Europe after the First World War, see: Paul Overy, *Light, Air & Openness. Modern Architecture Between the Wars* (London: Thames & Hudson, 2007), pp. 21–28.

208   Björn G. Björnsson, *Fyrsti arkitektinn*, pp. 14–15.

209   Today, the building hosts a nursing home, although most of its premises have undergone substantial changes. The portico is now in ruins. See: Björn G. Björnsson, *Fyrsti arkitektinn*, p. 184.

210   Rögnvaldur Ólafsson listed all the names of those who worked at the building site, from engineers to masons. See: Rögnvaldur Ólafsson, "Lýsing á hælinu," *Ársrit Heilsuhælisfélagsins* 2 (1912): p. 19.

211   "Þetta er fyrsta alíslenzka stórhýsið". "Heilsuhælið," *Ísafold* 36, no. 75 (November 17, 1909): p. 297.

212   "En aðalverk hans er Vífilstaðahælið". Thorvald Krabbe, "Rögnvaldur Ólafsson," *Tímarit Verkfræðingafélags Íslands* 2, no. 1 (March 1, 1917): p. 2.

213   Although the building's transversal section by Rögnvaldur Ólafsson suggests that the last floor should also be in concrete, cast in continuity with the vertical structures, the architect claimed that "the building's upper slab is in timber", and so was the timber roof structure, covered by corrugated iron. Rögnvaldur Ólafsson, "Lýsing á hælinu," p. 8.

214   BR, E25 KZ, Askja 2, Bréfabók 1906–1909, 448 and 450. January 25, 1909; BR, E25 KZ, Askja 2, Bréfabók 1909–1913, 39. March 24, 1909; 71. April 20, 1909; 86. May 3, 1909; 177. July 1, 1909; 310. September 17, 1909; 344. October 25, 1909.

215   BR, E25 KZ, Askja 2, Bréfabók 1906–1909, 475–76. February 5, 1909; BR, E25 KZ, Askja 2, Bréfabók 1909–1913, 53–54. April 3, 1909. Some troubles arose between Knud Zimsen and the building committee concerning their agreements. The engineer was extremely motivated in securing this economic opportunity. BR, E25 KZ, Askja 2, Bréfabók 1909–1913, 181–84, July 1909.

216   BR, E25 KZ, Askja 2, Bréfabók 1909–1913, 217–18. July 29, 1909.

217   BR, E25 KZ, Askja 2, Bréfabók 1909–1913, 299–300. September 19, 1909.

218   Especially in the German-speaking and Nordic countries, where the Monier patent influenced the building industry the most, reinforcement bars were often called "Monier iron"—*Monier-járn*. BR, E25 KZ, Askja 2, Bréfabók 1909–1913, 102. June 4, 1909.

219 Rögnvaldur Ólafsson, "Lýsing á hælinu," p. 19.

220 One newspaper article suggested that the Hennebique patent had been adopted to design the slabs of the sanatorium. In this case, too, it has not been possible to prove this information. See: "Heilsuhælið," *Ísafold* 36, no. 75 (November 17, 1909): p. 297.

221 ÞÍ, VHS, B-BDB/2, Örk 1. Fjós á Vífilsstöðum, March–April 1916.

222 "Jafntraust hús hefur aldrei verið reist hjer á landi; það stendur á klöpp og er alt ein klöpp". "Vífilsstöðum," *Lögrétta* 4, no. 53 (November 17, 1909): p. 210.

223 Seelow, *Die moderne Architektur in Island*, p. 73.

224 Björn G. Björnsson, *Fyrsti arkitektinn*, pp. 176–78; pp. 186–93.

225 "On est en Hyperborée. Cette côte, c'est la terre d'Islande, et cette ville en est la capitale: Reykjavík. ... Elle est entièrement construite en bois,—à part quatre édifices publics: la cathédrale, le palais de l'Assemblée (Althing), la banque et la prison". Pierre Piobb, "Une Capitale en bois: Reykjavík," *Lecture Modernes* 2, no. 22 (1902): p. 1353.

226 Gunnar Karlsson, *Iceland's 1100 Years. The History of a Marginal Society* (London: Hurst & Company, 2000), pp. 182–85; Guðjón Friðriksson, *Saga Reykjavíkur*, pp. 69–84. On the history of Reykjavík, see also: Kristín Ástgeirsdóttir, ed., *Reykjavík miðstöð þjóðlífs* (Reykjavík: Sögufélag, 1978); Páll Líndal, *Reykjavík 200 ára: saga höfuðborgar í myndum og máli* (Reykjavík: Hagall, 1986).

227 Páll Líndal, *Bæirnir byggjast* (Reykjavík: Skipulagsstjóri ríkisins og sögufélag, 1982), p. 104.

228 "Það skal hjer eptir bannað, að gjöra hús eða bæi af torfi, nema í úthverfum kaupstaðarins, og þó því að eins að byggingarnefndin veiti til þess samþykki". Lbs, Íslandssafn, Stjórnartíðindi fyrir Ísland 1894. A-deild. Lög um breytingu á opnu brjefi 29. maí 1839, um byggingarnefnd í Reykjavík, pp. 36–39.

229 Seelow, *Die moderne Architektur in Island*, pp. 162–63.

230 For a comparison, the first building regulations for urban settlements in Norway were emanated in 1896 and published in 1900: Arne Carlsen, *Den almindelige Bygningslovgivning* (Kristiania: H. Aschehoug & Co., 1900).

231 Sofia Nannini, "The City as a Gravel Pile: Building Codes, Concrete, and Urban Dwellings in Reykjavík (1903–45)," in *La città globale. La condizione urbana come fenomeno pervasivo / The Global City. The Urban Condition as a Pervasive Phenomenon*, edited by Marco Pretelli, Rosa Tamborrino, and Ines Tolic (Torino: AISU, 2021), pp. 182–92.

232 "Byggingarsamþyktin," *Reykjavík* 4, no. 32 (June 25, 1903): p. 4.

233 Lbs, Íslandssafn, Stjórnartíðindi fyrir Ísland 1903. B-deild. Byggingarsamþykkt fyrir Reykjavík [Building Code for Reykjavík], pp. 135–44.

234 Lbs, Íslandssafn, Stjórnartíðindi fyrir Ísland 1903. B-deild. Byggingarsamþykkt fyrir Reykjavík, Article 13, p. 137.

235 Lbs, Íslandssafn, Stjórnartíðindi fyrir Ísland 1903. B-deild. Byggingarsamþykkt fyrir Reykjavík, Article 16, p. 138.

236 Lbs, Íslandssafn, Stjórnartíðindi fyrir Ísland 1903. B-deild. Byggingarsamþykkt fyrir Reykjavík, Article 17, pp. 138–39.

237 "Ég hafði sett mjög strangar reglur um smíði steinhúsa, því að ég taldi, að með því væri verið að byggja fyrir framtíðina og því mikils um vert, að til þeirra væri sem bezt vandað". Lúðvík Kristjánsson, ed., *Úr bæ í borg*, p. 31.

238 "Torfbæi og torfhús má ekki byggja". Lbs, Íslandssafn, Stjórnartíðindi fyrir Ísland 1903. B-deild. Byggingarsamþykkt fyrir Reykjavík, Article 29, p. 143.

239 Peter Hallberg, *Halldór Laxness* (New York: Twayne Publishers, 1971), p. 192. On Laxness, see: Halldór Guðmundsson, *The Islander. A Biography of Halldór Laxness* (London: Maclehose Press, 2008).

240 Halldór Kiljan Laxness, *The Fish Can Sing*, trans. M. Magnusson (London: Vintage Digital, 2010). [*Brekkukotsannáll*]. First published in 1957. Laxness's critical stance in regard to the abandonment of turf houses, especially in rural areas, is also evident in the novel *Independent People*: Nannini, *Icelandic Farmhouses*, pp. 76–77.

241 Laxness, *The Fish Can Sing*, p. 246.

242 Laxness, *The Fish Can Sing*, p. 75.

243 "Hverju íbúðarhúsi skal fylgja óbyggð lóð, er ekki sje minni en hússtæðið". Lbs, Íslandssafn, Stjórnartíðindi fyrir Ísland 1903. B-deild. Byggingarsamþykkt fyrir Reykjavík, Article 17, pp. 138–39.

244 "Við hús, sem reist er nær lóðarmörkum en 5 áln., skal gjöra eldvarnarvegg út að nágrannalóð. ... Eldarnarveggi skal gjöra úr steini ... ". Lbs, Íslandssafn, Stjórnartíðindi fyrir Ísland 1903. B-deild. Byggingarsamþykkt fyrir Reykjavík, Article 20, p. 140.

245 "Timburbyggingar þurfa að hætta ... reisa aftur sambyggingar og þá líklega úr cementi og sandi". "Mesti húsbruni á Íslandi 1906," *Norðurland* 6, no. 8 (October 20, 1906): p. 27.

246 Rögnvaldur Ólafsson, "Um byggingarsamþykkt handa Reykjavíkurkaupstað," p. 31. The English translation was published together with the original text.

247 The event was usually referred to as "the Great Fire", *bruninn mikli*.

248 "Steinbær," *Morgunblaðið* 2, no. 212 (June 7, 1915): p. 1.

249 After the destruction caused by the fire, the new building code of Ålesund forbade all timber structures and promoted the use of masonry following a specific law called *Murtvangloven*. Helga Stave Tvinnereim, *Arkitektur i Ålesund 1904-1907: Oppattbygginga av byen etter brannen 23 januar 1904* (Ålesund: Aalsunds Museum, 1981).

250   "Framvegis má ekki byggja neitt hús í Reykjavíkurbæ úr öðru efni en steini eða steinsteypu, eða öðru efni, ekki ótraustara eða óeldtryggara, að dómi byggingarnefndar og bæjarstjórnar, nema þar sem opin bygging er, þ. e. þar sem hús eru ekki sett nær lóðarmörkum en 3,15 metrar, og minst 2 metrar frá götujaðri". Lbs, Íslandssafn, Stjórnartíðindi fyrir Ísland 1915. B-deild. Samþykt um viðauka við byggingarsamþykkt fyrir Reykjavík [Addition to the Building Code for Reykjavík], p. 152.

251   As an example, see the timber house at Grettisgata 26, built in 1904 a few months after the publication of the city's first building code. Hrefna Róbertsdóttir, *Gamli austurbærinn. Timburhúsabyggð í norðanverðu Skólavörðuholti frá byrjun 20. aldar* (Reykjavík: Árbæjarsafn, 1989), p. 21. In 1912, there were 19 concrete and 963 timber buildings in Reykjavík. Guðmundur Hannesson, *Um skipulag bæja* (Reykjavík: Háskóli Íslands, 1916), p. 13.

252   Jón Þorláksson, "Hvernig reynast steinsteypuhúsin?".

253   See the table in: Guðmundur Hannesson, *Um skipulag bæja*, p. 13. See also: Guðný Gerður Gunnarsdóttir, and Hjörleifur Stefánsson, *Kvosin*, p. 295.

254   Hörður Ágústsson, *Íslensk byggingararfleifð I*, p. 322. See also: Seelow, *Die moderne Architektur in Island,* pp. 82–85.

255   Icelandic "concrete classicism" was largely influenced by Danish neo-baroque historicism, such as the works by Ulrik Plesner (1861–1933), Carl Brummer (1864–1953), and Andreas Clemmensen (1852–1928). Seelow, *Die moderne Architektur in Island*, pp. 91–94; Hörður Ágústsson, *Íslensk byggingararfleifð I*, pp. 319–22 and pp. 355–64. Another source of influence might have been the Danish Bedre Byggeskik movement, which had a particular sway on Icelandic rural buildings: Nannini, *Icelandic Farmhouses*, pp. 91–92.

256   On Nordic classicism, see: Simo Paavilainen, *Nordisk klassicism 1910–1930* (Helsinki: Finlands Arkitekturmuseum, 1982); John Stewart, *Nordic Classicism: Scandinavian Architecture 1910–30* (London: Bloomsbury, 2018); Harry Charrington, "Nordic Visions of a Classical World," in *The Routledge Handbook on the Reception of Classical Architecture,* edited by Nicholas Temple, Andrzej Piotrowski, and Juan Manuel Heredia (Abingdon: Routledge, 2020), pp. 356–69.

257   Sigríður Björk Jónsdóttir, "Einar Erlendsson og reykvísk steinsteypuklassík," Dissertation in History, University of Iceland, 1995; Sigríður Björk Jónsdóttir, "Íslensk steinsteypuklassík í verkum Einars Erlendssonar," *Lesbók Morgunblaðsins* (September 26, 1998): pp. 10–12. On Finnur Thorlacius: Finnur Ó. Thorlacius, *Smiður í fjórum löndum* (Reykjavík: Alþýðuprentsmiðjan, 1961).

258   Hörður Ágústsson, *Íslensk byggingararfleifð I*, pp. 325–26. On rural concrete structures, see: Nannini, *Icelandic Farmhouses*, 47–51.

259   See, for example, the house "Galtafell" at Laufásvegur 46 (built by Einar Erlendsson in 1916) and the house at Skálholtsstígur 2 (built in 1927).

260   I would like to thank Mario Bevilacqua for suggesting this comparison. On Einar Erlendsson's Gamla Bíó, see: Hörður Ágústsson, *Íslensk byggingararfleifð I*, pp. 333 and 344.

261   On Icelandic traditionalist architecture in concrete, specifically inspired by the country's vernacular heritage, see: Nannini, *Icelandic Farmhouses*, pp. 62–70.

Chapter 3

Icelandic State Architecture: How Concrete Built a Nation (1916–50)

CONCRETE WAS THE FIRST DURABLE BUILDING
           MATERIAL OF THE ICELANDERS.

              Jónas Jónsson and Benedikt Gröndal, *Íslenzk bygging*, 1957[1]

Until the early twentieth century, Icelandic architecture had been molded by foreign influences. This architectural eclecticism derived from the contrast between public buildings—designed by a diverse group of academically trained Danish architects—and timber dwellings inspired by Scandinavian models and built by local carpenters. As the first generation of Icelandic architects emerged, this inner divergence did not disappear. On the contrary, between the mid nineteen-tens and the early nineteen-fifties, Icelandic architecture included a varied set of influences that coexisted. Those very decades were a pivotal moment for Icelandic political history: in December 1918, the country became an independent sovereign state—Konungsríkið Ísland, the Kingdom of Iceland—in personal union with the Kingdom of Denmark. This implied a substantial separation between Iceland and Denmark: Iceland's neutrality was declared and in 1920, the High Court of Reykjavík acquired the position of Supreme Court.[2] Because of this change in the political system, architecture was entrusted with the task of conveying representative and nationalistic values, acting as one of the cultural elements that could provide Iceland with a tangible image—echoing similar quests for a national architectural language in other Nordic countries such as Finland.[3] Icelandic national architecture did not settle on a single historicist image. Conversely, it adopted a mixed range of languages to pursue the realization of nationalistic meanings through its built heritage: historicists villas with a simplified classical language were built next to neo-Gothic cathedrals, and traditionalist projects emerged beside the first experiments with functionalist design.

The history narrated so far was shaped by master masons, engineers, farmers, and very few architects. As seen in the first chapter, Danish architects in charge of Icelandic public buildings rarely visited the country. At the beginning of Iceland's concrete age and until the mid-nineteen-tens, the only practicing architect on the island was Rögnvaldur Ólafsson. The decade-long task of planning and constructing rural buildings was first overseen by engineers and building experts, and only in 1937 was architect Þórir Baldvinsson (1901–1986) entrusted by the Agricultural Bank with the coordination of the architectural designs for farmhouses.[4] One might even wonder if in the first half of the twentieth century Icelandic architectural history was shaped by architects at all. The first Icelandic engineer returned home from Copenhagen in 1893, and the Icelandic society had to wait until 1919 to welcome an Icelandic architecture graduate. This quarter-century gap gave the country's building industry enough time to experience a technological revolution: by 1919, the Icelandic concrete age had fully and drastically changed local building traditions. Concrete did not only become the most widely available building material, but it was also the target of technical experiments and a conveyor of cultural meanings.

In order to retrace the technological developments and the pivotal significance of concrete within Icelandic architecture before the Second World War, this chapter will focus on the career of Guðjón Samúelsson, state architect between 1919 and 1950, and the single most influential protagonist of the Icelandic architectural scene throughout the first half of the twentieth century.[5] His vast influence originated from his position as state architect of the Kingdom of Iceland, with which he was entrusted in April 1920, after graduating from the Royal Danish Academy of Fine Arts in Copenhagen. Active from the declaration of independence until 1950, the year of this death, Guðjón Samúelsson relentlessly worked on hundreds of public projects of various kinds—housing, churches, hospitals, schools, public buildings—and was supported by dozens of assistants. Some of these buildings still define the cityscape of, for example, Reykjavík or Akureyri, and other historical landmarks such as Reykholt and Þingvellir.[6] Fig. 1

Guðjón Samúelsson oversaw most public buildings erected between the late nineteen-tens and the late nineteen-forties. His approach to architecture was manifold, at the same time experimental and pragmatic. The position as state architect invested his task with political meaning, as he was entrusted with seeking an architecture which could represent Iceland as an autonomous entity with cultural characteristics distinct from Denmark. His first projects were strongly influenced by historicist models and by Scandinavian national-romantic architecture—in particular by his professor Martin Nyrop (1849–1921) and Finnish architect Eliel Saarinen (1873–1950). In the early nineteen-twenties, he made some suggestions for an acropolis of Icelandic culture on the Skólavörðuholt hill, envisioned as a neoclassical square with a church with a Greek-cross plan at its center.[7]

Throughout the variety of languages adopted by the state architect during his long career, the materiality of concrete connected all his projects. This technology became the state architect's only means of expression for the creation of Icelandic civic and religious architecture. Most likely he had not learned about concrete construction during his academic education in Denmark, yet as soon as he returned to Iceland, he got himself involved in the engineering debate being conducted by the Icelandic Engineers' Society. Like his predecessor Rögnvaldur Ólafsson, Guðjón Samúelsson immediately became a member of the Society, published many articles in its journal, and collaborated shoulder to shoulder with many engineers in the years to come.[8] His interest in technical matters also emerged from his readings: for example, he

enthusiastically reviewed a booklet on concrete construction published by Guðmundur Hannesson in 1921.[9] Over the years, Guðjón Samúelsson benefitted from the support of conservative politicians, especially of Jónas Jónsson (1885–1968), also known as Jónas Jónsson frá Hriflu, member of the liberal and agrarian Progressive Party and a very controversial figure of Icelandic political and cultural history.[10] After the architect's death in 1950, his career was praised with a laudatory monograph edited by Jónas Jónsson and Benedikt Gröndal (1924–2010).[11]

Guðjón Samúelsson was not the only practicing architect in the decades before independence: in addition to a great number of master masons active as designers and builders, he was also surrounded by colleagues who by the nineteen-thirties became interested in the emerging *Neues Bauen* and acted as vehicles of the Modern Movement in Iceland.[12] Among them was Sigurður Guðmundsson (1885–1958), whose production was not exempt from the all-pervading use of concrete to the extent that this characteristic was even noticed and appreciated by British architecture critic Philip Morton Shand (1880–1960) in a series of articles published in *The Concrete Way* journal.[13] Shand's knowledge of the Icelandic context might have been the reason behind the publication of Sigurður Guðmundsson's villa for Haukur Thors (1930–31) in the 1941 third edition of *Gli elementi dell'architettura funzionale* by Alberto Sartoris (1901–1998). Ten photographs of Icelandic buildings are held at Sartoris' archive and were personally annotated by Shand.[14]

Fig. 1
Portrait of Guðjón Samúelsson with his father Samúel Jónsson. Photograph by Sigfús Eymundsson, ca. 1900.

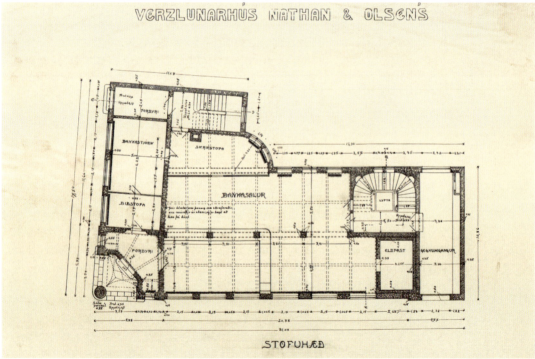

Fig. 2
Guðjón Samúelsson, Nathan & Olsen office building, Reykjavík (1916–17). Postcard.

Fig. 3
Guðjón Samúelsson, Nathan & Olsen office building, Reykjavík (1916–17). Plan of ground floor.

However, despite Iceland's involvement in the Modern Movement, it was Guðjón Samúelsson who most contributed to the construction of an architectural identity for the Icelandic nation in the first half of the twentieth century. The eclectic and experimental ways in which he employed concrete—reinforced and unreinforced, cast or prefabricated, structural or decorative—were specifically addressing the construction of a national architectural language. The multifaceted architecture of the state architect left many examples still visible today, yet lost its energy soon after the end of the war and the establishment of the Republic of Iceland.

Guðjón Samúelsson's earliest Icelandic projects were carried out while he was taking a break from his studies in architecture. He happened to be in Reykjavík after the fire had destroyed most of the city center, and he was given the chance to design the first building to emerge from the deserted plots of land near the parliament house. His project for the Nathan & Olsen office building (1916–17) bore strong resemblance to some notable Finnish examples, such as the Pohjola Insurance or the Telephone Company buildings in Helsinki,[15] and to some Jugendstil projects recently built in Ålesund.[16] Fig. 2

However, by choosing to cover the concrete walls with a cement plaster, Guðjón Samúelsson entirely avoided the debate which most characterized the Finnish and Norwegian projects—that is the use of local natural stone to clad the facades of civic buildings, which imbued them with meanings of national identity.[17] On the contrary, he turned to the increasingly local knowledge on concrete, so that the construction was overseen by master masons Jens Eyjólfsson and Kristin Sigurðsson (1881–1944).[18] The building had cast-in-place concrete walls, and only the underground and ground levels used a reinforced concrete frame. Fig. 3

CONCRETE TO MOLD THE ICELANDIC LANDSCAPE

Before completing his studies, in 1915–16, Guðjón Samúelsson drafted the project for the museum and studio of the popular sculptor and painter Einar Jónsson (1874–1954).[19] Guðjón Samúelsson envisaged the building as a small yet massive concrete fortress, with evident similarities to Eliel Saarinen's monumental proposal for the Finnish house of parliament.[20] Fig. 4

Guðjón Samúelsson's proposal was later revisited by Einar Erlendsson, and Einar Jónsson's participation in the design enhanced the building's sculptural look, to the point that the final version had many of the sculptural qualities already present in a handmade clay model made by the sculptor. Located on top of Skólavörðuholt hill in Reykjavík,

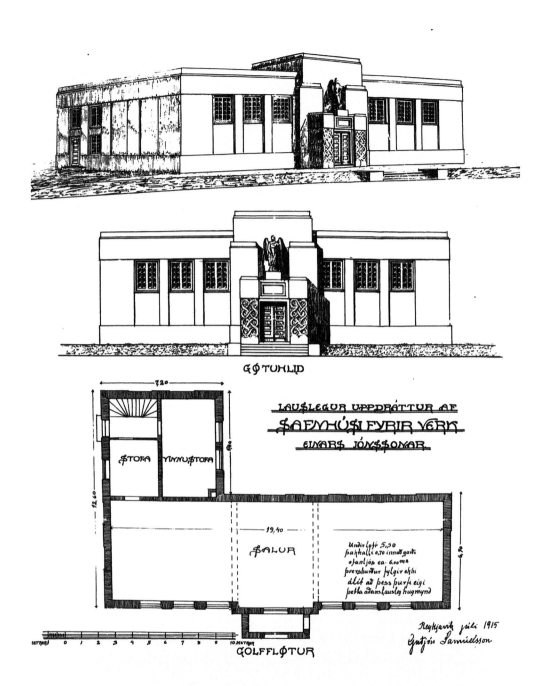

Fig. 4
Guðjón Samúelsson, Project for the
Einar Jónsson Museum (1915).

the museum was inaugurated in June 1923 and was soon compared to "a sort of basaltic pipe organ in a strange future church".[21] Its heavy presence, overlooking the whole city from a rocky hill, could not be ignored, and it was a starting point for many future works of the state architect. For the first time in Icelandic architectural history, the sculptural qualities of concrete were made evident, and they were employed to create an architectural monumentality with an expressionist character. The medium's plasticity even transformed ordinary architectural elements into giant sculptures, such as the spiral staircase on the rear courtyard. The malleable features of the material made the building resemble a piece of Icelandic landscape, completely different from any other architecture present on the island.[22] Fig. 5

Guðjón Samúelsson's most famous design trademark can be found in a series of projects developed since the mid-twenties that revolve around the ornamental motif usually known as *stuðlabergsstíll*—basaltic style—, at times also referred to as *hamrastíll*, or cliff style.[23] The term originated from Iceland's typical basalt formations, which sometimes reach such massive dimensions as to become true national landmarks, such as the formations at Reynisfjara, near Vík í Mýrdal, or the Svartifoss waterfall in South Iceland.[24] The association of such basaltic formations with art and architecture first appeared in some Icelandic newspaper articles published in the early twenties, initially connected to the artworks by Einar Jónsson.[25] Many of his sketches and sculptures highlighted the basaltic motif, obsessively repeated as a sort of metaphor of the Icelandic landscape, the idea of a geological primitive hut, or, in the case of the bas-relief dedicated to politician Jón Sigurðsson, even as a metaphor of the Icelandic people.[26] Figs. 6–8

From the late nineteen-twenties onwards, Guðjón Samúelsson frequently adopted and implemented the basaltic ornament into his designs, and it soon became the most popular signature of the new, national architecture. A hint of his fascination for the basaltic formation can be seen in a drawing for the main facade of the State Hospital, designed and built in 1925–31 in Reykjavík. In this elevation, dated January 1926, the main pediment at the center surrounds a drawing of a typical, pyramid-like Icelandic mountain with basaltic columns on top. Although the bas-relief was not ultimately built according to this specific design, it is interesting to notice the prominent position given to the Icelandic landscape in a building as important to Icelandic society as the National Hospital.[27] Fig. 9

Consistent experiments with basaltic sculptural ornament began with the construction of Landakotskirkja—the Catholic church at Landakot, on a hill overlooking the center of Reykjavík. The building was

Fig. 5
Einar Erlendsson and Einar Jónsson,
The Einar Jónsson Museum and Studio,
Reykjavík (1916–23).

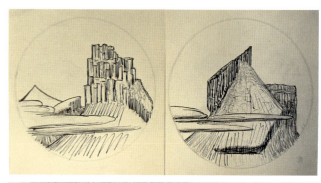

Fig. 6
Einar Jónsson, Sketches of Icelandic mountains, undated.

Fig. 7
Einar Jónsson, *Jól* [Christmas], 1917.

Fig. 8
Einar Jónsson, *Brautryðjandinn* [The Pioneer], Reykjavik (1931).

designed by Guðjón Samúelsson and built in 1925–29.[28] The church was envisaged as a massive neo-Gothic concrete building with three naves and a bell tower above the entrance.[29] Fig. 10

The choice of a neo-Gothic model for Guðjón Samúelsson's church mainly derived from the request of the vicariate, and it may be explained as an architectural outcome of early twentieth-century medievalism which had also infested other Nordic countries.[30] In a country boasting its own medieval culture and literature with pride, and yet without any physical remains of that supposed golden age, Guðjón Samúelsson's neo-Gothic church reflected a specific Icelandic medievalism which seemed to be halfway between that of the "found" and that of the "made" Middle Ages.[31] Icelandic national identity had its roots in a distinctive medieval past, whose timber cathedrals had not, however, created lasting physical ruins in the landscape. As Jónas Jónsson wrote in 1927, "If the Icelanders had learned how to build in stone during the Catholic golden age, there would now be superb cathedrals in Skálholt and Hólar, and beautiful small Gothic churches would adorn every district".[32] Guðjón Samúelsson's choice of a neo-Gothic design could have been a way to praise the Icelandic medieval past and also a way to create an alternative historical image for Reykjavík's urban landscape. Gothic forms, furthermore, might have been generally associated with

Fig. 9
Guðjón Samúelsson, Project for the National Hospital. Elevation, January 1926.

150

Fig. 10
Guðjón Samúelsson,
Catholic church at Landakot,
Reykjavík (1925–29).

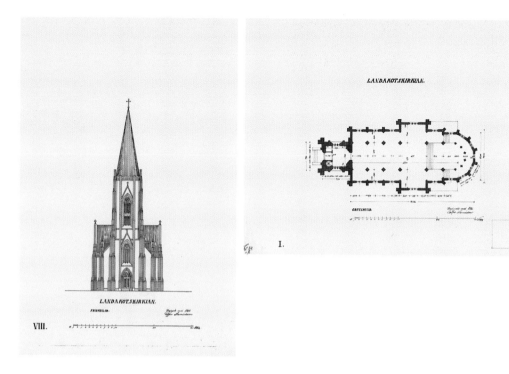

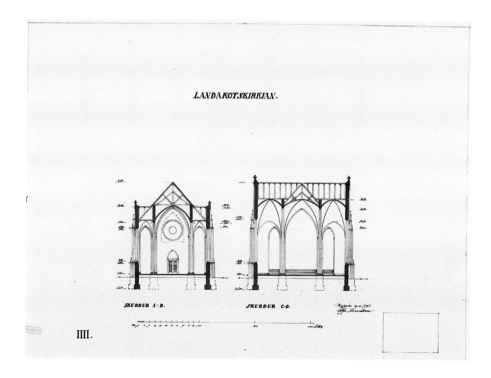

Fig. 11
Guðjón Samúelsson, Project for the church at Landakot, Reykjavík. Elevation. May 1926.

Fig. 12
Guðjón Samúelsson, Project for the church at Landakot, Reykjavík. Plan. May 1926.

Fig. 13
Guðjón Samúelsson, Project for the church at Landakot, Reykjavík. Cross sections. May 1926.

CHAPTER 3 153

Fig. 14
The church at Landakot under construction, 1928.

Fig. 15
The church at Landakot under construction, 1927.

ICELANDIC STATE ARCHITECTURE

the idea of an almost mythical Germanic culture of which Iceland claimed to be the cradle.[33] This choice was not left untouched by harsh criticism, especially by Halldór Laxness, who wrote that "Gothic churches in concrete are another example of a misunderstanding in architecture".[34] Figs. 11–13

Guðjón Samúelsson's church at Landakot was one of the many examples of neo-Gothic and eclectic concrete churches built at the beginning of the twentieth century—both in Europe and overseas.[35] From a structural point of view, the church included several technical novelties in the Icelandic use of concrete.[36] The works were overseen by master mason Jens Eyjólfsson. The inner pillars were made of cylindrical cast hollow blocks, molded in iron formwork. The blocks were prefabricated, piled up around iron reinforcement bars, and the inner hole filled with concrete. The groined vaults, instead, were made of lightweight concrete with pumice as its main aggregate, stretching out over a wire net. Anticipating a specific finishing technique, which will be discussed later in this chapter, fragments of Iceland spar were embedded in the outer walls of the building, thus allowing particular light effects.[37] Figs. 14–15

The church at Landakot was the first architectural project where the basaltic ornament was deliberately adopted as a design choice. The bulky outer pillars, acting as buttresses, were molded to recall the shapes of basaltic formations. As the photographs of the building site show, the whole design was the result of an elaborate intertwining of wooden formworks used for the vertical walls and the basaltic decorations of the pillars.[38] As soon as the construction came to an end, the authorship of the basaltic decoration was debated. Traces of the same sculptural pattern had been seen in Reykjavík before, specifically on the facade of the Egill Jacobsen store at Austurstræti 9, designed by Jens Eyjólfsson in 1920–21. However, the state architect reclaimed the authorship of this concrete pattern, asserting that it was thanks to him that a surface decoration had achieved the sculptural look and dimensions able to transform a building into a piece of the Icelandic landscape.[39] The national meanings behind the basaltic ornament surely derived from Guðjón Samúelsson's intense quest for an architecture which struggled to be considered as wholly Icelandic, and which could represent the country's cultural and natural richness.[40] Figs. 16–17

After the construction of the church at Landakot, concrete and basaltic-like decorations became the trademark of several public projects by Guðjón Samúelsson. The most prominent examples are the National Theatre, designed and built over a quarter of a century from 1925–50,[41] and Hallgrímskirkja, the Lutheran church dedicated to Icelandic poet and Lutheran minister Hallgrímur, first designed in 1937

Fig. 16
Church at Landakot,
Detail of the basalt decoration.

Fig. 17
Jens Eyjólfsson, Egill Jacobsen store,
Austurstræti 9, Reykjavík (1920–21).

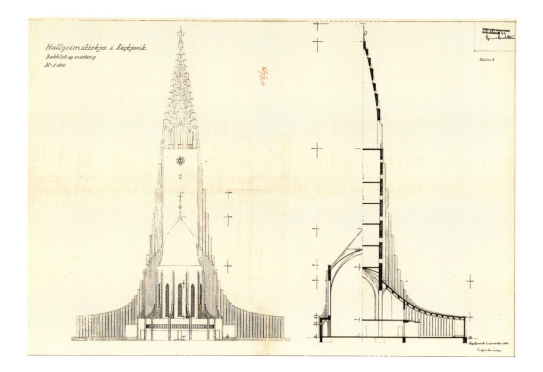

and eventually completed decades later, in 1986.[42] While in these two cases the basaltic motif emerges with particular intensity, simplified, more geometrical variations of the same ornament can also be found in the church of Akureyri (1934–40) and the church of Laugarnes (1940–49).[43] In spite of the long construction process, Hallgrímskirkja eventually became Guðjón Samúelsson's most renowned project and also one of Reykjavík's landmarks thanks to its special position on top of the Skólavörðuholt hill. The church is considered a "conclusion of Guðjón Samúelsson's quest towards a national Icelandic architecture"[44] and it is Iceland's most popular building both in scholarly writings and tourist guides.[45] Fig. 18

However, it is perhaps in the main hall of the National Theatre that the imitation of the basaltic formations reached its peak. There, Guðjón Samúelsson created a three-dimensional effect of concrete basaltic columns hanging from the ceiling, resembling the natural geological formations surrounding the Svartifoss waterfall. Figs. 19–21

Jónas Jónsson was one of the main supporters of Guðjón Samúelsson's basaltic architecture. He created a narrative to support the state architect's authorship over this sculptural pattern and enthusiastically promoted the link between architecture and the natural landscape. He claimed that Guðjón Samúelsson had been influenced by the

Fig. 18
Guðjón Samúelsson, Rear elevation and section for Hallgrímskirkja, Reykjavík, 1942.

Fig. 19
Guðjón Samúelsson, Project for the National Theatre. Pencil drawing.

Fig. 20
The theatre hall under construction.
Guðjón Samúelsson, "Íslenzk byggingarlist," *Tímarit Verkfræðingafélags Íslands* 18, no. 6 (December 1933): p. 75.

Fig. 21
Basalt formations at the Svartifoss waterfall.

basaltic formations in Hofsós, Skagafjörður, which became a model for his buildings.⁴⁶ This association was particularly highlighted in Jónas Jónsson's volume dedicated to the works of Guðjón Samúelsson, where he often juxtaposed the images of the state architect's designs and photographs of Icelandic geological formations. Fig. 22

He used several metaphors: the church of Hallgrímur was "like a basaltic eruption",⁴⁷ the National Theatre was "a palace of elves, where the stones could talk and spoke strange languages. They [the inhabitants of Reykjavík] marveled at that dark cliff with the characteristics of Icelandic mountains."⁴⁸ Drawing on Icelandic folklore such as the legend of *huldufólk* [hidden people], Jónas Jónsson described the state architect's buildings in a way that made them look similar to the imaginary paintings by artist Ásgrímur Jónsson (1876–1958), often starring the Icelandic landscape as if inhabited by elves.⁴⁹ Guðjón Samúelsson also mentioned the parallelism between the theatre and "the palace of an elf king" in one of his articles.⁵⁰ The reference to a magical world of elves may also be linked to the first play with which the theatre was opened in 1950: *Nýarsnóttin* [New Year's Eve] written in 1872 by Indriði Einarsson (1885–1939).⁵¹ Fig. 23

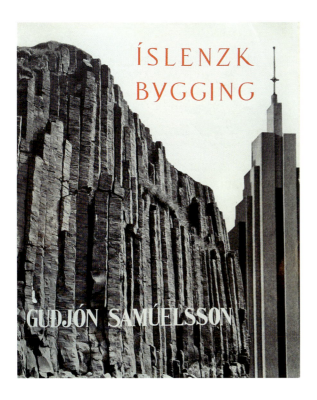

Fig. 22
Jónas Jónsson and Benedikt Gröndal, *Íslenzk bygging*, 1957. Book cover.

Despite Guðjón Samúelsson's ambition to create a national architecture based on the idealized image of the Icelandic landscape, the invention of the basaltic ornament was not completely detached from the architectural developments on the Continent. Already in the eighteen-forties, basaltic rocks were a source of fascination in the sketches of John Ruskin, who recognized the "expressive character" of Gothic architecture in relation with the geological forms.[52]

The most influential building was the Grundtivg's Church in Copenhagen, a refined brickwork designed by Danish architect Peder-Vilhelm Jensen-Klint (1853–1930) in 1913 and built in 1921–40.[53] Not only was this church a prime source of inspiration for Guðjón Samúelsson, but as early as 1916, the building had already been compared to "basaltic formations" by Danish architect Carl Petersen (1873–1923).[54] Fig. 24

Fig. 23
Ásgrímur Jónsson, *Álfakirkja* [Elf Church]. Watercolor (1905).

Fig. 24
P. V. Jensen-Klint, Grundtvig's Church, Copenhagen (1921–40).

Other references might have been Eliel Saarinen's national-romantic projects such as the Finnish parliament house (1908) or the railway station in Helsinki, inaugurated in 1919. Furthermore, one could also find echoes of the crystalline utopias of German expressionism.[55] Guðjón Samúelsson's designs might also be evocative of contemporary art déco decorations.[56] They could also be compared to massive pipe organs, as Einar Jónsson's studio and museum had been described at its inauguration—a rather recurring metaphor, featured in other cases of sacred buildings of the nineteen-thirties, such as the church of Pontinia (1934–35) by Italian architect Oriolo Frezzotti (1888–1965).[57]

Regardless of the intense debate it generated, the actual number of buildings characterized by the basaltic ornament is actually quite low. Guðjón Samúelsson quickly transitioned to a slightly different architectural language, defined by Jónas Jónsson as *lýðveldisstíllinn* [the republic style]. The term referred to many of Guðjón Samúelsson's public buildings of the late nineteen-twenties and the mid-nineteen-thirties, preceding the establishment of the Republic of Iceland. Less monumental and sculptural, they were characterized by marked vertical lines and usually flat roofs, and they might have been influenced by the new architecture of Guðjón Samúelsson's younger colleagues. These projects became very widespread throughout the country as ordinary public buildings like schools and swimming pools.[58] Emerging as an architect only after Iceland's recognition as a sovereign state in 1918, Guðjón Samúelsson focused on representing the country by means of its public buildings. After 1918, however, Iceland was *de facto* independent from Denmark.[59] This implied, perhaps, that local experiments with a national architectural language did not serve a specific political purpose and were soon replaced by more functional projects. Fig. 25

Fig. 25
Guðjón Samúelsson, School in Reykholt (1929–31). Photograph by Vigfús Sigurgeirsson, ca. 1950–56.

Guðjón Samúelsson's neo-Gothic and basaltic designs could be indeed seen as examples of an architectural expression which was "born as a myth".[60] Seelow identified the true peculiarity of the Icelandic basaltic architecture in its late emergence, if compared to the European movements it might have been inspired by. It is, however, important to highlight another specificity of Guðjón Samúelsson's sculptural decorations—a technical one, that is the all-encompassing use of concrete for its accomplishment. From a construction point of view, the role of concrete in the development of this ornament was undeniable: acting as a liquid stone, concrete could be molded and modeled freely enough to obtain shapes that imitated Icelandic nature, or even emulated the elaborate brickwork achievements, as with Grundtvig's Church. The complex design behind many basaltic ornaments in concrete was often the result of an intricate structure of wooden formworks, which helped cast the structure and the decoration at the same time. Such attention given to wood-working could have been linked to the knowledge of timber construction shared by many Icelandic builders, who had worked extensively with timber before the popularity of concrete rose in the mid-nineteen-tens.

Drawing on Sixten Ringbom's study on the use of natural stones in Nordic architecture, Seelow claimed that the adoption of the "basaltic style" helped Icelandic builders embrace the idea that a national architecture could refer to a national material—at least metaphorically.[61] Considering the importance of concrete in the actual definition and realization of such a sculptural trademark, one may even argue that at this point the national material of Iceland was not a specific natural stone or its metaphor but concrete itself. Icelandic concrete may be considered one of the many "national concretes" of twentieth-century architectural history.[62] Figs. 26–27

GEOLOGY AND THE SURFACE OF CONCRETE: THE ORIGINS AND DECLINE OF *STEINING*

Early twentieth-century Icelandic architecture was not affected by any specific debate regarding a "new national style focused […] on the nature and authenticity of materials", as it had been the case in other Nordic countries since the nineteenth century.[63] Timber, on the one hand, was not as largely available as in Scandinavia; at the same time, natural stones and their use in architecture were not at the center of attention, whereas the topic had kept many architects occupied in Norway, Sweden, and Finland.[64] Nevertheless, Icelandic builders were

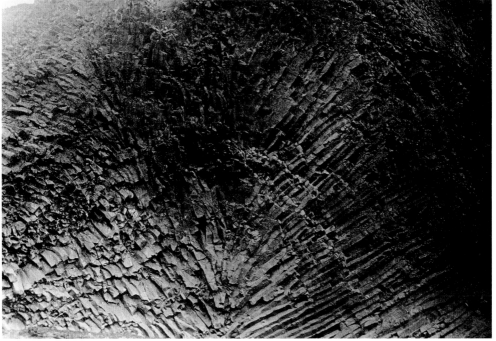

Fig. 26
Guðjón Samúelsson, Hallgrímskirkja, Reykjavík (1937–86). Detail.

Fig. 27
The "fan". Basalt.
Hljóðarklettar near Ásbyrgi, ca. 1900.

not indifferent to this issue: already in the eighteen-seventies, Sverrir Runólfsson had strived for a construction method employing Icelandic stones, such as rough lava and basalt. However, not only had Icelandic stones always been very hard to quarry and work, thus preventing their steady use as building material, but they were also historically linked to the buildings designed by Danish architects since the eighteenth century. When Guðjón Samúelsson started working in Iceland, concrete was everywhere: it had established itself as the most popular building technique in the country, out of necessity and thanks to the efforts of many Icelandic engineers and construction experts. There was another step to take: how to transform a common and rather anonymous technique into a national material? How to let the richness of the Icelandic landscape emerge from bare concrete walls? If imitating the basaltic formations was basically a matter of architectural design and proper placement of the formwork, how did Icelandic builders achieve a truthful metamorphosis of cast concrete into Icelandic natural stones? Instead of cladding the concrete structures with stone slabs, Guðjón Samúelsson—together with many Icelandic architects and builders—was looking for a different solution. The goal was to solve both this and also other practical problems: to hide the flaws and inaccuracies of rough concrete surfaces and protect them from the harsh weather. Fig. 28

In the years of Guðjón Samúelsson, most building sites employed timber formwork to cast concrete structures.[65] This development may sound counterintuitive, considering the scarcity of wood in the country and the high importation costs. However, many building companies specialized in timber had been active in Iceland since the late nineteenth century. With the rise of concrete construction they adapted to the necessities of the new technique, thus producing formwork. The Völundur company, for example, which had specialized in timber structures, advertised the production and sale of timber formwork in the nineteen-twenties.[66] Similarly, timber planks for formwork were increasingly advertised in many journals and newspapers: they were usually sold by those very traders who also offered cement, corrugated iron, and other building materials.[67] Much information on how formwork was conceived in the first decades of the century can be found in Guðmundur Hannesson's 1921 handbook on concrete and also in his 1942 volume on Icelandic construction history.[68] The author listed four different kinds of formwork in use in Iceland: *Sveinatungumót*, the moveable formwork named after the Sveinatunga farm; *flekamót*, a formwork made of timber planks and without vertical supports; *Reykjavíkurmót* (or *þiljamót*), the "formwork of Reykjavík", very popular in the city, with vertical and diagonal supports, and another moveable

formwork called *tangarmót*, "pincers formwork". Eventually, the "formwork of Reykjavík" became the most popular method for casting concrete: it was based on the use of metal elements to connect the two outer vertical supports. When the connections were made of wire, they would be left within the concrete walls and hidden when smoothing its surface. At times, the connections were instead made of cylindrical iron bars, which would be pulled out from the walls, creating small holes both in the timber supports and the concrete. Since the late nineteen-twenties, a few brands of wood-wool boards were publicized in Icelandic newspapers, such as the Austrian Heraklith and the American Masonite, which could be used both as formwork and insulation.[69] After the Second World War, most building technology changed: a greater variety of materials and tools became available, such as cranes and moveable formwork in metal and steel.[70]

Many imperfections on concrete surfaces derived from the use of formwork—maybe it was not properly placed or made of reused material.[71] Yet it was not only the formwork that caused imperfections on the surface: the reason often was the inaccurate mixing ratio of the components and sometimes also the large amount of water added to the mixture.[72] Until the early nineteen-twenties, concrete was usually mixed by hand, poured into the formwork using barrels, and levelled with paddles. To facilitate this task, some builders started adding greater amounts of water in order to produce a less dense mixture, which, however, resulted in weaker structures.[73] Concrete mixers first appeared in the mid-nineteen-tens, yet in the countryside such machines were mostly amateurishly constructed and usually powered by horses. Overall, bare concrete surfaces were usually uneven and rough, exposed to the severe weather conditions of the country. Cement plasters were typically applied to the exterior surfaces, yet with mixed outcomes in terms of waterproofing and aesthetics.[74] By the early

Fig. 28
Horse-powered concrete mixer in use in the countryside, ca. 1940–42.

nineteen-thirties, Guðjón Samúelsson arrived at a solution: turning a common pebbledash render into *steining*, his own patented, all-Icelandic, and largely debated finishing technique.

The state architect first experimented with his own version of a concrete render in 1930, as he was supervising the works for the National Theatre in Reykjavík.[75] The theatre was one of the most expensive architectural projects ever built in the country.[76] Icelandic engineer Jón Gunnarsson (1900–1973), who graduated from the Massachusetts Institute of Technology in 1931, becoming the first Icelandic engineer ever to be trained at an American institution, strongly criticized the way the structural works on the National Theatre had been carried out. The vertical structures, completed by 1933, were massive, unreinforced, 70-centimeter thick concrete walls. Only the horizontal structures, calculated by engineer Steinn Steinsen (1891–1981), were reinforced.[77] Jón Gunnarsson blamed it on the fact that Icelandic concrete buildings were being treated as if they had been built of turf, therefore requiring massive vertical structures.[78] Furthermore, not only were the vertical structures exceedingly thick, but there were also many inaccuracies in the placement of the formwork.

Cement finishings had already been in use in Iceland since the early nineteen-twenties, as the exterior surfaces had always been "the greatest trouble" of Icelandic concrete construction.[79] Outer concrete walls were usually coated with a cement plaster made with one part cement and two parts sand, a few centimeters thick.[80] Due to cold temperatures, however, the cement plaster tended to come off the concrete walls, which were often subject to cracks.[81] Within this context, the emergence of *steining* was due to two unrelated factors: the worldwide economic downturn that had struck Iceland, causing a halt in the construction of the theatre, and the severe winters which exposed the concrete surfaces to the rigors of snow and strong winds. By 1933, the theatre was completed, yet it remained empty of furniture and finishing. Fig. 29

Fearing permanent damage, engineer and then Mayor of Reykjavík Jón Þorláksson suggested that rough concrete surfaces be protected by cement and gravel render. However, another issue had started occupying the minds of Icelandic builders: leaving the concrete surface unfinished, or even coating them with another gray layer of cement, was not considered aesthetically pleasing. In 1903, Jón Þorláksson had already suggested the use of sand "of different colors" to decorate concrete cast stones.[82] In 1926, artist Guðmundur Einarsson (1895–1963) proposed the coating of concrete buildings with white quartz powder, "as if they were made of light gray marble".[83] Later, in 1942, Guðmundur Hannesson claimed that the color of concrete was "exceptionally ugly", therefore the builders had to prevent the "drowned rat effect" created by cement plasters.[84] When it came to protecting and decorating the surfaces of the theatre, in order to avoid a bleak gray layer on the whole building, Guðjón Samúelsson first proposed using Norwegian Mineralit render, known in Iceland as *mineralpuss*.[85] Common in Iceland since the early nineteen-thirties, Mineralit consisted of a mix of ground granite and mortar, applied on the outer walls and cleaned with hydrochloric acid: a version of what is generally known as roughcast.[86] Mineralit was often advertised in the Norwegian press, especially for its similarity to real granite ashlars.

Due to the economic downturn, by 1933, the import of foreign materials was too expensive, and this additional restriction inspired Guðjón Samúelsson to experiment with local geological resources.[87] The theatre was entirely rendered with a sort of pebbledash made of a selection of Icelandic rocks, such as obsidian, quartz, rhyolite, and Iceland spar.[88] If, at first, the decision was triggered by economic and structural reasons, the final result pointed in a completely different direction: transforming a cheap yet necessary finishing technique into an ode to the Icelandic landscape and a precious enrichment of the country's public architecture. Figs. 30–32

Fig. 29
The National Theatre under construction. Photograph by Loftur Guðmundsson, 1932.

Fig. 30
The National Theatre, main facade.

Figs. 31, 32
The National Theatre, detail of the *steining* render.

Considering its components and application, Guðjón Samúelsson's *steining* bore a strong resemblance to the widespread British pebbledash, in use in Iceland since the nineteen-twenties.[89] Roughcast and pebbledash are lime- or cement-based renders which were particularly popular in Scotland and England.[90] Both techniques share the use of pebbles and a cement or lime mortar, yet they are slightly different: the roughcast implies that pebbles are directly mixed with the mortar and then applied on the surface. To make pebbledash, a thin layer of mortar is first spread on a limited area of the wall, then the ground stones are quickly applied with the help of a trowel.

In 1934, Guðjón Samúelsson desperately tried to patent his *steining* coating in Iceland by sending his documentation to the Ministry of Industry.[91] In particular, he highlighted a few characteristics that would make his *steining* different from common pebbledash and more suitable to cold climates.[92] He insisted that the binding agent for the underlays should be cement only, in order to make it as resistant as possible against the Icelandic climate. A first layer had to be applied to the whole surface, and its mortar had to be composed of 1 part cement and 2 ½ parts hard sand. The second layer, for which the mixing ratio had to be 1 : 2, was spread on a small area at a time with a thickness of around 4mm. Hard stones were chosen, ground, and applied on the outer layer by hand with a trowel. After a few days, the whole surface could be washed with normal or slightly acid water.

In May 1935, the Icelandic Ministry refused filing the patent.[93] By 1939, however, the architect managed to file patents in both Denmark (1937) and the UK (1939), and afterwards he resubmitted the patent documents in Iceland.[94] He was supported by several politicians, including Þorsteinn Briem (1885–1949), former minister of industry and transport and member of parliament.[95] Despite the political support, the state architect's patent proposal was strongly opposed by Múrarafélag Reykjavíkur [The Reykjavík Master Masons' Society].[96] The Society refused to see such a common surface render under a private patent. By the end of the decade, *steining* had become very widespread in Reykjavík, and the adoption of a patent would have much increased its price, already at least twice as expensive as an ordinary cement plaster.[97] The architect filed the Icelandic patent in 1941, but the property issue was later brought to court and the patent was revoked by the Icelandic government in 1945.[98] This event was followed by the annulment of the Danish and British versions, and the argument was eventually resolved by letting the technique fall into the realm of the common finishing methods available for Icelandic builders.[99] The issue reflected the complex relationship between Icelandic workers and the few educated experts who struggled to leave their own mark on the development of local architecture.

Regardless of Guðjón Samúelsson's failure in filing the patent, *steining* did boast a different characteristic if compared to ordinary pebbledash. It was "uniquely Icelandic", and this Icelandicness originated from the selection of rocks decorating the buildings' surfaces.[100] These very rocks could transform an ordinarily rendered surface into a vibrant architecture which praised the geological richness of the country. In 1940, the state architect claimed that "Iceland seemed to be the poorest among all countries when it comes to building materials". Although the situation had already changed with the arrival of cement, he labeled gray concrete buildings as "unartistic", as they did not match as perfectly with the Icelandic landscape as did the traditional turf houses.[101] Therefore, by coating the surfaces with obsidian, quartz, and other local geological resources, a plain and dull material was transformed into the Icelandic landscape itself.

Dark obsidian was mainly mined near the Törfajökull glacier in the south, or in the Þingeyjarsýsla county in the north-east, and transported to Reykjavík by ship.[102] The presence of pointed obsidian fragments in the *steining* mixture resulted in very dark shades on the concrete surface, as in the case of the National Theatre. Shiny quartz was mined in the Mosfellsbær area, near Reykjavík. Its deposits were discovered mostly in the vicinity of some gold mines which had been active since 1909.[103] An interesting application of both obsidian and quartz can be seen on the facade of the church in Akureyri, in northern Iceland. Dark obsidian splinters were used to mark the edges of the pillars, while pale quartz pieces covered the rest of the surface. Fig. 33

The most precious material to be found in the *steining* render is ground Iceland spar. Usually, however, only the cheapest and most opaque fragments of Iceland spar were used for coating purposes.[104] Today, a few buildings still boast the original *steining* render and pebble mix. One of them is the modern villa commissioned by chemist Trausti Ólafsson and designed by master mason Guttormur Andrésson (1895–1958) in 1934, whose *steining*-rendered walls include translucent Iceland spar, black obsidian, and other volcanic rocks.[105] Since 1937, ground seashells—*skjeliamulning*—also became part of the *steining* tradition. They were introduced to produce a shiny finish, which was cheaper than crystals.

The utmost synthesis of this geological variety can be seen in the main building of the University of Iceland, part of the campus designed and built by Guðjón Samúelsson in 1934–40.[106] Fig. 34

Fig. 33
The church of Akureyri, detail of the *steining* render.

Fig. 34
Guðjón Samúelsson, Main building of the University of Iceland, Reykjavík (1934–40).

"In no other building on Earth can be found a similar decoration", claimed Jónas Jónsson, referring to the diversified application of *steining* both on the outside and inside.[107] The concrete render was one of the main topics of the rector's inauguration speech, proudly asserting that the building was a symbol of Iceland's construction materials.[108] Also, the state architect's specific interest in the surface renders was reported in the daily construction report.[109] The decoration of the concrete surface was achieved both with regular *steining* for the outer walls and the ceilings and by cladding the inner walls with precast slabs.[110] The rendering of the whole building took more than one year, and it absorbed much of Guðjón Samúelsson's energy. He personally supervised all trials on the renders and even located the precise spot on the Reykjanes peninsula from where to collect seashells for the *steining* blend.[111] While the stones were usually ground with the help of grinders, seashells had to be first separated from shingles, and this was done by hand by "three girls" on site.[112]

The vestibule's walls were covered with seashell-rendered slabs, whereas the ceiling was coated with calcite fragments of Iceland spar, surrounded by ground obsidian on a blue cement field. Figs. 35–36

The main doorway was rendered with a mixture of ground obsidian together with greenish rhyolite. The floor was covered with dolerite, whereas the main hall's vestibule was clad with red rhyolite slabs. The altar of the university chapel was decorated with clear Iceland crystals; the whole outer facade was rendered with a quartz-based *steining* blend, for which approximately 7 tons of quartz were employed.[113] The final result had a very powerful effect. Not only did the local aggregates generate a polychromy able to elegantly decorate a somber and austere building, but this symphony of stone fragments became an architectural mirror of the Icelandic geology and, consequently, a built eulogy to the island's natural landscape. Given the political interest in the technique, which emerged in the hectic years moving towards Iceland's declaration of independence, *steining* was ultimately not limited to technical matters, but it also acquired nationalistic meanings. Since its emergence in the early nineteen-thirties, *steining* has become so popular that overall it was used to cover thousands of buildings.[114]

Radical changes had occurred in Icelandic building traditions since the end of the Second World War, which altered the country's economy and allowed more imports of foreign goods and materials. At first, some builders experimented with imported rocks to be added to the *steining* blend. One example is the Heilsuverndarstöð Reykjavíkur [Reykjavík Health Center] by architect Einar Sveinsson (1906–1973), built in 1949–55. The reddish facade is entirely rendered with a *steining* mix of

Fig. 35
Guðjón Samúelsson, Drawing of the *steining* render on the ceiling above the entrance of the building, ca. 1930–39.

Fig. 36
Detail of the *steining* render on the ceiling above the main entrance.

ICELANDIC STATE ARCHITECTURE

German red marble and Icelandic calcite.[115] By the beginning of the nineteen-sixties, however, *steining* was eventually abandoned and replaced by plastered pre-cast structures, or by using *völun*, that is cast concrete treated with chemical retarders, allowing the concrete aggregates to emerge on the surface.[116] Only during the nineteen-nineties was the technique resumed, with the aim of restoring most of the architectural heritage dating back to the years of Guðjón Samúelsson.[117]

As became apparent from the state architect's failure in obtaining a patent, *steining* and ordinary pebbledash were technically much too similar. Icelandic *steining* had much in common with other contemporary finishing renders, such as ordinary pebbledash common in Great Britain or the Belgian *cimorné* in use in Flanders until the early nineteen-sixties.[118] Despite the characteristics it shared with contemporary techniques, *steining* stemmed from a distinct history and was granted a completely different future. When it was first employed, it physically reflected the country's material shortage and the national pride for the development of Icelandic architecture. When it was rediscovered in the nineteen-nineties, *steining* was not treated as a burden from the past—as postwar pebbledash is sometimes considered today in the United Kingdom—but as a key quality of Iceland's twentieth-century built heritage.[119] *Steining* can be placed on the thin line that divides nature and artificiality, once again expressing one of the many dichotomies that characterize concrete, as Adrian Forty writes.[120] Although his invention did not differ enough from other render techniques to be granted a patent, Guðjón Samúelsson was able to imbue it with a variety of meanings that could change the way one would look at his concrete surfaces. The use of this coating technique was particularly evocative of several elements of Icelandic construction: economic struggle, resource scarcity, geology, nationalism, and architectural experimentations were all condensed into a single yet expressive layer of concrete render.

AFTER 1944:
THE AMERICANIZATION OF ICELANDIC ARCHITECTURE

The Second World War was a pivotal watershed in Icelandic history. In April 1940, Denmark was occupied by Germany, and one month later, Iceland was occupied first by British forces and subsequently by troops from the United States.[121] The Allied occupation helped overcome the economic downturn that had shaken Iceland since the early nineteen-thirties, and yet the presence of such a vast military force had profound social and cultural consequences.[122] Furthermore, the German occupation of Denmark further distanced Iceland from the Danish kingdom. In May 1944 a referendum took place, and on June 17, the day of Jón Sigurðsson's birthday, the new Republic of Iceland was officially celebrated at Þingvellir.[123] Icelandic independence was not born out of a revolution, but it had developed through a slow transformation of the country's institutions since the establishment of home rule in 1904 and the Act of Union in 1918. Nevertheless, the declaration was undoubtedly a much-expected event, and it became a turning point in Iceland's recent history.[124]

The reaction of Icelandic engineers to the declaration of independence, as published in July 1944 in the journal of the Engineers' Society, defied a predictable nationalistic rhetoric.[125] Beyond the overall satisfaction regarding the new political situation, Icelandic engineers overcame merely nationalistic arguments and instead celebrated independence by pointing out the important contribution of Danish and Nordic engineering to Icelandic technical expertise. They thanked foreign institutions such as the Polytechnic School of Denmark, a "role model" for the recently opened degree courses in engineering at the University of Iceland, launched in 1940. The internationality and openness of Icelandic engineers stemmed from their varied academic education and experiences. However, their reaction addressed a very important topic: that Iceland was independent from a political point of view, but it was still much dependent on foreign technical knowledge, materials, and machinery. One of the achievements of the postwar years was the need of becoming independent regarding one key imported good: cement.

Architecture and construction were deeply affected by the political and economic changes brought on by the worldwide events of the nineteen-forties. Since the beginning of the decade, most vernacular building techniques were slowly being replaced by international construction methods. In 1944, Reykjavík hosted Iceland's first conference and exhibition on building techniques, which addressed several issues regarding housing, planning, and the production of building materials.[126] New building materials were introduced to the public, such as locally-produced pumice slabs and blocks to be employed for insulating purposes.[127]

Since the occupation by military troops in 1940, the population of Reykjavík had started to increase rapidly and the need for housing exploded. As a result, many people started living in the barracks built by the British and American soldiers. This "barrack life" had a tangible impact on the Icelandic population until the late nineteen-sixties.[128] For years, a rather high number of inhabitants were registered as homeless.[129] In order to address such critical conditions, in 1942 the City

Council of Reykjavík planned the construction of a number of five-story apartment buildings first on the eastern outskirts of the city, which were then replicated in several areas. The project was carried out by a team led by architect Einar Sveinsson, who drew inspiration from a number of different housing projects built in the Nordic countries in the nineteen-thirties.[130] The height of these buildings implied that concrete was finally going to be used as suggested by Rögnvaldur Ólafsson almost thirty years before—"to build more densely"—and that the obsolete building code of 1903 had to be fully revised. These buildings were among the first examples of reinforced concrete structures applied on a large scale for housing purposes. Fig. 37

Already discussed by Einar Erlendsson at the 1944 conference, the new building code for Reykjavík was issued in 1945.[131] The code stressed the use of concrete as the only building method allowed in the city—timber and other materials were subjected to a particular permit that could only be granted by the building commission. The code also defined precise guidelines on the type of cement, the quality and the storage of the aggregates, the design mix, production, and application of concrete, of the formwork and the reinforcement bars, and a whole chapter was devoted to concrete structures. In particular, the very weak design mix

Fig. 37
Einar Sveinsson and Ágúst Pálsson,
Apartment building at Hringbraut 35–49,
Reykjavík (1942).

required by the 1903 building code changed greatly: in the new code, reinforced concrete for walls and foundations could not be weaker than 1 : 3 : 3. The code did not mention turf farms anymore: willing to forget its vernacular past, Reykjavík was moving towards the future faster than ever, and its new building code became the written promise for a scientific use of building materials. In the same years, rural buildings also underwent a material revolution, and turf construction was permanently abandoned in the countryside.[132]

Construction was now going to be only in the hands of professional architects and engineers, established building companies, and master masons' societies, whose contributions led to a comprehensive modernization of the building industry. However, this process was by no means fast and without obstacles. In October 1948, architect Einar Sveinsson published a long article in the *Morgunblaðið* newspaper acknowledging the many weaknesses of Icelandic concrete construction.[133] He asked publicly for the direct attention of the government in building matters and, more importantly, promoted further research on concrete aggregates and cement production.

Einar Sveinsson's voice was not unimportant, and his key role in the postwar architectural debate was a sign that the times had largely changed since the early nineteen-forties. Graduated from the Technische Hochschule in Darmstadt in 1932, he had been city architect of Reykjavík since 1934, director of city planning, and member of the building commission.[134] Guðjón Samúelsson acted as state architect until his death in 1950, and yet his position had weakened in time as the number of active architects increased, as did their role in city and planning commissions. Despite the large dimensions of the state architect office, by the nineteen-forties there were also many private practitioners in the country.[135] Originating from Byggingameistarafélag Íslands, established in 1926, Akademíska arkitektafélag—the Iceland Architects' Society—was founded in 1936, with Guðjón Samúelsson as its first president. This event separated, at least formally, the activities and responsibilities of architects from those of engineers.[136]

By 1944, Icelandic architecture was not in the hands of Guðjón Samúelsson alone anymore. In the first years of the Republic of Iceland, many public buildings emerged in the capital, such as schools, churches, and the headquarters of the National Museum, whose somber and functional design had become the face of the "Reykjavík of the future", as defined by architect Þórir Baldvinsson.[137] Fig. 38

Besides the shared use of concrete and the *steining* render, these buildings defined a point of departure from Guðjón Samúelsson's eclectic production. When he passed away in 1950, he was remembered through plentiful obituaries which appeared in several newspapers and journals.[138] After his death, the position of state architect was appointed to his longtime collaborator Einar Erlendsson.[139] With the death of Guðjón Samúelsson, however, one of Icelandic architecture's most debated chapters ended, that of the search for a national architectural language. The idea of a basaltic architecture was put aside; its forms oddly and anachronistically reappeared on Reykjavík's highest point only with the late consecration of Hallgrímskirkja in 1986. *Steining* and the geological metaphor it embodied also slowly disappeared, only to be rediscovered again at the end of the century.

The American sway left a mark on Iceland during the hectic postwar years. The availability of building materials drastically changed, and Icelandic professionals were being educated not only in Europe but also in the United States and Canada.[140] On top of that, the increasing population demanded a greater number of housing projects, which saturated Reykjavík and its outskirts and enlarged many urban settlements throughout the country.[141] Moreover, economic and social influence deriving from the United States had become a key factor in Iceland's development since 1940 and lasted throughout the Cold War.[142] The effects of such a pervading process of Americanization—as defined by Jean Louis Cohen—were also seen in Iceland's building industry and architectural culture.[143] Examples can be found in many areas: from the diffuse advertisement of North American building materials and machinery in Icelandic technical journals to the 1964 design proposal for the Reykjavík City Hall, envisaged as a curtain-wall skyscraper.[144] The influence of the United States can mainly be seen on the outskirts of Reykjavík and other settlements, and their low-density neighborhoods are easily comparable to North American suburbia.[145] The fascination for detached houses in Icelandic postwar society was portrayed by author Svava Jakobsdóttir in her short novel *Leigjandinn* [The Lodger].[146]

It is sometimes difficult to find any connections between the architectural and construction histories narrated so far and the transformations that occurred in Icelandic architecture during the second half of the twentieth century. At the same time though, as a robust *fil rouge* which connects late nineteenth-century rural experiments to today's architectural studios, concrete was a legacy which the postwar years did not set aside. The process was slow and not without obstacles. In 1942, some members of the Icelandic Engineers' Society complained about the lack of regulations regarding reinforced concrete structures.[147] The Society highlighted the absence of detailed regulations again in 1955.[148] Throughout the twentieth century, cement—the "magic potion" described by Knud Zimsen[149]—, and concrete—a "revolution"[150] of the local architectural practice—lived up to the expectations of Icelandic builders. Rooted in a rural past, Icelandic concrete went through a great variety of amateurish trials, academic research, architectural experimentations, and national rhetoric, until it established itself as the main construction technique for building postwar Iceland.

Fig. 38
Sigurður Guðmundsson,
National Museum of Iceland,
Reykjavík (1945–52).

CHAPTER 3　　　　　　　　　181

ICELANDIC STATE ARCHITECTURE

ENDNOTES

1   "Steinsteypan var fyrsta varanlega byggingarefni Íslendinga." Jónas Jónsson and Benedikt Gröndal, eds., *Íslenzk bygging. Brautryðjandastarf Guðjóns Samúelssonar* (Reykjavík: Norðri, 1957), p. 108.

2   On the Act of Union, see: Gunnar Karlsson, *The History of Iceland*, pp. 280–84; Guðmundur Hálfdanarson, *Íslenska þjóðríkið*, pp. 135–38. Helgi Skúli Kjartansson, *Ísland á 20. öld*, pp. 71–77.

3   Ritva Tuomi, "On the Search for a National Style," *Abacus* 1 (Helsinki: Museum of Finnish Architecture, 1979), pp. 57–96; Malcolm Quantrill, *Finnish Architecture and the Modernist Tradition* (London: E. & F.N. Spon, 1995), pp. 1–27; Fabienne Chevallier and Anja Kervanto Nevanlinna, "La nation finlandaise, entre mémoire et projet," in *Idée nationale et architecture en Europe, 1860–1919: Finlande, Hongrie, Roumanie, Catalogne,* edited by Jean-Yves Andrieux, Fabienne Chevallier, and Anja Kervanto Nevanlinna (Rennes: Presses universitaires de Rennes, 2006), pp. 207–19; Charlotte Ashby, "The Pohjola Building: Reconciling Contradictions in Finnish Architecture," in *Nationalism and Architecture*, edited by Raymond Quek and Darren Deane, with Sarah Butler (Farnham: Ashgate, 2012), pp. 135–46.

4   Nannini, *Icelandic Farmhouses*, pp. 70–92. See also: Ólafur J. Engilbertsson and Pétur H. Ármannsson, eds., *Þórir Baldvinsson* (Reykjavík: Sögumiðlun, 2021).

5   Seelow, *Die moderne Architektur in Island*, pp. 107–53; Pétur H. Ármannsson, *Guðjón Samúelsson húsameistari* (Reykjavík: Hið íslenska bókmenntafélag, 2020).

6   Reykholt was one of the most important Icelandic settlements during the Middle Ages. In particular, it was the residence of famous historian and poet Snorri Sturluson. Geir Waage, *Reykholt: sagan* (Reykholt: Snorrastofa, 1996).

7   Seelow, *Die moderne Architektur in Island*, pp. 168–73; Pétur H. Ármannsson, *Guðjón Samúelsson húsameistari*, 135–43. See also: Ólafur Rastrick, *Háborgin. Menning, fagurfræði og pólitík í upphafi tuttugustu aldar* (Reykjavík: Háskólaútgáfan, 2013).

8   Among his articles, see: Guðjón Samúelsson, "Íslensk húsagerð og skipulag bæja," *Tímarit Verkfræðingafélags Íslands* 15, no. 1 (1930): pp. 1–8; Guðjón Samúelsson, "Íslenzk byggingarlist. Nokkrar opinberar byggingar á árunum 1916–1934," *Tímarit verkfræðingafélags Íslands* 6, no. 18 (1933): pp. 53–82.

9   Guðmundur Hannesson, *Steinsteypa. Leiðarvísir fyrir alþýðu og viðvaninga* (Reykjavík: Iðnfræðafjelag Íslands, 1921); Guðjón Samúelsson, "Steinsteypa," *Morgunblaðið* 10, no. 131 (April 10, 1923): p. 4. On Guðmundur Hannesson's booklet, see: Nannini, *Icelandic Farmhouses*, pp. 58–59.

10 Ólafur Rastrick, *Háborgin*, pp. 185–91; Ólafur Rastrick and Benedikt Hjartarson, "Cleaning the Domestic Evil – On the Degenerate Art Exhibition in Reykjavík, 1942," in *A Cultural History of the Avant-Garde in the Nordic Countries*, edited by Benedikt Hjartarson (Leiden: Brill, 2019), pp. 879–902.

11 Jónas Jónsson and Benedikt Gröndal, eds., *Íslenzk bygging*.

12 The reception and development of functionalism in Iceland was thoroughly presented by Seelow, *Die moderne Architektur in Island*, pp. 175–236 and 265–311. See also: Hörður Ágústsson, "Tid för framsteg," in *Nordisk Funktionalism*, edited by Gunilla Lundahl (Stockholm: Arkitektur Forlag AB, 1980), pp. 76–79; Júlíana Gottskálksdóttir. "Byggingarlist," in *Í deiglunni 1930–1944. Frá Alþingishátíð til lýðveldisstofnunar* (Reykjavík: Mal og Menning, 1994), pp. 155–64; Pétur H. Ármannsson, "The Development of Reykjavík in the 1920s and 1930s and the Impact of Functionalism," in *Nordisk Funksjonalisme*, edited by Wenche Findal (Oslo: Ad Notam Gyldendal, 1995), pp. 45–62; Guðmundur Gunnarsson, ed., *Icelandic Architecture* (Aarhus: Arkitektskolen i Aarhus, 1996); Pétur H. Ármannsson, "Reconstruction in Prosperity. An Introduction to Modern Architecture in Iceland," *Docomomo Journal: Nordic Countries* 19 (1998): pp. 46–48; Pétur H. Ármannsson, "Social Aspects and Modern Architecture in Iceland," in *Modern Movement Scandinavia: Vision and Reality*, edited by Ola Wedebrunn (Copenhagen: Fonden til udgivelse af arkitekturtidskrift, 1998), pp. 99–105.

13 Philip Morton Shand, "Concrete's Furthest North," *The Concrete Way*, incorporating *The Road Maker* 7, no. 6 (May/June 1935): pp. 330–35; Sigurður Guðmundsson, "Three New Concrete Buildings in Iceland," in "In Concrete. Third Series– XXVI," *The Concrete Way*, incorporating *The Road Maker* 9, no. 2 (September/October 1936): pp. 100–103; "A Concrete Sheepfold at Réttir, Iceland", in "In Concrete. Third Series–XX," *The Concrete Way*, incorporating *The Road Maker* 8, no. 2 (September/October 1935): p. 98.

14 Antoine Baudin, ed., *Photography, Modern Architecture and Design. The Alberto Sartoris Collection. Objects from the Vitra Design Museum* (Lausanne: EPFL Press, 2005), p. 84. On Sigurður Guðmundsson's career, see: Pétur H. Ármannsson, ed., *Sigurður Guðmundsson Arkitekt* (Reykjavík: Listasafn Reykjavíkur, 1997); Seelow, *Die moderne Architektur in Island*, pp. 175–95. On Sartoris's book, see: Cinzia Gavello, *Alberto Sartoris attraverso "Gli elementi dell'architettura funzionale". Genesi e fortuna critica di un libro* (Milano: FrancoAngeli, 2020).

15 The Pohjola Insurance Building was designed and built by Herman Gesellius (1874–1916), Armas Lindgren (1874–1929), and Eliel Saarinen in 1899–1901; the Telephone Company Headquarters in Helsinki by Lars Sonck (1870–1956) were built in 1904–05. For the comparison between these projects and Guðjón Samúelsson's office building, see: Seelow, *Die moderne Architektur in Island*, p. 113. On the Pohjola building, see: Fabienne Chevallier, *L'œuvre d'Eliel Saarinen en Finlande et la question de l'architecture nationale de 1898 à 1909* (Paris: Publications de la Sorbonne, 2001), pp. 141–52.

16 See, for example, the Svane Apoteket by architect Hagbarth Schytte-Berg (1860–1944), built in 1905–07, or the building at Notenesgate 9 by architect Karl Norum (1852–1911), built in 1906–07.

17 Sixten Ringbom, *Stone, Style and Truth: The Vogue for Natural Stone in Nordic Architecture 1880–1910* (Helsinki: Suomen muinaismuistoyhdistyksen aikakauskirja, 1987).

18   Atli Magnus Seelow, "Verslunarhús Nathan & Olsen við Austurstræti. Hornsteinn Guðjóns Samúelssonar að nýjum miðbæ Reykjavíkur," *Saga. Tímarit Sögufélags* 50, no. 1 (2012): pp. 9–21.

19   On Einar Jónsson's life and career, see: Ólafur Kvaran, *Einar Jónsson myndhöggvari* (Reykjavík: Hið íslenska bókmenntafélag, 2018).

20   Seelow, *Die moderne Architektur in Island*, pp. 110–11. Saarinen's sway on Guðjón Samúelsson is indisputable: some sketches found in the state architect's library collection are a proof of this influence. Guðjón Samúelsson used to copy some projects by Saarinen published in the *Moderne Bauformen* journal, available in Copenhagen during his study years. Pétur H. Ármannsson, *Guðjón Samúelsson húsameistari*, pp. 40–42 and 46–49. On Saarinen's parliament building for Finland and its mountain-like qualities, see: Kurt. W. Forster, "Berg und Tal in Bauten der Neuzeit," in *Felsengärten, Gartengrotten, Kunstberge. Motive der Natur in Architektur und Garten*, edited by Uta Hassler (München: Hirmer, 2014), pp. 48–49.

21   "... eins og stuðlabergs-orgel í einhverja furðulega framtíðarkirkju." Guðmundur Finnbogason, "Listasafn Einars Jónssonar opnað í dag," *Morgunblaðið* 10, no. 1932 (June 24, 1923): p. 2.

22   Ólafur Kvaran, *Einar Jónsson myndhöggvari*, pp. 180–83 and 189–91.

23   Seelow, *Die moderne Architektur in Island*, pp. 123–26.

24   Basalt formations are common in other contexts in the North Atlantic, such as the Scottish island of Staffa in the Inner Hebrides, where massive basaltic formations have been a tourist site since the early nineteenth century and were often likened to manmade architecture. See: Jan Pieper, "Werke der 'Baumeisterin Natur' in Schilderungen der Romantik," in *Felsengärten, Gartengrotten, Kunstberge*, pp. 136–53.

25   Ágúst H. Bjarnason, "Íslenzkir listamenn. Einar Jónsson, myndasmiður," *Iðunn* 8 no. 3–4 (January/April 1922): pp. 214–34; H. Franzson, "Íslenzk húsgerðarlist," *Skólablaðið* 1, no. 4 (April 17, 1926): pp. 12–13; Jónas Jónsson, "Byggingar VIII," *Samvinnan* 23, no. 1 (March 1929): pp. 72–76.

26   The work is titled *Brautryðjandinn* [The Pioneer] and it is part of Einar Jónsson's monument to the politician and leader of the independence movement, Jón Sigurðsson. The monument includes a statue, made in 1911, which was moved in front of the parliament house in 1931. When moved, a new base by Guðjón Samúelsson was added, together with the bas-relief.

27   On the construction of the hospital, see: Pétur H. Ármannsson, *Guðjón Samúelsson húsameistari*, pp. 144–52.

28   Jónas Jónsson and Benedikt Gröndal, *Íslenzk bygging*, pp. 54–57; Seelow, *Die moderne Architektur in Island*, pp. 116–18. See the paragraphs by Gunnar F. Guðmundsson, "Þættir úr byggingarsögu Kristskirkju", and by Pétur H. Ármannsson "Lýsing kirkjunnar" and "Byggingarlist kirkjunnar" in the chapter "Kristskirkja í Landakoti," in *Fornar kirkjur í Reykjavík. Dómkirkjan, Fríkirkjan, Krirstskirkja. Kirkjur Íslands* (Reykjavík: Hið íslenska bókmenntafélag, 2012), pp. 193–223; Pétur H. Ármannsson, *Guðjón Samúelsson húsameistari*, pp. 180–88.

29   The bell tower should have been topped by a tall spire, which eventually was not built. See the drawings: ÞÍ, Húsameistari ríkisins. Bréfa- og teikningasafn, Safn A(D), flokkur 21, verkefni H–L, Örk 30. A model for Guðjón Samúelsson's project might have been the church of the Abbaye royale in Celles-sur-Belles, whose tall central tower, slender inner pillars, and pointed groined vaults strongly influenced the final Icelandic design: Gunnar Guðmundsson, "Kristskirkja í Landakoti," pp. 202–03.

30   Guðjón Samúelsson's earliest design (1920) envisaged a Romanesque church with round arches and coated in white plaster. See: "Kristskirkja í Landakoti," pp. 195–96. On medievalism in twentieth-century Finnish architecture, see: Tuomi, "On the Search for a National Style," pp. 81–85. On the "Gothic", "Old Norse", or "Dragon Style" revival in Sweden and Norway, see: Lane, *National Romanticism and Modern Architecture in Germany and the Scandinavian Countries*, pp. 62–69.

31   As Louise d'Arcens writes, medievalism can be either of the "'found' Middle Ages" or of the "'made' Middle Ages", the former emerging "through contact with, and interpretation of, the 'found' or material remains of the medieval past", and the latter encompassing "texts, objects, performances, and practices that are not only post-medieval in their provenance but imaginative in their impulse and founded on ideas of 'the medieval' as a conceptual rather than a historical category". Louise D'Arcens, "Introduction. Medievalism: Scope and Complexity," in *The Cambridge Companion to Medievalism*, edited by Louise D'Arcens (Cambridge: Cambridge University Press, 2016), p. 2.

32   "Ef íslendingar hefðu kunnað að byggja úr steini á blómaöld kaþólskunnar myndu nú standa veglegar dómkirkjur í Skálholti og á Hólum og fagrar gotneskar smákirkjur prýða hverja sveit". Jónas Jónsson, "Landakotskirkja," *Tíminn* 11, no. 57 (December 23, 1927): p. 216. The most prominent examples of medieval timber buildings in Iceland were the churches of Skálholt and Hólar, the two main sites of the Icelandic Church. See: Gunnar Karlsson, *The History of Iceland*, pp. 38–43. On the churches and their archaeological remains, see: Kristján Eldjárn, Hakon Christie, and Jón Steffensen, *Skálholt: fornleifarannsóknir 1954–58* (Reykjavík: Lögberg, 1988); Hörður Ágústsson, *Skálholt: kirkjur* (Reykjavík: Hið íslenska bókmenntafélag, 1990); Hjörleifur Stefánsson, Kjell H. Halvorsen, and Magnús Skúlason, eds., *Af norskum rótum*, pp. 16–19.

33   On Gothic architecture as the expression of a Germanic "genius", often with racist undertones, see: Irene Cheng, "Structural Racialism in Modern Architectural Theory," in *Race and Modern Architecture: A Critical History from the Enlightenment to the Present*, edited by Irene Cheng, Charles L. Davis II, and Mabel O. Wilson (Pittsburgh: University of Pittsburgh Press, 2020), pp. 138–42.

34   "'Gotneskar' kirkjur úr steinsteypu eru enn eitt dæmi misskilnings í byggingarlist." Halldór Laxness, "Sálarfegurð í mannabústöðum," in *Húsakostur og híbýlaprýði*, edited by Hörður Bjarnarson et al. (Reykjavík: Mál og menning, 1939), p. 118. See also: Seelow, *Die moderne Architektur in Island*, p. 236.

35   See, for example, the essay by Stephanie Van de Voorde and Roony De Meyer, "L'application innovante du béton armé dans la construction d'églises en Belgique. Béton sacré ou usine à prière?," in *Édifice & Artifice*, pp. 587–96. See also the Canadian cases discussed in Barry Magrill, "Pouring Ecclesiastical Tradition into a Modern Mould," *Journal of the Society for the Study of Architecture in Canada* 37, no. 1 (2012): pp. 3–15. Many eclectic churches in reinforced concrete were also published in the *Beton und Eisen* journal: Leopold Bauer, "Die katholische Pfarrkirche in Bielitz," *Beton und Eisen* 10, no. 11 (July 1911): pp. 229–32; F. v. Perko, "Die evangelische Kirche in Innsbruck," *Beton und Eisen* 6, no. 2 (1907): pp. 36–38.

36   Jónas Jónsson, "Landakotskirkja," pp. 216–17; "Landakotskirkjan nýja," *Morgunblaðið* 15, no. 121 (May 27, 1928): p. 5; Guðjón Samúelsson, "Kaþólska kirkjan," *Morgunblaðið* 15, no. 163 (June 7, 1928): 6; Jónas Jónsson, "Byggingar VIII," pp. 72–76.

37   The surface render has been removed during later restorations. See: "Kristkirkja í Landakoti," p. 212.

38   In the project report, Guðjón Samúelsson asserted that the pillars and the arches had to be built in reinforced concrete. ÞÍ, Húsameistari ríkisins. Bréfa- og teikningasafn, B/210, Örk 1, 1926–1996. Ýmsar kirkjur. However, the detailed drawings related to the reinforcement are not present in the National Archives. According to Guðmundur Hannesson, the first application of reinforcement bars in cast-in-place concrete walls occurred in the Kjartan Thors house, designed by Sigurður Guðmundsson in 1927. Guðmundur Hannesson, *Húsagerð á Íslandi*, p. 258. On reinforced concrete, see the series of articles by Jón Þórlaksson, "Steinsteypa til íbúðarhúsagerðar I," *Tímarit Verkfræðingafélags Íslands* 17, no. 4 (1932): pp. 34–45 and in *Tímarit Verkfræðingafélags Íslands* 17, no. 5 (1932): pp. 49–53; 18, no. 1 (1933): pp. 12–14; 18, no. 3 (1933): p. 32.

39   The dispute appeared in pages of the *Morgunblaðið* newspaper, as Guðjón Samúelsson responded to an article published on the newly built church: "Landakotskirkjan nýja," *Morgunblaðið* 15, no. 121 (May 27, 1928): p. 5; Guðjón Samúelsson, "Kaþólska kirkjan," *Morgunblaðið* 15, no. 163 (July 17, 1928): p. 6.

40   Seelow, *Die moderne Architektur in Island*, p. 118.

41   On the National Theatre, see: Jónas Jónsson, *Þjóðleikhúsið: þættir úr byggingarsögu* (Reykjavík: Ísafoldprentsmiðja, 1953), p. 118; Hörður Ágústsson, *Íslensk byggingararfleið I*, pp. 350–51; Seelow, *Die moderne Architektur in Island*, pp. 127–33; Pétur H. Ármannsson, *Guðjón Samúelsson húsameistari*, 246–59. The project was published in: Guðjón Samúelsson, "The National Theatre, Reykjavík, Iceland," *The Builder* 180, no. 5650 (June 1951): pp. 784–85.

42   Jónas Jónsson and Benedikt Gröndal, *Íslenzk bygging*, pp. 62–67; Seelow, *Die moderne Architektur in Island*, pp. 144–51; Sigurður Pálsson, *Mínum drottni til þakklætis: saga Hallgrímskirkju* (Reykjavík: Hallgrímskirkja, 2015); Pétur H. Ármannsson, *Guðjón Samúelsson húsameistari*, pp. 316–36.

43   Jónas Jónsson and Benedikt Gröndal, *Íslenzk bygging*, pp. 58–61; Seelow, *Die moderne Architektur in Island*, pp. 138–43.

44   Seelow, *Die moderne Architektur in Island*, p. 144.

45   Hallgrímskirkja is one of the very few Icelandic buildings featured in Marian C. Donnelly, *Architecture in the Scandinavian Countries* (Cambridge, Mass./London: MIT, 1982), p. 333.

46   Jónas Jónsson, Benedikt Gröndal, *Íslenzk bygging*, p. 109. See also Jónas Jónsson's positive reception of the church at Landakot: Jónas Jónsson, "Landakotskirkja," *Tíminn* 11, no. 57 (December 23, 1927): pp. 217–18.

47   Jónas Jónsson, "Hallgrímskirkja í Reykjavík," *Tíminn. Jólablað* (December 23, 1942): pp. 9–10.

48   "Það var álfahöll, þar sem steinarnir höfðu mál og töluðu annarlegar tungur. Þeir undruðust þennan dökka klett með einkennum íslenzkra fjalla." Jónas Jónsson, *Þjóðleikhúsið: þættir úr byggingarsögu*, p. 118.

49   On Ásgrímur Jónsson, one of the most prominent Icelandic painters at the beginning of the century, see: Júlíana Gottskálksdóttir, *Ljósbrigði: Safn Ásgríms Jónssonar* (Reykjavík: Listasafn Íslands, 1996).

50   Guðjón Samúelsson, "Íslenzk byggingarlist. Nokkrar opinberar byggingar á árunum 1916–1934," p. 75. Elves are a key part of Icelandic folklore and are present in many folktales. See: Einar Ólafur Sveinsson, *The Folk-stories of Iceland* (London: Viking Society for Northern Research, 2003), pp. 170–82.

51   The protagonist of the play is Áslaug, an elf-woman and representative of the hidden people. According to Icelandic mythology, elves were considered to live in the Icelandic mountains, inhabiting Iceland since its geological formation. From the figure of Áslaug originated the Icelandic tradition of the *fjallkona* (mountain woman) related to the national celebration. See: Terry Gunnel, "The Development and Role of the *Fjallkona* (Mountain Woman) in Icelandic National Day Celebrations and Other Contexts," in *Ritual Year 11: Traditions and Transformations*, edited by Guzel Stolyarova, Irina Sedakova, and Nina Vlaskina (Moscow: T8, 2016), pp. 28–29. On the idea of a "supernatural landscape" embedded in Icelandic history and traditions, see: Miriam Mayburd, "The Hills Have Eyes: Post-Mortem Mountain Dwelling and the (Super)Natural Landscape in the *Íslendingasögur*," *Viking and Medieval Scandinavia* 10 (2014): pp. 129–54.

52   Adrian Forty, *Words and Buildings: A Vocabulary of Modern Architecture* (New York: Thames & Hudson, 2000), pp. 128–29.

53   On the design and construction of the church, see: Steen Eiler Rasmussen, *Nordische Baukunst* (Berlin: Verlag Ernst Wasmuth, 1940), pp. 62–71; Thomas Bo Jensen, *P.V. Jensen-Klint: The Headstrong Master Builder* (London: Routledge, 2009), pp. 288–391.

54   Petersen writes about "basaltformationer" [basaltic formations] when describing the model of the church. Carl Petersen, "Grundtvig-Kirken," *Berlingske Tidende* 168, no. 216 (August 3, 1916): p. 3. The article is also quoted in: Jensen, *P.V. Jensen-Klint*, p. 290.

55   Seelow has traced many comparisons between Guðjón Samúelsson's buildings and projects that might have been influential: Seelow, *Die moderne Architektur in Island*, pp. 110, 124, 132, 149. To this list one may also add some designs by Hans Poelzig (1869–1936) representing ideal, crystal-like architectures, such as the model for a chapel in Karlsruhe and some sketches for the Majolikakapelle in Munich (1921). Wolfgang Pehnt, *Die Architektur des Expressionismus* (Stuttgart: Verlag Gerd Hatje, 1998), p. 85; "Majolikakapelle München," in *Hans Poelzig. Der zeichnerische Nachlass* (Berlin: Galerie Bassenge, 2014), p. 78. A striking representation of an utopian architecture envisaged as a basaltic-like sculpture was sketched around 1920 by Dutch architect Johannes Christiaan Van Epen (1880–1960). Pehnt, *Die Architektur des Expressionismus*, p. 31.

56   See, for example, the top of the Chrysler Building in New York City (1930), which is often quoted as a possible reference: Seelow, *Die moderne Architektur in Island*, p. 148; Pétur H. Ármannsson, *Guðjón Samúelsson húsameistari*, p. 336.

57   The church boasts a central concrete bell tower in the shape of a tall pipe organ; its verticality is surprisingly similar to Guðjón Samúelsson's churches. It is impossible to detect if Guðjón Samúelsson was familiar with this project or, in general, with the architectural production of the Italian fascist regime. In summer 1935, Guðjón Samúelsson traveled to Europe to collect ideas for the construction of the university campus to be built in Reykjavík, visiting Norway, Denmark, Germany, and the UK. During his travels, he might have been in contact with journals and reports on contemporary buildings and architectural projects, including examples from Italy.

58   Jónas Jónsson and Benedikt Gröndal, *Íslenzk bygging*, p. 111. See some examples in: Seelow, *Die moderne Architektur in Island*, pp. 209–10.

59   Guðmundur Hálfdanarson, "Severing the Ties", pp. 246–47.

60   Wolf Tegethoff, "Art and National Identity," in *Nation, Style, Modernism. CIHA Conference Papers*, edited by Jacek Purchla and Wolf Tegethoff (Cracow/Munich: International Cultural Centre/Zentralinstitut für Kunstgeschichte, 2006), p. 17.

61   Seelow, *Die moderne Architektur in Island*, p. 124.

62   On "national concretes", meaning the specific ways in which concrete conveys national characteristics, see: Forty, *Concrete and Culture*, pp. 119–42.

63   Lane, *National Romanticism and Modern Architecture in Germany and the Scandinavian Countries*, p. 174.

64   See, for example, the claim that granite was a "Nordic" stone with a character matching the inhabitants of the Nordic countries. Ringbom, *Stone, Style, and Truth*, p. 50. See also: Atli Magnus Seelow, "Exploring Natural Stone and Building a National Identity: The Geological Exploration of Natural Stone Deposits in the Nordic Countries and the Development of a National-Romantic Architecture," *Arts* 6, no. 6 (2017).

65   Jón Þorláksson, "Nýtt byggingarlag. Steyptir steinar, tvöfaldir veggir," p. 290.

66   See an example of the company's advertisement in: "Völundur," *Vísir* 12, no. 126 (June 6, 1922): p. 4.

67   One of them was engineer Jón Þorláksson, who extensively traded building materials in Iceland through his company J. Þorláksson & Norðmann. See for example the advertisement in: "Byggingar-efni," *Morgunblaðið* 12, no. 23 (August 9, 1925): p. 1.

68   Guðmundur Hannesson, *Steinsteypa*, pp. 66–76; Guðmundur Hannesson, *Húsagerð á Íslandi*, pp. 259–61.

69   See the advertisement of Heraklith in: *Morgunblaðið* 16, no. 81 (April 10, 1929): p. 4. See the advertisement of Masonite in: *Morgunblaðið* 21, no. 24 (January 28, 1934): p. 8.

70   An example is the *skriðmót* formwork, in timber or metal, that is moveable thanks to a hydraulic lifting system. See: Lýður Björnsson, *Steypa lögð og steinsmíð rís*, pp. 145–50. The categories of *þiljumót* and *flekamót* still exist today: the former refers to formwork with greased timber planks and timber vertical structures; the latter instead refers to formwork with a metal structure, supporting greased horizontal timber planks. I would like to thank expert *múrari* Jakob Maríasson for the precious information and Arlene Lucianaz for her help in the translation.

71   Advertisement on "old formwork" can be found in many newspapers until the nineteen-forties. "Steypumótaviður," *Morgunblaðið* 14, no. 125 (June 3, 1927): p. 4.

72   Guðmundur Hannesson, *Húsagerð á Íslandi*, pp. 261–64.

73   Guðmundur Hannesson, *Húsagerð á Íslandi*, pp. 255–57.

74   Guðmundur Hannesson, *Húsagerð á Íslandi*, p. 265.

75   Jónas Jónsson, *Þjóðleikhúsið*, 67–70. See also: Sofia Nannini, "Icelandic Concrete Surfaces: Guðjón Samúelsson's *Steining* (1930–50)," in *Iron, Steel and Buildings: the Proceedings of the Seventh Conference of the Construction History Society*, edited by James W. P. Campbell et al. (Cambridge: The Construction History Society, 2020), pp. 541–52.

76   For the overall costs of the building, see: Jónas Jónsson, *Þjóðleikhúsið*, pp. 98–105.

77   ÞÍ, Húsameistari ríkisins. Bréfa- og teikningasafn, Mappa 2, Geymsla 7. Örk 410, drawings of horizontal reinforced concrete structures (1930–33). Reinforced concrete pillars are located only in the foundations.

78   Jón Gunnarsson, "Veggir steinhúsa," *Alþýðublaðið* 3, no. 193 (August 21, 1931): pp. 3–4. See also: Jón Gunnarsson, "Blöndun steinsteypu og meðferð hennar," *Eimreiðin* 37, no. 3 (1931): pp. 255–64. See also: Jakob F. Ásgeirsson, *Jón Gunnarsson: ævisaga* (Reykjavík: Ugla, 2018), pp. 67–69.

79   Guðmundur Hannesson, *Húsagerð á Íslandi*, p. 264.

80   See, for example, the description of the coating of the National Hospital, designed by Guðjón Samúelsson. "Alt húsið skal húðað utan úr cementsblöndu 1–2, cement og sands um 20 cm á þykt …" [The whole building will be coated with a cement mix 1–2, cement and sand, around 2cm thick …]. ÞÍ, Húsameistari ríkisins, Bréfa- og teikningasafn, B/9, Landspítalinn. Örk 1.

81   On top of that, cement coating was considered too expensive. See: Jón Gunnarsson, "Hví er verið að "pússa" steinhúsin?," *Tíminn* (July 25, 1931): p. 4.

82   Jón Þorláksson, "Nýtt byggingarlag," p. 301.

83   Guðmundur Einarsson, "Háborgin," *Eimreiðin* 32, no. 3 (1926): p. 244.

84   Guðmundur Hannesson, *Húsagerð á Íslandi*, p. 265.

85   Kornelíus Sigmundsson, "Hrafntinnu-kvartshúðunin," *Tímarit iðnaðarmanna* 12, no. 3 (1939): p. 33.

86   Sigurður Guðmundsson had applied Mineralit to two villas built in Reykjavík in 1930–31. See: Seelow, *Die moderne Architektur in Island*, p. 242.

87   Jónas Jónsson and Benedikt Gröndal, *Íslenzk bygging*, p. 68.

88   Guðjón Samúelsson, "Íslenzk byggingarlist," p. 76.

89   Pebbledash in Icelandic was commonly known as *perluákast*. Guðmundur Hannesson reported that the technique was first used by architect Sigurður Guðmundsson in 1927. Guðmundur Hannesson, *Húsagerð á Íslandi*, p. 265.

90   Thanks to their rustic look, they were largely employed by architects of the Arts and Crafts movement. Applications of roughcast renders can be found at Hill House, built in 1902–04 by Charles Rennie Mackintosh (1868–1928) and Margaret Macdonald (1864–1933) and coated with a Scottish version of roughcast called *harling*, and at 22 Hampstead Way (1908–09) in North London, designed by Mackay Hugh Baillie Scott (1865–1945). On render and coating techniques in England, see: Alison Henry and John Stewart, eds., *Practical Building Conservation: Mortars, Renders, and Plasters* (London: Ashgate, 2012).

91   See the correspondence between Guðjón Samúelsson and the Ministry of Industry and Transportation in: Alþingi, Þingsskjal A (1941), "370 Tillaga til Þingsályktunar. Flm. Jónas Jónsson."

92   Alþingi, "370 Tillaga til Þingsályktunar". Attachment I–II, letter by Guðjón Samúelsson to the Ministry of Industry and Transportation, November 16, 1934.

93   Alþingi, "370 Tillaga til Þingsályktunar". Attachment III, letter by Páll Pálmason, representative of the Ministry of Industry and Transportation to Guðjón Samúelsson, May 16, 1935.

94   Guðjón Samúelsson, "Fremgangsmaade til Behandling af Yderfladerne af Bygninger og andre Bygningsværker, navnlig af Beton," Patent DK 56543, June 29, 1937; Guðjón Samúelsson, "Improvements in or relating to Treating the Surfaces of Buildings and other Structures, particularly of Concrete," Patent GB 516,064, December 21, 1939.

95   Attachment IX, letter by Þorsteinn Briem to the Ministry of Industry and Transportation, March 14, 1940. Alþingi, "370 Tillaga til Þingsályktunar".

96   The Society was founded in 1933. Björn Sigfússon, *Múrarasaga Reykjavíkur* (Reykjavík: Múrarasamtökunum í Reykjavík, 1951).

97   Attachment XI, letter by the Directorate of the Reykjavík Master Masons' Society to the Ministry of Industry and Transportation, December 3, 1940. Alþingi, "370 Tillaga til Þingsályktunar".

98   Lýður Björnsson, *Steypa lögð og steinsmíð rís*, pp. 110–11.

99   Ári Trausti Guðmundsson and Flosi Ólafsson, *Steinuð Hús. Varðveisla, viðgerðir, endurbætur og nýsteining* (Reykjavík: Húsafriðunarnefnd ríkisins, 2003), p. 18.

100   Ári Trausti Guðmundsson and Flosi Ólafsson, *Steinuð Hús*, p. 6.

101   Attachment VIII, letter by Guðjón Samúelsson to the Ministry of Industry and Transportation, May 27, 1940. Alþingi, "370 Tillaga til Þingsályktunar".

102   Ári Trausti Guðmundsson and Flosi Ólafsson, *Steinuð Hús*, pp. 24–25.

103 Ári Trausti Guðmundsson and Flosi Ólafsson, *Steinuð Hús*, pp. 22–23.

104 Sveinn Þórðarson, "Saga silfurbergsins," pp. 106–07.

105 I would like to thank Rúnar and Edda at the Eric The Red Guesthouse in Reykjavík for inviting me to visit the villa and sharing Bergþóra Góa Kvaran's research on the building with me.

106 Jónas Jónsson and Benedikt Gröndal, *Íslenzk bygging*, pp. 68–75; Páll Sigurðsson, *Úr húsnæðis- og byggingarsögu Háskóla Íslands* (Reykjavík: Háskóli Íslands, 1986–1991); Seelow, *Die moderne Architektur in Island*, pp. 134–37; Pétur H. Ármannsson, *Guðjón Samúelsson húsameistari*, pp. 277–93.

107 "Er þvílíkt skraut ekki til í neinu öðru húsi á jörðinni." Jónas Jónsson and Benedikt Gröndal, *Íslenzk bygging*, p. 128.

108 "Ræða rektors," *Árbók Háskóla Íslands*, Academic Year 1939–40 (Reykjavík: Prentsmiðjan Gutenberg, 1940), pp. 59–60.

109 The construction log was partially reprinted in: Páll Sigurðsson, ed., *Úr húsnæðis- og byggingarsögu Háskóla Íslands*, p. 326.

110 Slabs were cast in glass containers: the front side was polished, the slabs were hooked and cemented onto the walls. Jónas Jónsson and Benedikt Gröndal, *Íslenzk bygging*, p. 128.

111 Páll Sigurðsson, ed., *Úr húsnæðisog byggingarsögu Háskóla Íslands*, p. 326.

112 Páll Sigurðsson, ed., *Úr húsnæðisog byggingarsögu Háskóla Íslands*, p. 327.

113 Páll Sigurðsson, ed., *Úr húsnæðisog byggingarsögu Háskóla Íslands*, p. 324.

114 Ári Trausti Guðmundsson and Flosi Ólafsson, *Steinuð hús*, p. 4.

115 Seelow, *Die moderne Architektur in Island*, p. 243.

116 Ári Trausti Guðmundsson and Flosi Ólafsson, *Steinuð hús*, pp. 38–39. On similar finishes, see: Henry Langdon Childe, *Concrete Finishes and Decoration* (London: Concrete Publication Limited, 1964), pp. 60–61.

117 The main building of the University of Iceland was restored in 1995, as was the National Theatre in 2006–08. Both renovation works were carried out under the supervision of the National Architectural Heritage Board, and in 2003, the Cultural Heritage Agency of Iceland published a booklet on *steining* and its restoration by geologist Ári Trausti Guðmundsson and master mason Flosi Ólafsson. For these occasions, some closed mines were reopened for the collection of quartz and Iceland spar. Ári Trausti Guðmundsson and Flosi Ólafsson, *Steinhuð hús*, p. 23.

118 Liesbeth Dekeyser, Ann Verdonck, and Hilde De Clercq, "*Cimorné* Cement Render With Opalescent Glass Granules: A Decorative Façade Finish Developed by Innovative Craftsmanship in the Interwar Period," *Journal of Architectural Conservation* 19, no. 2 (2013): pp. 86–102; Liesbeth Dekeyser, "*Cimorné* Interwar Decorative Cement Render: A Historical and Technical Approach Towards Restoration Guidelines," PhD Dissertation, Faculty of Engineering, Vrije Universiteit Brussel, 2015.

119 Laura Barnett, "Grey, Lumpy, Impossible to Remove – But Pebbledash Isn't All Bad," *Guardian* (April 21, 2010), https://www.theguardian.com/lifeandstyle/2010/apr/21/pebbledash-homesnick-clegg, accessed May 16, 2023.

120 Forty, *Concrete and Culture*, pp. 43–68.

121 In 1940, approximately 25,000 British soldiers were stationed in Iceland; starting in 1941, around 60,000 American soldiers reached the country. These numbers were very high if compared to the small local population: in 1941, Iceland's population was about 120,000. Foreign troops were mostly deployed in Reykjavík and the Reykjanes peninsula, near the village of Keflavík, where the American troops opened a military base and an airport, which became Iceland's international civil airport in 1987. For a short account of the occupation years of Iceland during the Second World War, see: Gunnar Karlsson, *The History of Iceland*, pp. 313–18. See also: Helgi Skúli Kjartansson, *Ísland á 20. öld*, pp. 213–39; Pétur Hrafn Árnason and Sigurður Líndal, eds., *Saga Íslands XI*, pp. 68–84.

122 Guðmundur Hálfdanarson, "The Beloved War. The Second World War and the Icelandic National Narrative," in *Nordic Narratives of the Second World War*, edited by Henrik Stenius, Mirja Österberg, and Johan Östling (Lund: Nordic Academic Press, 2011), pp. 79–100; Valur Ingimundarson, *The Rebellious Ally. Iceland, the United States, and the Politics of Empire 1945–2006* (Dordrecht: Republic of Letters, 2011); Sigurður Gylfi Magnússon, *Wasteland With Words: A Societal History of Iceland* (London: Reaktion, 2010), pp. 238–45.

123 Gunnar Karlsson, *The History of Iceland*, pp. 319–23.

124 Guðmundur Hálfdanarson, *Íslenska þjóðríkið*, p. 138.

125 Finnbogi R. Þorvaldsson, "Endurreisn lýðveldis á Íslandi," *Tímarit Verkfræðingafélag Íslands* 29, no. 2 (July 1944): p. 17.

126 Arnór Sigurjónsson, ed., *Byggingarmálaráðstefnan 1944. Erindi og umræður* (Reykjavík: Landssamband iðnaðarmanna, 1946).

127 Vikurfélagið H. F., *Nokkur orð um vikur* (Reykjavík: Vikurfélagið, 1952).

128 Eggert Þór Bernharðsson, *Undir Bárujárnsboga. Braggalíf í Reykjavík 1940–1970* (Reykjavík: JPV Forlag, 2000).

129 Seelow, *Die moderne Architektur in Island*, pp. 315–17; Jón Rúnar Sveinsson, *Society, urbanity and housing in Iceland* (Gävle: Meyer Information & Publishing Ltd., 2000). See also a contemporary account on housing policies in Iceland in: Björn Björnsson, *Húsnæðismál og byggingarstarfsemi í Reykjavík 1928–1947* (Reykjavík, 1948). On urban living conditions in the first decades of the century, see: Sigurður Gylfi Magnússon, *Wasteland With Words*, pp. 174–86.

130 These housing blocks are at Hringbraut 37–47 (built in 1942–44), Skúlagata 64–80 (built in 1944–48), and Langahlíð 19–25 (built in 1945–49). Seelow, *Die moderne Architektur in Island*, pp. 319–26.

131 Einar Erlendsson, "Byggingarsamþykktir," in *Byggingarmálaráðstefnan 1944*, pp. 117–28;

Lbs, Íslandssafn, Stjórnartíðindi fyrir Ísland 1945. B-deild. Byggingarsamþykkt fyrir Reykjavík, pp. 357–75.

132   Nannini, *Icelandic Farmhouses*, p. 73 and pp. 83–85.

133   Einar Sveinsson, "Húsnæðisvandamálin og íbúðarbyggingar Reykjavíkurbæjar. Byggingarmátinn," *Morgunblaðið* 23, no. 237 (October 8, 1948): pp. 6 and 12.

134   Pétur H. Ármannsson, ed., *Einar Sveinsson: arkitekt og húsameistari Reykjavíkur* (Reykjavík: Kjarvalsstaðir, 1995); Seelow, *Die moderne Architektur in Island*, pp. 418–19.

135   Between 1919 and 1950, Guðjón Samúelsson had a total of 39 collaborators. Seelow, *Die moderne Architektur in Island*, 107. For biographic information on twentieth-century Icelandic architects, see: Haraldur Helgason, ed., *Arkitektatal* (Reykjavík: Þjóðsaga, 1997).

136   The founding members were Ágúst Pálsson (1893–1967), Sigurður Guðmundsson, Bárður Ísleifsson (1905–2000), Eiríkur Einarsson (1907–69), Einar Sveinsson, and Gunnlaugur Halldórsson (1909–1986). See: "Nýtt félag húsagerðameistara," *Þjóðviljinn* 1, no. 19 (November 21, 1936): p. 1.

137   "Reykjavík framtíðarinnar". On the many public projects designed outside of the state architect office, see: Seelow, *Die moderne Architektur in Island*, pp. 329–53.

138   H. Kr., "Guðjón Samúelsson. Húsameistari ríkisins," *Tíminn* 34, no. 95 (May 3, 1950): pp. 5 and 7; Geir Zoëga, "Guðjón Samúelsson. Húsameistari ríkisins," *Tímarit verkfræðingafélag Íslands* 35, no. 3 (June 1950): pp. 25–26. Like many of the engineers discussed in Chapter 2, he was described as a "pioneer" for Icelandic society.

139   "Húsameistari ríkisins settur," *Þjóðviljinn* 15, no. 102 (May 11, 1950): p. 8. The office continued its activity for many decades, until it was revoked in 1996. The position was restored in 2015 with the purpose of managing the real estate properties of the government, such as the prime minister's office. "Stéfan Thors settur húsameistari ríkisins," https://www.ruv.is/frett/stefan-thors-settur-husameistari-rikisins, accessed May 17, 2023.

140   The first census of Icelandic engineers was published in 1956. By then, several younger engineers had already graduated from North American institutions, such as MIT, IIT, McGill, Cornell, and others. See: Jón E. Vestdal, *Verkfræðingatal: æviágrip íslenzkra verkfræðinga og annarra félagsmanna Verkfræðingafélags Íslands* (Reykjavík: Sögufélag, 1956).

141   Bjarni Reynarsson, *Borgir og borgarskipulag* (Reykjavík: Skrudda, 2014), pp. 233–43.

142   On the relations between Iceland and the United States, see: Valur Ingimundarson, *Í eldlínu kalda stríðsins. Samskipti Íslands og Bandaríkjanna 1945–1960* (Reykjavík: Vaka-Helgafell, 1996); Valur Ingimundarson, *The Struggle for Western Integration. Iceland, the United States, and NATO During the First Cold War* (Oslo: Institut for forsvarsstudier, 1999).

143   "The actual transformation of European (and other) societies in the American image … Americanization is one of the principal modalities of modernization." Jean Louis Cohen, *Scenes of the World to Come. European Architecture and the American Challenge 1893–1960* (Paris: Flammarion/Montréal: CCA, 1995), p. 15.

144   "Ráðhús Reykjavíkinga við Tjörnina," *Morgunblaðið* 51, no. 8 (January 11, 1964): pp. 1, 8, and 17.

145   Bjarni Reynarsson, "The Planning of Reykjavík, Iceland; Three Ideological Waves – A Historical Overview," *Planning Perspectives* 14 (1999): p. 65.

146   Svava Jakobsdóttir, *Leigjandinn* (Reykjavík: Helgafell, 1969).

147   Árni Pálsson, "Normur um járnbenta steypu," *Tímarit Verkfræðingafélags Íslands* 27, no. 2 (1942): pp. 15–16.

148   Sigurður Thoroddsen, "Um steinsteypugerð í Reykjavík," *Tímarit Verkfræðingafélags Íslands* 40, no. 5 (1955): pp. 78–80. The news was echoed by the press: the *Þjóðviljinn* newspaper titled "Icelanders use more concrete than others, but they handle it worse": "Íslendingar nota meiri steinsteypu en aðrir en kunna verr með hana að fara," *Þjóðviljinn* 21, no. 25 (January 31, 1956): p. 4.

149   Lúðvík Kristjánsson, ed., *Við fjörð og vík*, p. 128.

150   "Þessi byggingarmáti var alger bylting í húsagerð hjer á landi …" [This building method was a total revolution in the construction of the country …]. Einar Sveinsson, "Húsnæðisvandamálin og íbúðarbyggingar Reykjavíkurbæjar. Byggingarmátinn," p. 6.

Epilogue

When Iceland Became Inhabitable

THIS PLACE ISN'T FIT FOR HABITATION;
 EVERYTHING IS AGAINST IT:
  COMMON SENSE, THE WIND,
   THE LAVA. STILL, WE'VE LIVED HERE ALL THESE
    YEARS, ALL THESE CENTURIES, STUBBORN AS
THE LAVA, SILENT WITHIN HISTORY AS THE MOSS THAT GROWS
OVER ROCK AND CHANGES IT INTO SOIL, SOMEONE SHOULD STUFF US,
    PIN MEDALS ON US, WRITE A BOOK ABOUT US. US?

Jón Kalman Stefánsson, *Fish Have No Feet*, 2016[1]

Iceland's intrinsic scarcity of building materials and its unwelcoming environment had been at the core of many of the island's descriptions, from Adam of Bremen's account until early twentieth-century travel reports. Since the very beginning of the "concrete age", a new goal became evident: that Iceland would launch its own cement production, thus making concrete a locally produced good. However, producing cement in Iceland was not easy: the island has scarce geological sources of calcium carbonite, such as limestone, and clay. Combining technological and political arguments, the debate covered more than three decades and required a thorough study of local sources which could be employed for cement production.[2]

Initially, the debate was mainly limited within the Icelandic Engineers' Society. At the beginning of the nineteen-twenties, its members started publishing detailed studies on the possibilities of producing cement in the country.[3] The issue was acknowledged at a political level in 1935, when the parliament issued a grant to support further research on the topic, inviting foreign and local engineers to contribute. The topic was resumed after the Second World War: in 1949, the Sementsverksmiðja ríkisins [State Cement Works] was founded, and it was decided to build the new plant in Akranes, north of Reykjavík, and on the Faxaflói Bay—strategically situated not far from the capital. Other locations were taken into consideration, especially Öndunarfjörður and Patreksfjörður in the Westfjords, but were considered too distant from the capital.[4] The

Fig. 1
The State Cement Works in Akranes.
Photograph by Björn Björnsson, 1960.

reason behind this choice was that Akranes was both close to seashells deposits, which needed dredging from the bottom of the bay and were sources of calcium carbonite, and to argillaceous rhyolite deposits. Gypsum would be still imported from abroad.[5] The political influence of the United States was behind the financing of the State Cement Works. Through loans from the International Cooperation Administration, the cement factory was officially inaugurated in June 1958.[6] Fig. 1

The inauguration of the plant was an occasion for rhetoric speeches comparable to those pronounced fourteen years before, on the day of the declaration of independence. In Akranes, President Ásgeir Ásgeirsson (1894–1972) claimed that "the history of Icelandic construction had mainly been a tragedy" until the end of the nineteenth century, and it was changed only by the discovery of Portland cement. Laying the cornerstone of the State Cement Works also meant laying a cornerstone for the "construction history of the future".[7] Minister of Industry Gylfi Þorsteinsson Gíslason (1917–2004) added that "many would consider uninhabitable a country without building materials. Many would consider unbelievable that a culture could develop among people living within earth and gravel. And many would also consider unthinkable that such people could be independent".[8] Both politicians remembered the starting point of Iceland's concrete history: Iceland's first concrete house, the farm at Sveinatunga built in 1895, was touted as a mythic national achievement. Subsequently, they both wished that the cement works would become a key protagonist in the future of the country. As the *Tíminn* journal had titled a few years before, the plant would become "the mother of the future buildings in Iceland."[9]

More than 130 years after the first reports on pozzolana deposits and more than 110 years after the first application of Portland cement in the country, Icelandic politicians and engineers finally considered Iceland as independent within the realm of the construction industry. However, the experience of local cement production was short-lived, and the State Cement Works halted production in 2012. Despite the closing down of the plant, Iceland's ability to produce its own cement is still considered a pivotal historic moment in the country's recent history and worth of a national narrative in an official location. In 2020, a sack of Icelandic cement was on display as part of a temporary exhibition at the National Museum in Reykjavík.[10] Fig. 2

The Icelandic concrete *saga* was not a history of sensational events, it was far less tumultuous than the many volcanic eruptions that often shake the island. On the contrary, it was a slow process, comprised of many small steps. The history of Icelandic concrete was made up of countless experiments, knowledge transfers, errors, debates, myths, failures. In the end, those very stages became the mirror of a society experiencing fast-paced transformations. Concrete superseded building traditions which were hundreds of years old. For some time, a few builders tried to immortalize the shapes of vernacular turf farms, using concrete as a link between past images and present needs.[11] Most of all, concrete created a new image for twentieth-century Iceland, it allowed a complete renovation of its living conditions and drastically transformed its society. The history of concrete is, for Iceland, a history of material and social change. The most active promoters of this change were the first Icelandic engineers, who were often described as trailblazers of the country's construction history. This was their main legacy: literally and metaphorically creating a road towards better living conditions and the material independence needed to employ long-lasting building techniques. If one single image could be chosen as an allegory for their pivotal role in twentieth-century Icelandic history, that image would be the "pioneer" sketched several times by artist Einar Jónsson. What Einar Jónsson depicted was a human figure breaking the hard basaltic rocks of Iceland, making a new road on which to walk on—perhaps the road towards modernization, with all its consequences. Fig. 3

However, the Icelandic concrete *saga* was also a collective history. No single individual was responsible for its outcomes: this history was shaped by several figures who contributed with their own expertise. Their contributions were not anonymous; however, with a few exceptions, these actors are little known. This is the peculiarity of the Icelandic concrete tradition: although prompted by distinct groups of people—master masons, farmers, politicians, engineers, architects—, it was not fully embodied by a single person, nor by a single professional category. On the contrary, it was backed by the whole Icelandic population.

Fig. 2
Cement sack of the State Cement Works on display at the National Museum of Iceland, 2020.

For many technological, environmental, and social reasons, concrete had a more evident role in Icelandic construction and architectural histories than it had in the other Nordic countries. Concrete acted as a motor for the country's material metamorphosis; its transformative power also promoted deep social and cultural changes. It improved local living conditions and allowed the construction of symbolic buildings for the Icelandic society; at the same time, concrete took on new meanings which are evident in various areas of the Icelandic cultural production. Until the first decades of the twentieth century, turf construction was a pivotal element of Icelandic culture. When concrete replaced turf, not only did it open a new chapter in Iceland's construction history, but it also became a part of the country's culture, to the present day.

The fact that the Icelandic concrete age has not ended yet can be appreciated by walking in the suburbs of Reykjavík or by visiting other towns and villages in the country. The history narrated in this book laid the foundations for nearly the whole Icelandic built environment since the postwar decades. Already in 1960, more than two thirds of residential houses were in concrete, less than a third in timber, and only one percent of housing units were turf farms.[12] This trend continued in the following decades: by 1982, concrete houses accounted for 93.9% of the country's residential units. The industrialization of concrete construction changed Icelandic postwar architecture. One example above all was the widespread use of precast concrete panels for many housing

Fig. 3
Einar Jónsson, *Banebryderen* [The trailblazer], 1907.

projects all around the country, one of its earliest examples being the construction of the residential neighborhood in Breiðholt, Reykjavík.[13]

Concrete did not only establish itself as the preferred material for construction companies, but it also became the trademark of many Icelandic architects.[14] Notable examples are the works by architect Högna Sigurðardóttir (1929–2017), who studied and worked in Paris and was one of the first Icelandic architects to pioneer the use of *béton brut* in the country.[15] In the last three decades, Studio Granda emerged as one of the most active architecture offices of the country, and its use of concrete stretches from monumental buildings to smaller experimental works.[16] In 1992, they completed the Reykjavík Town Hall, with massive concrete pillars reflecting in the Tjörnin Pond. In 2014, the studio designed and built a residential country house at Garður, in southern Iceland. The building can be seen as a sort of contemporary Icelandic turf house: it was built partially underground, flanked by earth abutments, yet enclosed by cast concrete walls and an arched concrete ceiling. In parallel with Guðjón Samúelsson's experimentations on *steining*, the terrazzo floor finishing includes basalt and shell fragments.[17] Fig. 4

The restoration of twentieth-century concrete heritage has been one of the most pressing topics of Icelandic architecture in the past decades, especially in the city of Reykjavík. Studio Granda restored Sigurður Guðmundsson's harbor warehouse Hafnarhúsið (1933–39) into the Reykjavík Art Museum (1997–2000). Hornsteinar Architects restored the former National Library, now House of Culture (1997–2000), and they also completed the expansion of the National Museum (1997–2004).[18] Arkís Architects renovated Guðjón Samúelsson's commercial building of Nathan & Olsen, now Apotek Hotel (2013–14).[19] In 2017,

Fig. 4
Studio Granda,
Reykjavík City Hall (1987–92).

Kurtogpi Architects restored the small concrete studio of Icelandic artist Ásmundur Sveinsson (1893–1982), built in 1933 by architect Sigurður Guðmundsson, and in the same year, they also renovated the former herring factory known as Marshall Húsið.[20] In recent years, the concrete structure of Hallgrímskirkja has been in a state of almost constant renovation, to the point that restoration works on the church have been considered an "eternal task".[21] The eminence of concrete in the Icelandic context is also highlighted by the work of Steinsteypufélag Íslands [The Icelandic Concrete Society], founded in 1971, as the last society dedicated to concrete construction to be founded in the Nordic countries.[22] Every few years, the Society awards a prize for Iceland's most appreciated architectural or infrastructural projects in concrete.[23]

The impact of concrete on Icelandic national culture cannot be overstated. Beyond architecture, concrete is all-pervading in many other areas of Icelandic culture, from artworks to literature. The material was largely used by Icelandic artists and sculptors Ásmundur Sveinsson (1893–1982) and Sigurjón Ólafsson (1908–1982). The former enthusiastically used concrete to build his second house and studio on the outskirts of Reykjavík, completed in 1959. As artist Einar Jónsson had done before him in the mid-nineteen-tens, Ásmundur Sveinsson designed his studio as a massive concrete sculpture, flanked by two cones and topped by a spherical dome.[24] Icelandic artist Sigurjón Ólafsson also experimented with concrete, with a particular focus on casting bas-reliefs.[25] One example is *Saltfiskstöflun* (1934–35), located on Rauðarárholt hill in Reykjavík—a large concrete sculpture dedicated to the stacking of salted fish. Fig. 5

He also used concrete to cast facade decorations, as in the Búrfell power station (1966–69). The main wall of the dam facing the water is covered with concrete panels, five meters high and more than sixty meters long, decorated by geometric reliefs dedicated to the relationship between humans and nature.[26] Sigurjón Ólafsson's bas-reliefs can also be found on facades of residential and commercial buildings in Reykjavík, such as on the south facade of an apartment building at Espigerði 2 (1973–74) and of the Sundaborg warehouses near the Sundahöfn harbor (1971–74).[27] In recent years, concrete is still present in many art exhibitions: contemporary artists such as Ingólfur Arnarsson and Brynhildur Þorgeirsdóttir have experimented with many abstract and sculptural works cast in concrete.[28]

The heritage of the Icelandic concrete age has been frequently portrayed by photographers, filmmakers and, most of all, by many Icelandic novelists. The presence of hundreds of concrete ruins all over the island emerges from the landscape photographs collected in *Metamorphosis* by Sigurgeir Sigurjónsson, in which the Icelandic nature is juxtaposed with ruins, buildings, and construction sites.[29] Literature is the field where the revolution in building tradition that occurred in the early twentieth century has emerged most. Decades after Laxness's masterpieces, many Icelandic authors still mention the social changes brought about by modern concrete dwellings. Einar Már Guðmundsson's novel *Fótspor á himnum* [Footprints in Heaven], published in 1997, is a nostalgic and disillusioned hymn to those who lived in the years when Reykjavík was still divided between turf farms and unlivable concrete

Fig. 5
Sigurjón Ólafsson, *Saltfiskstöflun*, 1934–35. Rauðarárholt, Reykjavík.

basements.[30] The destruction of traditional farms and their replacements in concrete are mentioned by Bergsveinn Birgisson in his novel *Svar við bréfi Helgu* [Reply to a Letter from Helga], published in 2010.[31]

Jón Kalman Stefánsson's novels often refer to architecture in the Icelandic nature and to the hardship of inhabiting that peculiar landscape.[32] In his book *Fiskarnir hafa enga fætur* [Fish Have No Feet], published in 2013, the author used concrete as a collective metaphor for human relationships and life:

> … and somewhere in Keflavík Jakob mixes concrete, he adds a little resin to the mix to bind it, to keep it from separating, to keep it from sliding down after it's been spread on a wall or used to fasten a weatherboard, so that it remains whole and thereby acquires a purpose. Needs just a small amount, hardly more than a capful in the concrete mixture, which is composed of numerous shovelsful of sand and cement, a certain amount of water, yet all it takes is one capful of resin for the mixture to remain bound together rather than slowly separate or crumble off the walls. After tossing the resin into the mixture, Jakob hesitates, watching the raw materials spin and combine, watching the resin disappear into the mixture. Why is it so easy to combine cement, sand and water into one, a whole, a unit, a purpose, all it takes is one capful, it isn't fair, because it seems so difficult to get life to hang together, this human life that you've got to drag around with you wherever you go, wherever you are.[33]

The fact that a contemporary novelist did not consider concrete as part of a distant technical world, but as a shared historical and social feature to be used for a literary metaphor, is clear evidence of the Icelandic concrete *saga* that has materialized since the mid-nineteen century. Today, the works of Icelandic artists, historians, directors, and novelists all tell the same story from different perspectives: for those inhabiting Iceland, concrete is everywhere and holds a variety of meanings. It is the cornerstone of the country's recent history; its presence is so widespread that it may be taken for granted and its origins may not even be questioned. The history of concrete construction and architecture in Iceland is a collective history that emerged during the nineteenth century and has influenced society to the present day, engaging engineers and farmers, architects and politicians. Concrete acted as a driving force for social and economic transformation in Iceland. It permanently connected the island to the global architectural practice, and it was seen as an opportunity to overcome the rigors of a rural past and embrace the comfort and contradictions of modernity.

ENDNOTES

1   Jón Kalman Stefánsson, *Fish Have No Feet*, trans. by Philip Roughton (London: MacLehose Press, Kindle Edition, 2016), chapter "Keflavík – present". [*Fiskarnir hafa enga fætur*].

2   Guðmundur Guðmundsson, *Sementsiðnaður á Íslandi í 50 ár* (Reykjavík: VFÍ, 2008); Lýður Björnsson, *Steypa lögð og steinsmíð rís*, pp. 133–44.

3   Helgi H. Eiríksson, "Íslenskar bergtegundir sem byggingarefni," *Tímarit Verkfræðingafélags Íslands* 6, no. 3 (1921): pp. 25–31; see also the research by Danish engineer Poulsen on Pozzolana deposits in Iceland: A. Poulsen, "Om Puzzolan og Portland Cement" *Tímarit Verkfræðingafélags Íslands* 14, no. 1 (1929): pp. 1–6. Research on pozzolanic deposits in Iceland continued in the postwar years. See: Hörður Jónsson and Haraldur Ásgeirsson, "Móberg Pozzolans," *Tímarit Verkfræðingafélags Íslands* 44, no. 5 (1959): pp. 71–78.

4   Guðmundur Guðmundsson, *Sementsiðnaður á Íslandi*, pp. 16–18.

5   Fillmore C. F. Earney, "Seashells and Cement in Iceland," *Marine Mining* 5, no. 3 (1986): pp. 307–20. The research behind the choice for a location and the cement production was first discussed in: Haraldur Ásgeirsson, "Framleiðsla portlandsements," *Tímarit Verkfræðingafélags Íslands* 31, no. 2 (1946): pp. 23–27; Jón E. Vestdal, "Hráefni til sementsframleiðslu og hagnýting þeirra," *Tímarit Verkfræðingafélags Íslands* 34, no. 5 (1959): pp. 58–76; Haraldur Ásgeirsson, "Staðsetning sementsverksmiðjunnar," *Tímarit Verkfræðingafélags Íslands* 34, no. 6 (1949): pp. 90–92; Jón E. Vestdal, "Sementsverksmiðjan á Akranesi," *Tímarit Verkfræðingafélags Íslands* 42, no. 4 (1957): pp. 46–55.

6   When the World Bank first refused to grant a loan to the Icelandic company in 1954, the Icelandic government replied that Iceland could accept an offer by the Soviet Union for an industrial development loan. In 1955, the International Cooperation Administration, a United States government agency, decided to grant two loans for the construction of the Icelandic plant. On the political debate behind the construction of the plant, see: Valur Ingimundarson, *Í eldlínu kalda stríðsins*, pp. 289–92; Guðmundur Guðmundsson, *Sementsiðnaður á Íslandi*, pp. 21–22.

7   "Þessi hornsteinn, sem geymir sögu verksmiðjunnar, er jafnframt hornsteinn í byggingarsögu framtíðarinnar. Saga húsagerðar á Íslandi er að mestu leyti raunasaga fram í lok síðustu aldar." Ásgeir Ásgeirsson, "Ávarp forseta Íslands," *Tímarit Verkfræðingafélags Íslands* 43, no. 4 (1958): p. 49.

8   "Margir mundu segja það land óbyggilegt, þar sem engin væru byggingarefni. Ýmsir mundu telja það ótrúlegt, að menning gæti þróazt með mönnum, sem búa í mold og grjóti. Og enn mundu margir álíta það óhugsandi, að slíkt fólk gæti verið sjálfstæð þjóð." Gylfi Þ. Gíslason, "Ræða," *Tímarit Verkfræðingafélags Íslands* 43, no. 4 (1958): p. 50.

9   "Sementsverksmiðjan, móðir framtíðarbygginganna á Íslandi," *Tíminn* 37, no. 140 (June 26, 1953): p. 1.

10   I would like to thank Arlène Lucianaz for letting me know about the temporary display of this item.

11   Nannini, *Icelandic Farmhouses*, pp. 59–70.

12   Lýður Björnsson, *Steypa lögð og steinsmíð rís*, p. 155.

13   Lýður Björnsson, *Steypa lögð og steinsmíð rís*, p. 175.

14   On Icelandic contemporary architectural culture, see: Peter Cachola Schmal, ed., *Iceland and Architecture?* (Berlin: Jovis Verlag, 2011). See also: Birgit Abrecht, *Discover Icelandic Architecture* (Reykjavík: Mál og menning, 2018).

15   Guja Dögg Hauksdóttir, "The Search of Meaning Through Concrete: Matter and Mind in the Work of Högna Sigurðardóttir," *The Journal of Architecture* 20, no. 3 (2015): pp. 489–509.

16   Studio Granda was founded by architects Margrét Harðardóttir and Steve Christer in 1987. Sheila O'Donnell and John Tuomey, *Í hlutarins eðli – The Nature of Things: Studio Granda* (Reykjavík: Kjarvalsstaðir, 1995); Annette W. LeCuyer, *Studio Granda: Dreams and Other Realities* (Ann Arbor: University of Michigan, 1998). See also the interview with the studio in: Schmal, ed., *Iceland and Architecture?*, pp. 74–121.

17   "Garður Landhouse / Studio Granda", *Archdaily*, February 21, 2017, https://www.archdaily.com/805562/gardur-landhouse-studio-granda?ad_medium=office_landing&ad_name=article.

18   Hornsteinar Architects, http://www.hornsteinar.is/, accessed May 18, 2023.

19   Tomas Lauri, ed., *Natural Elements: The Architecture of Arkís Architects* (Stockholm: Arvinius+Orfeus, 2020).

20   Kurtogpi Architects, https://www.kurtogpi.is/, accessed May 18, 2023.

21   Anna Kristín Pálsdóttir, "Steinsteypuskemmdir eilífðarverkefni," *RÚV*, August 12, 2015, https://www.ruv.is/frett/steypuskemmdir-eilifdarverkefni.

22   The Swedish Concrete Association [Svenska Betongföreningen] was founded in 1912; the Finnish Concrete Association opened in 1925 as Betongföreningen i Finland, now Suomen Betoniyhdistys; in Denmark, Dansk Betonforening was founded in 1947, now merged into Dansk Beton; Norsk Betongforening was established in Norway in 1955.

23   Steinsteypuverðlaun Steinsteypufélagsins, http://www.steinsteypufelag.is/steinsteypuverethlaunin.html, accessed May 18, 2023.

24   Pétur H. Ármannsson, "Salir Ásmundar," in *Ásmundur Sveinsson*, edited by Ólöf Kristín Sigurðardóttir (Reykjavík: Listasafn Reykjavíkur – Ásmundarsafn, 2017), pp. 172–83.

25   Birgitta Spur, ed., *Sigurjón Ólafsson: myndhöggvari* (Reykjavik: Styrktarsjóður Listasafns Sigurjóns Ólafssonar, 1985); Lise Funder and Birgitta Spur, eds., *Sculptor Sigurjón Ólafsson and His Portraits* (Reykjavík: Sigurjón Ólafsson Museum, 2008).

26   Sigurjón Ólafsson Museum, "Concrete in Flight," http://www.lso.is/08_Burfell/Burf_cat_e.pdf, accessed May 18, 2023.

27   Lýður Björnsson, *Steypa lögð og steinsmíð rís*, p. 156.

28   Ingólfur Arnarsson, *Jarðhæði/Ground Level* (Reykjavík Art Museum, November 3, 2018–February 10, 2019) and *Frumefni náttúrunnar/Natural Elements* by Brynhildur Þorgeirsdóttir (Ásmundur Sveinsson Museum, April 6, 2019–June 10, 2019).

29   Sigurgeir Sigurjónsson, *Metamorphosis* (Reykjavik: Prentmiðlun, 2017).

30   Einar Már Guðmundsson, *Fótspor á himnum* (Reykjavík: Mál og menning, 1997).

31   Bergsveinn Birgisson, *Reply to a Letter from Helga*, trans. by Philip Roughton (Las Vegas: AmazonCrossing, 2013). Original edition: *Svar við bréfi Helgu* (Reykjavík: Bjartur, 2010).

32   Sofia Nannini, "Narrare senza architettura. L'Islanda nei romanzi di Jón Kalman Stefánsson," in *Archiletture. Forma e narrazione tra architettura e letteratura*, edited by Andrea Borsari, Matteo Cassani Simonetti, and Giulio Iacoli (Milano: Mimesis, 2019), pp. 467–78.

33   Jón Kalman Stefánsson, *Fish Have No Feet*, chapter "Keflavík 1980". The original text goes as follows: "… og einhverstaðar í Keflavík hrærir Jakob í steypu, hann skvettir léttblendi út í svo blandan haldist saman, fari ekki í sundur, skríði ekki niður þegar búið er að smyrja henni á vegg, setja í vatnsbretti, til að hún haldist sem eining og öðlist þar með tilgang. Þarf bara smáskvettu, varla meira en tappa út í steypublönduna sem samanstendur þó af allnokkrum skóflum af sandi og sementi, slatta af vatni, en samt þarf ekki meira en tappa af léttblendi til að blandan haldist saman en skríði ekki í sundur, eða molni úr veggnum. Jakob hikar eftir að hafa skvett léttblendinu út í blönduna, horfir á hana snúast í hrærivélinni og blandast saman við steypuna, hverfa inn í hana. Afhverju er svona auðvelt að láta sement, sand og vatn bindast saman, verða eitt, að heild, einingu, tilgangi, það þarf bara einn tappa, það er ekki sanngjart, því það virðist svo erfitt að fá lífið til að hanga saman, þessa ævi manns sem maður þarf að burðast með hvert sem maður fer, hvar sem maður er." Jón Kalman Stefánsson, *Fiskarnir hafa enga fætur* (Reykjavik: Skynjun, 2013), pp. 234–35.

Appendix

References

Note: Icelandic authors have been listed alphabetically following the order of their first names, the last name usually being a patronymic [–*son*, –*dóttir*]. The titles of references in Nordic languages have been translated and inserted in brackets.

ARCHIVAL SOURCES

Alþingi. Alþingistíðindi — Parliament gazette

Borgarskjalasafn Reykjavíkur — Reykjavík City Archives [BR]
    Einkaskjalasafn nr. 25. Knud Zimsen [Private archive of Knud Zimsen]

    Teikningavefur Reykjavíkurborgar [City of Reykjavík – Drawings]

Det Kgl. Bibliotek — Royal Danish Library

Landsbókasafn Íslands – Háskólabókasafn — National and University Library of Iceland [Lbs]
    Handritasafn [Manuscript Department]

    Íslandssafn [Icelandic National Collection]

    Ritaukaskrá Landsbókasafnsins [Catalogue of the National Library]

    Stjórnartíðindi fyrir Ísland [Government gazette]

    Tímarit digital library, https://timarit.is/

Listasafn Einars Jónssonar — Einar Jónsson's Museum

Vegagerðin — Icelandic Road and Coastal Administration

Þjóðskjalasafn Íslands — National Archives of Iceland [ÞÍ]
    Húsameistari ríkisins. Bréfa- og teikningasafn [State Architect Fonds]

    Rentukammer. Bréfasafn [Danish Treasury. Letters]

    Stjórnarráð Íslands I. Skrifstofa. Bréfasafn [Ministry Offices of Iceland I. Letters]

    Stjórnarráð Íslands II. Skrifstofa. Bréfasafn [Ministry Offices of Iceland II. Letters]

    Teikningasafn [Drawing Collection]

    Vita- og hafnarmálastofnun. Bréfasafn [Institute for Lighthouses and Harbors. Letters]

PUBLISHED SOURCES

"A Concrete Sheepfold at Réttir, Iceland." In "In Concrete. Third Series–XX." *The Concrete Way*, incorporating *The Road Maker* 8, no. 2 (September/October 1935): 98.

Abrecht, Birgit. *Discover Icelandic Architecture*. Reykjavík: Mál og menning, 2018.

Adam of Bremen. *Gesta Hammaburgensis ecclesiae pontificum*, edited by Johann Martin Lappenberg. Second edition. Hannover: Impensis Bibliopolii Hahniani, 1876.

A. J. Johnson. "Framtíðar húsagjörð. Er hún ekki framkvæmanleg á Íslandi?" [Construction of the Future. Is it Not Practicable in Iceland?]. *Reykjavík* 9, no. 27 (1908): 105–06.

Albrecht, [?]. "Der Betonhohlstein, ein neues Baumaterial." *Beton und Eisen* 5, no. 7 (1906): 166–68.

"Alþing II." [Parliament II]. *Þjóðólfur* 39, no. 29 (July 8, 1887): 114.

"Alþingishúsið" [The House of Parliament]. *Þjóðólfur* 33, no. 3 (January 29, 1881): 9.

Andrés Kristjánsson. *Aldarsaga Kaupfélags Þingeyinga* [One Century of the Þingeyinga Cooperative]. Húsavík: Kaupfélag Þingeyinga, 1982.

Anna D. Ágústsdóttir and Guðni Valberg. *Reykjavík sem ekki varð* [The Reykjavík That Did Not Take Place]. Reykjavík: Crymogea, 2014.

Aprea, Salvatore. *German Concrete: The Science of Cement from Trass to Portland, 1819-1877*. Lausanne: EPFL Press, 2016.

Arnór Sigurjónsson, ed. *Byggingarmálaráðstefnan 1944. Erindi og umræður* [Building Conference 1944. Lectures and Discussions]. Reykjavík: Landssamband Iðnaðarmanna, 1946.

Ashby, Charlotte. "The Pohjola Building: Reconciling Contradictions in Finnish Architecture." In *Nationalism and Architecture*, edited by Raymond Quek and Darren Deane, with Sarah Butler, 135–46. Farnham: Ashgate, 2012.

Association of the Concrete Industry of Finland. *Tehdään betonista: Concrete in Finnish Architecture*. Helsinki: Garamond, 1989.

Auden, Wystan Hugh, and Louis MacNeice. *Letters from Iceland*. London: Faber and Faber, 1937.

Auður Hauksdóttir. "Language and the Development of National Identity: Icelanders' Attitudes to Danish in Turbulent Times." *Made in Denmark: Investigations of the Dispersion of 'Danishness'. KULT* 11 (2013): 65–94.

Árbók Háskóla Íslands [Yearbook of the University of Iceland]. Academic Year 1939–40. Reykjavík: Prentsmiðjan Gutenberg, 1940.

Avenier, Cédric. "Ciment naturel, la matière des moulages d'architecture au XIXe siècle." In *Édifice & Artifice. Histories constructives*, edited by Robert Carvais, André Guillerme, Valérie Nègre, and Joël Sakarovitch, 577–86. Paris: Picard, 2012.

Ágúst H. Bjarnason. "Íslenzkir listamenn. Einar Jónsson, myndasmíður" [Icelandic Artists: Sculptor Einar Jónsson]. *Iðunn* 8 no. 3–4 (January/April 1922): 214–34.

Ári Trausti Guðmundsson and Flosi Ólafsson. *Steinuð Hús. Varðveisla, viðgerðir, endurbætur og nýsteining* [Houses with *Steining*. Conservation, Fixing, Improving, and New *Steining*]. Reykjavík: Húsafriðunarnefnd ríkisins, 2003.

Árni Pálsson. "Normur um járnbenta steypu" [Norms on Reinforced Concrete]. *Tímarit Verkfræðingafélags Íslands* 27, no. 2 (1942): 15–16.

Ásdís Hlökk Theodórsdóttir and Sigurður Svavarsson, eds. *Aldarspegill. Samtal við Guðmund Hannesson* [The Mirror of the Century. A Dialogue with Guðmundur Hannesson]. Reykjavík: Skipulagsstofnun og Hið íslenska bókmenntafélag, 2016.

Ásgeir Ásgeirsson. "Ávarp forseta Íslands" [Speech of the President of Iceland]. *Tímarit Verkfræðingafélags Íslands* 43, no. 4 (1958): 49.

Á. Ó. [Árni Óla]. "Kalknám í Esjunni og kalkbrennsla í Reykjavík" [Lime Production in Reykjavík]. *Lesbók Morgunblaðsins* 24, no. 39 (October 23, 1949): 461–64.

Bailes, Alyson, Margrét Cela, Katla Kjartansdóttir, and Kristinn Schram. "Iceland: Small but Central." In *Perceptions and Strategies of Arcticness in Sub-Arctic Europe,* edited by Andris Sprūds and Toms Rostoks, 75–97. Riga: Latvian Institute of International Affairs, 2014.

"Bankahúsið nýja" [The New Bank]. *Ísafold* 32, no. 27 (May 13, 1905): 106.

"Bankastjóri" [Bank Director]. *Ísafold* 25, no. 6 (February 2, 1898): 21.

Baudin, Antoine, ed. *Photography, Modern Architecture and Design. The Alberto Sartoris Collection. Objects from the Vitra Design Museum.* Lausanne: EPFL Press, 2005.

Bauer, Leopold. "Die katholische Pfarrkirche in Bielitz." *Beton und Eisen* 10, no. 11 (July 1911): 229–32.

Bech, C [?]. "Jærnbeton, særlig dets Anvendelse ved Vandbygningsarbejder" [The Use of Reinforced Concrete in Water Works]. *Ársrit Verkfræðingafjelags Íslands* (1914): 6–7.

Bender, Henning, and Morten Pedersen. *Aalborg og cementen* [Aalborg and Cement]. Aalborg: Aalborgbogen, 2006.

Bergsteinn Jónsson. *Bygging Alþingishússins 1880–1881* [The Construction of the House of Parliament 1880–1881]. Reykjavík: Bókaútgáfa menningarsjóðs og þjóðvinafélagsins, 1972.

Bergsveinn Birgisson. *Svar við bréfi Helgu.* Reykjavík: Bjartur, 2010. English edition: *Reply to a Letter from Helga*, translated by Philip Roughton. Las Vegas: AmazonCrossing, 2013.

Bevilacqua, Mario. "Prima di Grandjean: rilievi e incisioni di architettura a Firenze tra Cinquecento e Settecento." In *Tra Firenze e Rio. Auguste Grandjean de Montigny (1776–1850) e la riscoperta dell'architettura del Rinascimento toscano,* edited by Mario Bevilacqua, 29–43. Firenze: Didapress, 2019.

"Billigere bygninger" [Cheaper Buildings]. *Bergens Tidende* 49, no. 107 (1916): 5.

Bjarni Reynarsson. "The Planning of Reykjavík, Iceland: Three Ideological Waves – A Historical Overview." *Planning Perspectives* 14, no. 1 (1999): 49–67.

Bjarni Reynarsson. *Borgir og borgarskipulag: þróun borga á Vesturlöndum, Kaupmannahöfn og Reykjavík* [Cities and City Planning: Urban Development in the Western Countries, Copenhagen, and Reykjavík]. Reykjavík: Skrudda, 2014.

Björn Björnsson. *Húsnæðismál og byggingarstarfsemi í Reykjavík 1928–1947* [Housing and Construction in Reykjavík 1928–1947]. Reykjavík, 1948.

Björn G. Björnsson. *Fyrsti arkitektinn. Rögnvaldur Ágúst Ólafsson og verk hans* [The First Architect. Rögnvaldur Ágúst Ólafsson and His Work]. Reykjavík: Hið íslenska Bókmenntafélag, 2016.

Björn Sigfússon. *Múrarasaga Reykjavíkur* [History of Reykjavík's Master Masons]. Reykjavík: Múrarasamtökunum í Reykjavík, 1951.

Bregnsbo, Michael, and Kurt Villads Jensen, eds. *The Rise and Fall of the Danish Empire.* Cham: Palgrave Macmillian, 2022.

Bromley, R. G. "Field Meeting: Bornholm, Denmark, 28 August to 4 September 2000". *Proceedings of the Geologists' Association* 111, no. 1 (2002): 77–88.

"Brúagjörð yfir Þjórsá og Ölfusá" [The Construction of Bridges on the Þjórsá and Ölfusá Rivers]. *Víkverji* 1, no. 20 (1873): 77–78.

"Byggingar-efni" [Building Materials]. *Morgunblaðið* 12, no. 23 (August 9, 1925): 1.

"Byggingarsamþyktin" [The Building Code]. *Reykjavík* 4, no. 32 (June 25, 1903): 4.

"Byggt og búið í gamla daga" [Built and Inhabited in the Old Days]. *Tíminn* 63, no. 151 (July 7, 1979): 8.

Calder, Barnabas. *Architecture: From Prehistory to Climate Emergency.* Harmondsworth: Penguin Books, 2021.

Carlsen, Arne. *Den almindelige Bygningslovgivning*. Kristiania: H. Aschehoug & Co., 1900.

Carvais, Robert. "Plaidoyer pour une histoire humaine et sociale de la construction." In *Édifice & Artifice. Histoires constructives*, edited by Robert Carvais, André Guillerme, Valérie Nègre, and Joël Sakarovitch, 31–43. Paris: Picard, 2008.

Cederberg, John. "De første bygninger og bygværker af beton og jernbeton i Danmark" [The First Buildings and Structures in Concrete and Reinforced Concrete in Denmark]. *Fabrik og Bolig* 2 (1999): 3–37.

Charrington, Harry. "Nordic Visions of a Classical World." In *The Routledge Handbook on the Reception of Classical Architecture,* edited by Nicholas Temple, Andrzej Piotrowski, and Juan Manuel Heredia, 356–69. Abingdon: Routledge, 2020.

Cheng, Irene. "Structural Racialism in Modern Architectural Theory." In *Race and Modern Architecture: A Critical History from the Enlightenment to the Present*, edited by Irene Cheng, Charles L. Davis II, and Mabel O. Wilson, 134–52. Pittsburgh: University of Pittsburgh Press, 2020.

Chevallier, Fabienne. *L'œuvre d'Eliel Saarinen en Finlande et la question de l'architecture nationale de 1898 à 1909.* Paris: Publications de la Sorbonne, 2001.

Chevallier, Fabienne, and Anja Kervanto Nevanlinna. "La nation finlandaise, entre mémoire et projet." In *Idée nationale et architecture en Europe, 1860–1919: Finlande, Hongrie, Roumanie, Catalogne* edited by Jean-Yves Andrieux, Fabienne Chevallier, and Anja Kervanto Nevanlinna. 207–19. Rennes: Presses universitaires de Rennes, 2006.

Childe, Henry Langdon. *Concrete Finishes and Decoration.* London: Concrete Publication Limited, 1964.

Christiani & Nielsen: Twenty Five Years of Civil Engineering, 1904–1929. Copenhagen: Krohns Bogtrykkeri, 1929.

Cohen, Jean Louis. *Scenes of the World to Come. European Architecture and the American Challenge 1893–1960*. Paris: Flammarion/Montréal: CCA, 1995.

Cohen, Jean Louis, and G. Martin Moeller Jr., eds. *Liquid Stone: New Architecture in Concrete.* Basel: Birkhäuser, 2006.

D'Arcens, Louise, ed. *The Cambridge Companion to Medievalism*. Cambridge: Cambridge University Press, 2016.

Dekeyser, Liesbeth, Ann Verdonck, and Hilde De Clercq. "*Cimorné* Cement Render with Opalescent Glass Granules: A Decorative Façade Finish Developed by Innovative Craftsmanship in the Interwar Period." *Journal of Architectural Conservation* 19, no. 2 (2013): 86–102.

Dekeyser, Liesbeth. "*Cimorné* Interwar Decorative Cement Render: A Historical and Technical Approach Towards Restoration Guidelines." PhD Dissertation, Faculty of Engineering, Vrije Universiteit Brussel, 2015.

Delhumeau, Gwenaël. *L'invention du béton armé: Hennebique, 1890–1914*. Paris: Norma, 1999.

Donnelly, Marian C. *Architecture in the Scandinavian Countries*. Cambridge, Massachusetts: MIT University Press, 1992.

Earney, Fillmore C. F. "Seashells and Cement in Iceland." *Marine Mining* 5, no. 3 (1986): 307–20.

Eggert Þór Bernharðsson. *Undir Bárujárnsboga. Braggalíf í Reykjavík 1940–1970* [Under a Corrugated Iron Arch. Barrack Life in Reykjavík Between 1940 and 1970]. Reykjavík: JPV Forlag, 2000.

Eggert Þór Bernharðsson, ed. *Safnahúsið 1909–2009: Þjóðmenningarhúsið* [Safnahúsið 1909–2009: The House of National Culture]. Reykjavík: Þjóðmenningarhúsið, 2009.

Einar Már Guðmundsson. *Fótspor á himnum* [Footprints in Heaven]. Reykjavík: Mál og menning, 1997.

Einar Ólafur Sveinsson. *The Folk-stories of Iceland*. London: Viking Society for Northern Research, 2003.

Einar Sveinsson. "Húsnæðisvandamálin og íbúðarbyggingar Reykjavíkurbæjar. Byggingarmátinn" [The Issue of Housing and Residential Buildings in Reykjavík. The Building Method]. *Morgunblaðið* 23, no. 237 (October 8, 1948): 6 and 12.

Ellenberger, Íris. "Somewhere Between 'Self' and 'Other': Colonialism in Icelandic Historical Research." In *Nordic Perspectives on Encountering Foreignness*, edited by Anne Folke Henningsen, Leila Koivunen, and Taina Syrjämaa, 99–114. Turku: University of Turku, 2009.

Emil Jónsson. "Thorvald Krabbe" [Thorvald Krabbe, Obituary] *Tímarit Verkfræðingafélags Íslands* 38, no. 5 (1953): 111–112.

Faber, Tobias. *Dansk Architektur* [Danish Architecture]. Copenhagen: Arkitektens Forlag, 1977.

"Fangelsi" [Prison]. *Víkverji* 2, no. 1 (June 16, 1874): 117–18.

Fiandaca, Ornella. *Le béton armé "système Hennebique" a Messina fra XIX e XX secolo: dalle sperimentazioni pre-terremoto del brevetto alle sue declinazioni antisismiche*. Ariccia: Aracne, 2014.

Finnbogi Guðmundsson. *Úr sögu Safnahússins við Hverfisgötu* [On the History of the *Safnahús* in Hverfisgata]. Reykjavík: Sérprentun úr Árbók Landsbókasafnið, 1980.

Finnbogi Guðmundsson, ed. "Þrjú bréf Rögnvalds Ág. Ólafssonar til Guðmundar Finnbogasonar." [Three Letters by Rögnvaldur Ólafsson to Guðmundur Finnbogason]. *Árbók Landsbókasafn Íslands* 10 (1984): 53–60.

Finnbogi R. Þorvaldsson. "Endurreisn lýðveldis á Íslandi" [The Renaissance of the Republic in Iceland]. *Tímarit Verkfræðingafélags Íslands* 29, no. 2 (1944): 17.

Finnur Ó. Thorlacius. *Smiður í fjórum löndum. Endurminningar* [Builder in Four Countries. A Memoir]. Reykjavík: Bókaútgáfan Logi, 1961.

Finsen, Helge, and Esbjørn Hiort. *Gamle Stenhuse i Island fra 1700-tallet* [Old Stone Houses in Iceland from the Eighteenth Century]. Copenhagen: Arkitektens Forlag, 1977.

Finsen, Helge, and Esbjørn Hiort. *Steinhúsin gömlu á Íslandi* [Old Stone Houses in Iceland]. Translated by Kristján Eldjárn. Reykjavík: Bókaútgáfan Iðunn, 1978.

F. L. Smidth-Koncernen. *Cementbranchens konkurrenceforhold* [Competitive Relations in the Cement Business]. Copenhagen: S. L. Møllers Bogtrykkeri, 1959.

"Fnjóskárbrúin" [The Bridge over the Fnjóská River]. *Norðri* 3, no. 22 (June 2, 1908): 88.

"Fnjóskárbrúin" [The Bridge over the Fnjóská River]. *Norðri* 3, no. 26 (June 30, 1908): 103.

"Fnjóskárbrúin hrunin!" [The Bridge over the Fnjóská River Collapses!]. *Austri* 18, no. 25 (July 9, 1908): 88.

"Fnjóskárbrúin" [The Bridge over the Fnjóská River]. *Óðinn* 5, no. 2 (May 1, 1909): 12.

Forchhammer, Johann Georg. *Om Færöernes geognostiske Beskaffenhed* [On the Geological Nature of the Faroe Islands]. Copenhagen: Martv. Frid. Popps Bogtrykkerie, 1824.

Forchhammer, Johann Georg. *Danmarks geognostiske Forhold* [The Geological Features of Denmark]. Copenhagen: Schultz, 1835.

Forchhammer, Johann Georg. *Om de bornholmske Kulformationer* [On Coal Formations in Bornholm]. Copenhagen: Videnskabernes Selskab, 1837.

Forchhammer, Johann Georg. *Skandinaviens geognostiske Natur* [Scandinavia's Geological Nature]. Copenhagen: C. A. Reitzel, 1843.

Forster, Kurt W. "Berg und Tal in Bauten der Neuzeit." In *Felsengärten, Gartengrotten, Kunstberge. Motive der Natur in Architektur und Garten*, edited by Uta Hassler, 46–61. München: Hirmer, 2014.

Forty, Adrian. *Words and Buildings: A Vocabulary of Modern Architecture*. New York: Thames & Hudson, 2000.

Forty, Adrian. "A Material Without a History." In *Liquid Stone: New Architecture in Concrete*, edited by Jean Luis Cohen and G. Martin Moeller Jr., 34–45. Basel: Birkhäuser, 2006.

Forty, Adrian. *Concrete and Culture: A Material History*. London: Reaktion Books, 2012.

Foss, Alex. "Nyere Metodere i Cementfabrikationen, særlig Aalborg Portland-Cementfabrik" [Recent Methods in the Production of Cement, Particularly the Aalborg Portland Cement Plant]. *Den Tekniske Forenings Tidsskrift* 15 (1892): 178–82.

Funder, Lise, and Birgitta Spur, eds. *Sculptor Sigurjón Ólafsson and His Portraits.* Reykjavík: Sigurjón Ólafsson Museum, 2008.

Gargiani, Roberto, ed. *L'architrave, le plancher, la plate-forme: nouvelle historie de la construction.* Lausanne: Presses polytechniques et universitaires romandes, 2012.

Gargiani, Roberto. *Concrete from Archeology to Invention: 1700-1769. The Renaissance of Pozzolana and Roman Construction Techniques.* Lausanne: EPFL Press, 2013.

Gavello, Cinzia. *Alberto Sartoris attraverso "Gli elementi dell'architettura funzionale". Genesi e fortuna critica di un libro.* Milano: FrancoAngeli, 2020.

Geir Waage. *Reykholt: sagan* [Reykholt: The History]. Reykholt: Snorrastofa, 1996.

Geir Zoëga. "Jón Þorláksson" [Jón Þorláksson, Obituary]. *Tímarit Verkfræðingafélags Íslands* 20, no. 1 (1935): 1–2.

Geir Zoëga. "Guðjón Samúelsson" [Guðjón Samúelsson, Obituary]. *Tímarit Verkfræðingafélags Íslands* 35, no. 3 (1950): 25–26.

Geir Zoëga. "Sigurður Thoroddsen" [Sigurður Thorodssen, Obituary]. *Tímarit Verkfræðingafélags Íslands* 40, no. 6 (1955): 89–90.

Georg Ahrens. "Um sementsteypu" [On Concrete]. *Þjóðólfur* 37, no. 3 (January 17, 1885): 9–10.

Gilbreth, Frank Bunker. *Concrete System.* New York: The Engineering News Publishing Company, 1908.

Gísli Gunnarsson. *Monopoly Trade and Economic Stagnation: Studies in the Foreign Trade of Iceland, 1602–1787.* Lund: Ekonomisk-historiska föreningen, 1983.

Gísli Jónsson. *Saga Iðnaðarmannafélagsins í Reykjavík* [The History of the Craftsman Association in Reykjavík]. Reykjavík: Iðnaðarmannafélagið í Reykjavík, 1967.

"Götur og byggingar o. fl. í Reykjavík" [Streets, Buildings, etc. in Reykjavík]. *Reykvíkingur* 2, no. 4 (1892): 14–15.

Gry, Helge. *Geology of Bornholm.* Copenhagen: Theodor Sorgenfrei, 1960.

Guðjón Friðriksson. *Saga Reykjavíkur. Bærinn vaknar (1870–1940). Vol. 1* [History of Reykjavík. The City Awakens (1870–1940)]. Reykjavík: Iðunn, 1991.

Guðjón Friðriksson. *Saga Reykjavíkur. Bærinn vaknar (1870–1940). Vol. 2* [History of Reykjavík. The City Awakens (1870–1940)]. Reykjavík: Iðunn, 1994.

Guðjón Friðriksson. *Hér heilsast skipin: saga Faxaflóahafna* [The Ships Are Greeting Here. History of the Harbors in Faxaflói]. Akranes: Uppheimar, 2013.

Guðjón Samúelsson. "Steinsteypa" [Concrete]. *Morgunblaðið* 10, no. 131 (April 10, 1923): 4.

Guðjón Samúelsson. "Kaþólska kirkjan" [The Catholic Church]. *Morgunblaðið* 15, no. 163 (June 7, 1928).

Guðjón Samúelsson. "Íslensk húsagerð og skipulag bæja" [Icelandic Architecture and Urban Planning]. *Tímarit Verkfræðingafélags Íslands* 15, no. 1 (1930): 1–8.

Guðjón Samúelsson. "Íslenzk byggingarlist. Nokkrar opinberar byggingar á árunum 1916–1934" [Icelandic Architecture. Some Public Buildings in the Years 1916–1934]. *Tímarit verkfræðingafélags Íslands* 6, no. 18 (1933): 53–82.

Guðjón Samúelsson. "Fremgangsmaade til Behandling af Yderfladerne af Bygninger og andre Bygningsværker, navnlig af Beton." Patent DK 56543, June 29, 1937.

Guðjón Samúelsson. "Improvements in or Relating to Treating the Surfaces of Buildings and Other Structures, Particularly of Concrete." Patent GB 516,064, December 21, 1939.

Guðjón Samúelsson. "The National Theatre, Reykjavík, Iceland." *The Builder* 180, no. 5650 (June 1951): 784–85.

Guðmundur Björnsson. "Ræða landlæknis" [Speech of the Director of Public Health]. *Ársrit Heilsuhælisfélagsins* 1 (1909): 24–30.

Guðmundur Einarsson. "Háborgin" [The Acropolis]. *Eimreiðin* 32, no. 3 (1926): 244.

Guðmundur Finnbogason. "Listasafn Einars Jónssonar opnað í dag" [The Einar Jónsson Museum Opened Today]. *Morgunblaðið* 10, no. 1932 (June 24, 1923): 2.

Guðmundur Guðmundsson. *Sementsiðnaður á Íslandi í 50 ár* [Fifty Years of Cement Industry in Iceland]. Reykjavík: Verkfræðingafélag Íslands, 2008.

Guðmundur Gunnarsson, ed. *Icelandic Architecture.* Aarhus: Arkitektskolen i Aarhus, 1996.

Guðmundur Hannesson. "Hlý og rakalaus steinhús. Tillögur og leiðbeiningar" [Warm and Dry Concrete Houses. Suggestions and Guidelines]. *Búnaðarrit* 27, no. 1 (1913): 1–26.

Guðmundur Hannesson. *Um skipulag bæja* [On Town Planning]. Reykjavík: Háskóli Íslands, 1916.

Guðmundur Hannesson. *Skipulag sveitabæja* [Planning of Farmhouses]. Reykjavík: Þorsteinn Gíslason, 1919.

Guðmundur Hannesson. *Steinsteypa. Leiðarvísir fyrir alþýðu og viðvaninga* [Concrete. Guidebook for Common People and Beginners]. Reykjavík: Iðnfræðafjelag Íslands, 1921.

Guðmundur Hannesson. *Húsagerð á Íslandi* [Construction in Iceland]. Reykjavík: Prentsmiðjan Edda H. F., 1942.

Guðmundur Hálfdanarson. "Social Distinctions and National Unity: On Politics of Nationalism in Nineteenth-Century Iceland." *History of European Ideas* 21, no. 6 (1995): 763–79.

Guðmundur Hálfdanarson. "Þingvellir: An Icelandic 'Lieu de Mémoire'." *History and Memory* 12, no. 1 (2000).

Guðmundur Hálfdanarson. "Iceland: A Peaceful Secession." *Scandinavian Journal of History* 25, no. 1–2 (2000): 87–100.

Guðmundur Hálfdanarson. *Íslenska þjóðríkið: uppruni og endimörk* [Icelandic Nation State: Origins and Limits]. Reykjavík: Hið íslenska bókmenntafélag, 2001.

Guðmundur Hálfdanarson. "From Linguistic Patriotism to Cultural Nationalism: Language and Identity in Iceland." In *Language and Identities in Historical Perspective*, edited by Ann Katherine Isaacs, 55–67. Pisa: Pisa University Press, 2005.

Guðmundur Hálfdanarson. "Severing the Ties – Iceland's Journey from a Union with Denmark to a Nation-State." *Scandinavian Journal of History* 31, no. 3–4 (2006): 239–41.

Guðmundur Hálfdanarson. "Interpreting the Nordic Past: Icelandic Medieval Manuscripts and the Construction of a Modern Nation." In *The Uses of the Middle Ages in Modern European States. History, Nationhood and the Search for Origins*, edited by Robert Evans and Guy P. Marchal, 52–71. Basingstoke: Palgrave Macmillan, 2011.

Guðmundur Hálfdanarson. "The Beloved War. The Second World War and the Icelandic National Narrative." In *Nordic Narratives of the Second World War*, edited by Henrik Stenius, Mirja Österberg, and Johan Östling, 79–100. Lund: Nordic Academic Press, 2011.

Guðmundur Hálfdanarson. "Iceland Perceived: Nordic, European or a Colonial Other?" In *The Postcolonial North Atlantic. Iceland, Greenland and the Faroe Islands*, edited by Lill-Ann Körber and Ebbe Volquardsen, 39–66. Berlin: Nordeuropa-Institut der Humboldt-Universität, 2014.

Guðmundur Hálfdanarson and Ólafur Rastrick. "Culture and the Constitution of the Icelandic in the 19th and 20th Centuries." In *Power and Culture: Hegemony, Interaction and Dissent*, edited by Jonathan Osmond and Ausma Cimdina, 87–102. Pisa: Pisa University Press, 2006.

Guðmundur Magnússon. *Tækni fleygir fram. Tæknifræði á Íslandi og saga Tæknifræðingafélags Íslands* [Technology Advances. Technical Knowledge in Iceland and the History of the Icelandic Technical Society]. Reykjavík: Iðnsaga Íslendinga og hið íslenska bókmenntafélag, 2010.

Guðný Gerður Gunnarsdóttir and Hjörleifur Stefánsson. *Kvosin. Byggingarsaga miðbæjar Reykjavíkur* [*Kvosin*. Architectural History of the City Centre of Reykjavík]. Reykjavík: Torfusamtökin, 1987.

Guðrún Harðardóttir. *Þingeyrakirkja* [The Church at Þingeyrar]. In *Kirkjur Íslands*. Vol. 8 [Church of Iceland], 263–315. Reykjavík: Hið íslenska bókmenntafélag, 2006.

Guja Dögg Hauksdóttir. "The Search of Meaning Through Concrete: Matter and Mind in the Work of Högna Sigurðardóttir." *The Journal of Architecture* 20, no. 3 (2015): 489–509.

Gunnar Bollason. "Ágrip af sögu minningarmarka og steinsmíði á Ísland frá öndurveðu fram á 20. öld" [Outline of the History of Monuments and Stonemasonry in Iceland until the Twentieth Century]. *Árbók hins íslenszka fornleifafélags* 100 (2009): 5–41.

Gunnar Karlsson. *The History of Iceland*. Minneapolis: University of Minnesota Press, 2000.

Gunnar Karlsson. *Iceland's 1100 Years. The History of a Marginal Society*. London: Hurst & Company, 2000.

Gunnell, Terry. "The Development and Role of the *Fjallkona* (Mountain Woman) in Icelandic National Day Celebrations and Other Contexts." In *Ritual Year 11: Traditions and Transformations*, edited by Guzel Stolyarova, Irina Sedakova, and Nina Vlaskina, 22–40. Moscow: T8, 2016.

Gylfi Þ. Gíslason. "Ræða" [Speech]. *Tímarit Verkfræðingafélags Íslands* 43, no. 4 (1958): 50–52.

Hallberg, Peter. *Halldór Laxness*. New York: Twayne Publishers, 1971.

Halldór Guðmundsson. *The Islander. A Biography of Halldór Laxness*. London: Maclehose Press, 2008.

Halldór Kiljan Laxness. "Sálarfegurð í mannabústöðum" [The Beauty of Souls in Human Dwellings]. In *Húsakostur og híbýlaprýði*, edited by Hörður Bjarnarson, Sigurður Guðmundsson, Þórir Baldvinsson, Einar Sveinsson, Helgi Hallgrímsson, Skarphéðinn Jóhansson, Eiríkur Einarsson, Gunnlaugur Claessen, Aron Guðbrandsson, and Halldór Laxness, 115–21. Reykjavík: Mál og menning, 1939.

Halldór Kiljan Laxness. *Independent People*. Translated by J. A. Thompson. New York: Alfred A. Knopf, 1946. [*Sjálfstætt Fólk*]. First published in 1934–35.

Halldór Kiljan Laxness. *The Fish Can Sing*. Translated by Magnus Magnusson. London: Vintage Digital, 2010. [*Brekkukotsannáll*]. First published in 1957.

Hannes Hólmsteinn Gissurarson. *Jón Þorláksson. Forsætisráðherra* [Jón Þorláksson. Prime Minister]. Kópavogur: Almenna bókafélagið, 1992.

Hannes Lárusson. "The Icelandic Farmstead." *Almanach Warszawy* 10, 523–43. Warszawa: Muzeum Warszawy, 2016.

Hansen, Torben Seir. "Bornholm Cement. A Danish Example of Roman Cement." Lecture Presentation (2008). http://www.romanportland.net/files/doc/seminar2008/torben_seir_seminar2008s.pdf.

Haraldur Ásgeirsson. "Framleiðsla portlandsements" [Production of Portland Cement]. *Tímarit Verkfræðingafélags Íslands* 31, no. 2 (1946): 23–27.

Haraldur Ásgeirsson. "Staðsetning sementsverksmiðjunnar" [The Location of the Cement Plant]. *Tímarit Verkfræðingafélags Íslands* 34, no. 6 (1949): 90–92.

Haraldur Sigurðsson. *Ísland í skrifum erlendra manna um þjóðlíf og náttúru landsins. Ritaskrá* [Iceland in Foreign Writings Regarding the Country's Nature and Society. A Bibliography]. Reykjavík: Landsbókasafn Íslands, 1991.

Hassler, Uta, ed. *Was der Architekt von Stahlbeton wissen sollte: Ein Leitfaden für Denkmalpfleger und Architekten*. Zürich: gta Verlag, 2010.

Haugsted, Ida. "L. A. Winstrups rejse til Island" [L. A. Winstrup's Journey to Iceland]. *Architectura* 20 (1998): 67–93.

Haugsted, Ida. "Tømrer- og bygmester Bald & Søn på Island og Færøerne [Bald & Søn, Master Carpenters and Builders in Iceland and the Faroe Islands]. *Architectura* 36 (2014): 26–53.

"Heilsuhælið" [The Sanatorium]. *Ísafold* 36, no. 75 (November 17, 1909): 297.

Heimir Þorleifsson, ed. *Saga Reykjavíkurskóla: Historia Scholæ Reykjavicensis* [History of the Reykjavík School]. Reykjavík: Menningarsjóður, 1975–84.

Heinzerling, Friedrich, and Otto Intze. *Deutsches Normalprofil-Buch für Walzeisen zu Bau- und Schiffbau-Zwecken.* Aachen: Verlag Von Jos. La Ruelle, 1897.

Helga Maureen Gylfadóttir and Guðný Gerður Gunnarsdóttir. "Húsakönnun. Austurstræti – Pósthússtræti – Hafnarstræti – Lækjargata" [Research on the Built Heritage: Austurstræti – Pósthússtræti – Hafnarstræti – Lækjargata]. Reykjavík: Minjasafn Reykjavíkur, 2006.

Helgi Helgason. "Um steinsteypu" [On Concrete]. *Fróði* 4, no. 113 (1883): 265–67.

Helgi H. Eiríksson. "Íslenskar bergtegundir sem byggingarefni" [Icelandic Geological Resources as Building Material]. *Tímarit Verkfræðingafélags Íslands* 6, no. 3 (1921): 25–31 (translation into English on pp. 30–31).

Helgi Skúli Kjartansson. *Ísland á 20 öld* [Iceland in the Twentieth Century]. Reykjavík: Sögufélag, 2002.

"Helluþökin í Reykjavík" [Stone Roofs in Reykjavík]. *Þjóðólfur* 1, no. 5 (January 13, 1849): 23–24.

Henry, Alison, and John Stewart, eds. *Practical Building Conservation: Mortars, Renders, and Plasters.* London: Ashgate, 2012.

Hess, Ludwig. "Fnjóská-Brücke auf Island – Landungssteg im Hafen von Hundested." *Beton und Eisen* 8, no. 8 (1909): 188–89.

Hiort, Esbjørn. "Andreas Kirkerup's islandske kirke. Af Reykjavík Domkirkes bygningshistorie." [Andreas Kirkerup's Icelandic Church. On the Construction of the Cathedral of Reykjavík]. *Architectura. Arkitekturhistorisk Årsskrift* 2 (1980): 126–41.

Hiort, Esbjørn, and Hjörleifur Stefánsson. "Úr byggingarsögu dómkirkjunnar í Reykjavík." [On the Construction of the Cathedral in Reykjavík]. *Árbók Hins íslenzka fornleifafélags* 81 (1984): 27–48.

Hjörleifur Stefánsson. *Hegningarhúsið við Skólavörðustíg* [The Prison in Skólavörðustígur]. Reykjavík: Árbæjarsafn, 1984.

Hjörleifur Stefánsson, ed. *Bárujárn: verkmenning og saga* [Corrugated Iron: Technique and History]. Reykjavík: Minjavernd, 1995.

Hjörleifur Stefánsson, Kjell H. Halvorsen, and Magnús Skúlason, eds. *Af norskum rótum: gömul timburhús á Íslandi* [From Nordic Roots. Old Timber Houses in Iceland]. Reykjavík: Mál og menning, 2003.

Hjörleifur Stefánsson. *Af jörðu. Íslensk torfhús.* Reykjavík: Crymogea, 2013. English translation: *From Earth: Earth Architecture in Iceland.* Reykjavík: Gullinsnið, 2019.

Hjörleifur Stefánsson. *Hvílíkt torf – Tóm steypa! Úr torfhúsum í steypuhús* [What Sort of Turf – Empty Concrete! From Turf to Concrete Houses]. Reykjavík: Háskólaútgáfan, 2020.

Hrefna Róbertsdóttir. *Gamli austurbærinn. Timburhúsabyggð í norðanverðu Skólavörðuholti frá byrjun 20. aldar* [The Old *Austurbær*. Timber Buildings North of the Skólavörðustigur Hill Since the Beginning of the Twentieth Century]. Reykjavík: Árbæjarsafn, 1989.

Hughes, David, Simon Swann, and Alan Gardner. "Roman Cement. Part One: Its Origins and Properties." *Journal of Architectural Conservation* 13, no. (2007): 21–36.

"Húsabótarannsóknirnar" [Research on the Improvement of Houses]. *Ísafold* 27, no. 65 (October 20, 1900): 259.

Hörður Ágústsson. *Skálholt: kirkjur* [Skálholt: Churches]. Reykjavík: Hið íslenska bókmenntafélag, 1990.

Hörður Ágústsson. *Íslensk byggingararfleifð I: Ágrip af húsagerðarsögu 1750–1940* [Icelandic Architectural Heritage. An Outline of the History of Architecture 1750–1940]. Reykjavík: Húsafriðunarnefnd ríkisins, 2000.

Hörður Ágústsson. *Íslensk byggingararfleifð II: Varðveisluannáll 1863–1990. Verndunaróskir* [Icelandic Architectural Heritage. Annals of Preservation 1863–1990. Conservation Plans]. Reykjavík: Húsafriðunarnefnd ríkisins, 2000.

Hörður Jónsson and Haraldur Ásgeirsson. "Móberg Pozzolans." [Palagonite Pozzolana]. *Tímarit Verkfræðingafélags Íslands* 44, no. 5 (1959): 71–78.

"Húsameistari ríkisins settur" [The State Architect Nominated]. *Þjóðviljinn* 15, no. 102 (May 11, 1950): 8.

H.[?] Franzson. "Íslenzk húsgerðarlist" [Icelandic Architecture]. *Skólablaðið* 1, no. 4 (April 17, 1926): 12–13.

H. Kr. "Guðjón Samúelsson. Húsameistari ríkisins" [Guðjón Samúelsson: State Architect]. *Tíminn* 34, no. 95 (May 3, 1950): 5 and 7.

Idorn, Gunnar M. *Concrete Progress: From Antiquity to the Third Millennium.* London: Thomas Telford, 1997.

"Iðnskóli Reykjavíkur" [Technical School in Reykjavík]. *Bæjarskrá Reykjavíkur* (1905): 140.

"Iðnskólinn" [The Technical School]. *Reykjavík* 6, no. 15 (1905): 59.

"In Concrete. Third Series–XIII". *The Concrete Way*, incorporating *The Road Maker* 7, no. 1 (July–August 1934): 34–50.

Ingi Sigurðsson. "The Icelandic Enlightenment as an Extended Phenomenon." *Scandinavian Journal of History* 35, no. 4 (December 2010): 371–90.

"Innlendar fréttir" [News from Iceland]. *Þjóðólfur* 35 no. 3 (January 20, 1883): 7.

Iori, Tullia. *Il cemento armato in Italia. Dalle origini alla Seconda Guerra Mondiale*. Roma: Edilstampa, 2001.

"Íslendingar nota meiri steinsteypu en aðrir en kunna verr með hana að fara" [Icelanders Use More Concrete Than Others, but They Handle It Worse]. *Þjóðviljinn* 21, no. 25 (January 31, 1956): 4.

"Íslenzkur verkfræðingur." [Icelandic Engineer]. *Ísafold* 20, no. 39 (1893): 155.

Jahren, Per, and Tongbo Sui. *History of Concrete: A Very Old and Modern Material*. Singapore: World Scientific Publishing, 2017.

Jakob F. Ásgeirsson. *Jón Gunnarsson: ævisaga* [Jón Gunnarsson: A Biography]. Reykjavík: Ugla, 2018.

Jappe, Anselm. *Béton. Arme de construction massive du capitalisme*. Paris: Les Éditions L'échappée, 2020.

Jensen, Thomas Bo. *P.V. Jensen-Klint: The Headstrong Master Builder*. London: Routledge, 2009.

Jón G. Friðjónsson. *Mergur málsins. Íslensk orðatiltæki: uppruni, saga og notkun*. [The Core of the Language. Icelandic Idioms: Origin, History and Use]. Reykjavík: Mál og menning, 2006.

Jón Gunnarsson. "Hví er verið að "pússa" steinhúsin?" [Why are Concrete Houses Being Plastered?]. *Tíminn* (July 25, 1931): 4.

Jón Gunnarsson. "Þjóðleikhúsið" [The National Theatre]. *Tíminn* (August 8, 1931): 182.

Jón Gunnarsson. "Veggir steinhúsa" [Walls in Concrete Houses]. *Alþýðublaðið* (August 21, 1931): 3–4.

Jón Gunnarsson. "Blöndun steinsteypu og meðferð hennar" [The Mixing of Concrete and Its Application]. *Eimreiðin* 37, no. 3 (1931): 255–64.

Jón Guðnason. *Verkfræðingafélag Íslands: 1912–1962* [Icelandic Engineers' Society: 1912–1962]. Reykjavík: Verkfræðingafélag Íslands, 1962.

Jón Guðnason, ed. *Iðnbylting á Íslandi. Umsköpun atvinnulífs um 1880 til 1940* [Industrial Revolution in Iceland. Changes in the Working Life Between 1880 and 1940]. Reykjavík: Sagnfræðistofnun Háskóla Íslands, 1987.

Jón Hjaltalín. "Fjórða bréf" [Fourth Letter]. *Ný félagsrit* 12 (1852): 66.

Jón Hjaltalín. "Um híbýli manna" [On Housing]. *Heilbrigðistíðindi* 2, no. 5–6 (May–June 1872): 33–36.

Jón Hjaltalín. "Um híbýli manna" [On Housing]. *Heilbrigðistíðindi* 2, no. 7–8 (July–August 1872): 49–53.

Jón Hjaltalín. "Kalkbrennsla" [Lime Production]. *Heilbrigðistíðindi* 3, no. 7–8 (July–August 1872): 60–63.

Jón Hjaltalín. "Um steinlím og ýmsilegt, er þar að lýtur" [On Limestone]. *Þjóðólfur* 29, no. 1 (November 17, 1876): 3–4.

Jón Hjaltalín. "Um steinlím og ýmsilegt, er þar að lýtur" [On Limestone]. *Þjóðólfur* 29, no. 7 (January 18, 1877): 25–26.

Jón Hjaltalín. "Um byggingar, kalkbrennslu og steinsmíði" [On Buildings, Lime Production, and Stonemasonry]. *Heilbrigðistíðindi* 4, no. 1 (January 1879): 5–7.

Jón Jakobsson. "Landsbókasafnið" [The National Library]. *Lögrétta* 4, no. 16 (March 31, 1909): 61–62.

Jón Kalman Stefánsson, *Fiskarnir hafa enga fætur*. Reykjavík: Skynjun, 2013. English translation: *Fish Have No Feet: A Family History*. Translated by Philip Roughton. London: Maclehose Press, 2016.

Jón Rúnar Sveinsson. *Society, Urbanity and Housing in Iceland*. Gävle: Meyer Information & Publishing Ltd., 2000.

Jón Ólafur Ísberg, ed. *Iðnskóli í eina öld: Iðnskólinn í Reykjavík 1904–2004* [One Century of Technical School: The Technical School in Reykjavík 1904–2004]. Reykjavík: Hólar, 2004.

Jón E. Vestdal. "Hráefni til sementsframleiðslu og hagnýting þeirra" [Raw Materials for the Production of Cement and Their Use]. *Tímarit Verkfræðingafélags Íslands* 34, no. 5 (1949): 57–76.

Jón E. Vestdal. *Verkfræðingatal: æviágrip íslenzkra verkfræðinga og annarra félagsmanna Verkfræðingafélags Íslands* [Engineers' Census: Biographies of Icelandic Engineers and Other Members of the Icelandic Engineers' Society]. Reykjavík: Sögufélag, 1956.

Jón E. Vestdal. "Sementsverksmiðjan á Akranesi" [The Cement Plant in Akranes]. *Tímarit Verkfræðingafélags Íslands* 42, no. 4 (1957): 46–55.

Jón E. Vestdal. "Vígsla Sementsverksmiðju ríkisins á Akranesi" [Inauguration of the Cement Plant in Akranes]. *Tímarit Verkfræðingafélags Íslands* 43, no. 4 (1958): 52–56.

Jón Þorláksson. "Nýtt byggingarlag. Steyptir steinar, tvöfaldir veggir" [New Building Method. Cast Stones, Double Walls]. *Búnaðarrit* 17, no. 1 (1903): 277–302.

"Jon Þorláksson." *Norðurland* 2, no. 48 (1903): 191.

Jón Þorláksson. "Kuldinn og rakinn. Orsakir þeirra og ráðin við þeim" [Cold and Humidity. Their Causes and How to Deal with Them]. *Búnaðarrit* 18, no. 1 (1904): 98–131.

Jón Þorláksson. "Iðnskólinn í Reykjavík" [The Technical School in Reykjavík]. *Þjóðólfur* 56, no. 33 (1904): 132.

Jón Þorláksson. *Burðarþolfræði: Ágrip*. [Material Technology: An Outline]. Reykjavík: Iðnskólinn, 1909.

Jón Þorláksson. "Hvernig reynast steinsteypuhúsin?" [How Do Concrete Houses Stand the Test of Time?]. *Búnaðarrit* 25, no. 1 (1911): 207–27.

Jón Þorláksson. "Steinsteypa til íbúðarhúsargerðar" [Concrete in Residential Buildings]. *Tímarit Verkfræðingafélags Íslands* 17, no. 4 (1932): 33–45.

Jón Þorláksson. "Steinsteypa til íbúðarhúsargerðar" [Concrete in Residential Buildings]. *Tímarit Verkfræðingafélags Íslands* 17, no. 5 (1932): 49–53.

Jón Þorláksson. "Steinsteypa til íbúðarhúsargerðar" [Concrete in Residential Buildings]. *Tímarit Verkfræðingafélags Íslands* 17, no. 6 (1932): 61–73.

Jón Þorláksson. "Steinsteypa til íbúðarhúsargerðar" [Concrete in Residential Buildings]. *Tímarit Verkfræðingafélags Íslands* 18, no. 1 (1933): 12–14.

Jón Þorláksson. "Steinsteypa til íbúðarhúsargerðar" [Concrete in Residential Buildings]. *Tímarit Verkfræðingafélags Íslands* 18, no. 4 (1933): 32.

Jónas Jónsson. "Landakotskirkja" [The Church at Landakot]. *Tíminn* 11, no. 57 (December 23, 1927): 215–16.

Jónas Jónsson. "Byggingar. VIII" [Buildings. VIII]. *Samvinnan* 23, no. 1 (March 1929): 72–76.

Jónas Jónsson. "Hallgrímskirkja í Reykjavík [The Church of Hallgrímur in Reykjavík]. *Tíminn. Jólablað* [Christmas Edition]. (December 23, 1942): 9–10.

Jónas Jónsson. *Þjóðleikhúsið: þættir úr byggingarsögu* [The National Theatre. History of the Building]. Reykjavík: Ísafoldprentsmiðja, 1953.

Jónas Jónsson and Benedikt Gröndal, eds. *Íslenzk Bygging. Brautryðjandastarf Guðjóns Samúelssonar* [Icelandic Architecture. The Pioneering Work of Guðjón Samúelssonar]. Reykjavík: Norðri, 1957.

Júlíana Gottskálksdóttir. "Byggingarlist" [Architecture]. In *Í deiglunni 1930–1944. Frá Alþingishátíð til lýðveldisstofnunar* [In the Crucible. From the 1000th Anniversary of Alþingi to the Establishment of the Republic], 155–64. Reykjavík: Mal og Menning, 1994.

Júlíana Gottskálksdóttir. *Ljósbrigði: Safn Ásgríms Jónssonar* [The Ásgrímur Jónsson Museum]. Reykjavík: Listasafn Íslands, 1996.

"Kalk í Esjunni" [Lime on Mt. Esja]. *Víkverji* 1, no. 21 (August 28, 1873): 83.

"Kalksteinn" [Limestone]. *Fjallkonan* 17, no. 33 (August 25, 1900): 4.

Karlsen, Trygve. "Engineering Education in Norway." *European Journal of Engineering Education* 2, no. 1 (1977): 105–8.

Karlskov Skyggebjerg, Louise. "E. Suenson og tidlig materialelære i Danmark." *Historisk Beton* lecture series, released July 9, 2019. https://www.youtube.com/watch?v=WTT8Rbf7U_g.

Kirkjur Íslands. Fornar kirkjur í Reykjavík. Dómkirkjan, Fríkirkjan í Reykjavík, Kristkirkja í Landakoti [Churches of Iceland. The Cathedral of Reykjavík, The Free Church of Reykjavík, and the Church at Landakot]. Reykjavík: Hið íslenska bókmenntafélag, 2012.

Kissane, Michael J. "Seeing the Forest for the Trees: Land Reclamation in Iceland." *Scandinavian Review* 86, no. 1 (1998): 4–7.

Kiørboe, Frederik. "Landsbibliotek i Reykjavik (Landsbókasafn Íslands)" [The National Library of Iceland]. *Architekten* 1, no. 16 (1910): 169–74.

Kjartan Bergmann Guðjónsson. "Sverrir steinhöggvari" [Master Mason Sverrir Runólfsson]. *Tíminn* 2, no. 22 (June 9, 1963): 518.

Klitgaard-Nielsen, H. [?]. "Om Jærnbetonnormer for Island" [On Reinforced Concrete Norms for Iceland]. *Tímarit Verkfræðingafélags Íslands* 7, no. 4 (1922): 53–56.

"Klæðaverksmiðjan 'Iðunn'" [The Iðunn Wool Factory]. *Óðinn* 1, no. 1 (April 1, 1905): 4–6.

"Klæðaverksmiðjan 'Iðunn'" [The Iðunn Wool Factory]. *Þjóðólfur* 58, no. 49 (November 9, 1906): 188.

Knud Zimsen. *Skýrsla um rannsóknir stjórnarinnar til undirbúnings klæðaverksmiðju á Íslandi* [Report on the Governmental Research for the Construction of a Wool Factory in Iceland]. Copenhagen: J. H. Schultz, 1901.

Kolderup, Edvard. *Haandbog i husbygningskunst* [Architecture Handbook]. Kristiania: H. Aschehoug & Co. Forlag, 1891.

Kornelíus Sigmundsson. "Hræfntinnukvartshúðunin" [Quartz-Obsidian Plaster]. *Tímarit iðnaðarmanna* 12, no. 3 (1939): 33.

Krabbe, Thorvald Haraldsen. "Enn um íslenskt steypuefni." [On Icelandic Aggregates]. *Tímarit Verkfræðingafélags Íslands* 2, no. 2 (1917): 27–28.

Krabbe, Thorvald Haraldsen. *A Few Remarks on Icelandic Lighthouse Practise*. Reykjavík: Iceland Lighthouse Service, 1932.

Krabbe, Thorvald Haraldsen. *Island og dets tekniske udvikling gennem tiderne* [Iceland and Its Technical Development over Time]. Copenhagen: Danks-islandsk samfund, 1946.

Kristín Loftsdóttir and Katrín Anna Lund. "Þingvellir: Commodifying the 'Heart' of Iceland." In *Postcolonial Perspectives on the European High North*, edited by Graham Huggan and Lars Jensen, 117–41. London: Palgrave Macmillan, 2016.

Kristín Loftsdóttir. *Crisis and Coloniality at Europe's Margins*. Abingdon/New York: Routledge, 2019.

Kristín Ástgeirsdóttir, ed. *Reykjavík miðstöð þjóðlífs* [Reykjavík as the Centre of National Life]. Reykjavík: Sögufélag, 1978.

Kristján Eldjárn, Hakon Christie, and Jón Steffensen. *Skálholt: fornleifarannsóknir 1954–58* [Skálholt: Archeological Investigations 1954–58]. Reykjavík: Lögberg, 1988.

Kuban, Sabine. "Konstruieren in einer regellosen Zeit. Eisenbetonbemessung zwischen Monier-Broschüre und den ersten behördlichen Vorschriften (1887–1904)." In *Alltag und Veränderung. Praktiken des Bauens und Konstruierens*, edited by Werner Lorenz, Klaus Tragbar, Christoph Rauhut, Torsten Meyer, and Christina Krafczyk, 205–20. Dresden: Thelem, 2017.

Kugler, Franz. *Geschichte der Baukunst. Vol. 1–3*. Stuttgart: Verlag von Ebner & Seubert, 1856–59.

Kurrer, Karl-Eugen. *Geschichte der Baustatik*. Berlin: Ernst, 2002.

Kurrer, Karl-Eugen. "La dalle dans le système Monier." In *L'architrave, le plancher, la plate-forme: nouvelle historie de la construction*, edited by Roberto Gargiani, 544–552. Lausanne: Presses polytechniques et universitaires romandes, 2012.

Labonne, Henry. *L'Islande et l'archipel des Færoeer*. Paris: Libraire Hachette, 1888.

"Landstjórn" [National Government]. *Fréttir frá Íslandi* 7, no. 1 (1878): 5.

"Landsbókasafnið nýja." [The New National Library]. *Ísafold* 33, no. 46 (June 14, 1906): 182–183.

Lane, Barbara Miller. *National Romanticism and Modern Architecture in Germany and the Scandinavian Countries*. Cambridge: Cambridge University Press, 2000.

Lange, Preben. "Tigulsteinsgerð og móhnoð." [Brick Production and Peat Handling]. *Reykjavík* 5, no. 8 (1904): 30.

Lauri, Tomas, ed. *Natural Elements. The Architecture of Arkís Architects*. Stockholm: Arvinius+Orfeus, 2020.

LeCuyer, Annette W. *Studio Granda: Dreams and Other Realities*. Ann Arbor: University of Michigan, 1998.

Leifur Sveinsson. "Þættir úr sögu Timburverzlunarinnar Völundar h.f." [History of the Building Firm *Völundur*]. *Morgunblaðið* (February 25, 1979): 36–37.

Leopardi, Giacomo. *Poesie e prose, Vol. 2*. Milano: Arnoldo Mondadori Editore, 1988.

"Lög fjelagsins" [Society's Charter]. *Ársrit Verkfræðingafélags Íslands 1912/1913* 1 (1914): 3.

Leó Kristjánsson. "Úr sögu íslenska silfurbergsins" [On the History of Iceland Spar]. *Náttúrufræðingurinn* 76, no. 1–2 (2008): 37–48.

Leó Kristjánsson. *Iceland Spar and Its Influence on the Development of Science and Technology in the Period 1780–1930: Notes and References*. Reykjavík: Institute of Earth Sciences, University of Iceland, 2015.

Lucas, Gavin, and Angelos Parigoris. "Icelandic Archaeology and the Ambiguities of Colonialism." In *Scandinavian Colonialism and the Rise of Modernity: Small Time Agents in a Global Arena*, edited by Magdalena Naum and Jonas M. Nordin, 89–104. New York: Springer, 2013.

Lundahl, Gunilla, ed. *Nordisk Funktionalism* [Nordic Functionalism]. Stockholm: Arkitektur Forlag AB, 1980.

Lúðvík Kristjánsson, ed. *Við fjörð og vík. Brot úr endurminningum Knud Zimsens fyrrverandi borgarstjóra* [By the Fjord and the Bay. Some Memories of Former Mayor Knud Zimsen]. Reykjavík: Helgafell, 1948.

Lúðvík Kristjánsson, ed. *Úr bæ í borg: nokkrar endurminningar Knud Zimsens fyrrverandi borgarstjóra um þróun Reykjavíkur* [From Village to Town. Some Memories of Former Mayor Knud Zimsen on the Development of Reykjavík]. Reykjavík: Helgafell, 1952.

Lýður Björnsson. *Steypa lögð og steinsmíð rís. Sagt frá mannvirkjum úr steini og steypu* [Concrete Is Laid and Stonemasonry Is Rising. History of Stone and Concrete Structures]. Reykjavík: Hið íslenska bókmenntafélag, 1990.

Mackenzie, George Steuart. *Travels in the Island of Iceland*. Edinburgh: Thomas Allan and Company, 1811.

Magrill, Barry. "Pouring Ecclesiastical Tradition into a Modern Mould." *Journal of the Society for the Study of Architecture in Canada* 37, no. 1 (2012): 3–15.

Mamy, Henri. "L'Islande". *Le Génie Civil: revue générale des industries françaises et étrangères* 10, no. 19 (March 12, 1887): 301–03.

Mann, Charles C. *1493: Uncovering the New World Columbus Created*. New York: Alfred A. Knopf, 2005.

Mann, Charles C. "The Dawn of the Homogenocene." *Orion Magazine* 30, no. 3 (2011): 16–26.

"Mannalát" [Obituary]. *Ísafold* 27, no. 63 (October 10, 1900): 251.

"Mannalát" [Obituary]. *Þjóðviljinn* 14, no. 38 (October 30, 1900): 151.

Marx, Edwin. *Wände und Wandöffnungen*. Stuttgart: Arnold Bergsträsser Verlagsbuchhandlung, 1900.

Mayburd, Miriam. "The Hills Have Eyes: Post-Mortem Mountain Dwelling and the (Super)Natural Landscape in the *Íslendingasögur*." *Viking and Medieval Scandinavia* 10 (2014): 129–54.

"Mentasafnið" [The National Museum]. *Ísafold* 36, no. 24 (May 1, 1909): 93.

"Mesti húsbruni á Íslandi" [The Greatest Fire in Iceland]. *Norðurland* 6, no. 8 (October 20, 1906): 27.

"Merkir Íslendingar. Jón Hjaltalín" [Important Icelanders: Jón Hjaltalín]. *Morgunblaðið* 100, no. 98 (April 27, 2012): 39.

"Mikill húsbruni enn" [Another Great Fire]. *Ísafold* 33, no. 50 (August 4, 1906): 199.

"Mjölnir." *Reykjavík* 5, no. 12 (1904): 45.

"Myndirnar" [The Images]. *Sunnanfari* 8, no. 3 (June 1, 1900): 22.

Mörsch, Emil. *Der Eisenbetonbau: seine Theorie und Anwendung*. Neustadt: Wayss & Freytag, 1908.

Nannini, Sofia. "Narrare senza architettura. L'Islanda nei romanzi di Jón Kalman Stefánsson." In *Architetture. Forma e narrazione tra architettura e letteratura*, edited by Andrea Borsari, Matteo Cassani Simonetti, and Giulio Iacoli, 467–78. Milano: Mimesis, 2019.

Nannini, Sofia. "Icelandic Concrete Surfaces. Guðjón Samúelsson's *Steining* (1930–50)." In *Iron, Steel and Buildings: The Proceedings of the Seventh Conference of the Construction History Society*, edited by James W. P. Campbell, Nina Baker, Karey Draper, Michael Driver, Michael Heaton, Yiting Pan, Natcha Ruamsanitwong, and David Yeomans, 541–52. Cambridge: The Construction History Society, 2020.

Nannini, Sofia. "The City as a Gravel Pile: Building Codes, Concrete, and Urban Dwellings in Reykjavík (1903–45)." *La città globale. La condizione urbana come fenomeno pervasivo / The Global City. The Urban Condition as a Pervasive Phenomenon*, edited by Marco Pretelli, Rosa Tamborrino, and Ines Tolic, 182–92. Torino: AISU, 2021.

Nannini, Sofia. "Hennebique Moves North: The First Applications of Reinforced Concrete in Iceland (1907–10)." In *Storia della costruzione. Percorsi politecnici*, edited by Edoardo Piccoli, Mauro Volpiano, and Valentina Burgassi, 161–72. Torino: Politecnico di Torino, 2021.

Nannini, Sofia. *Icelandic Farmhouses: Identity, Landscape, and Construction (1790–1945)*. Firenze: Firenze University Press, 2023.

Newby, Frank, ed. *Early Reinforced Concrete.* Aldershot: Ashgate, 2001.

"Nú stækkar landið" [The Country Grows Larger]. *Morgunblaðið* 61, no. 121 (July 12, 1974): 14–15.

"Nýr fjelagsmaður" [New Member]. *Tímarit Verkfræðingafélags Íslands* 4, no. 3 (1919): 32.

"Nýr verkfræðingur" [A New Engineer]. *Þjóðviljinn* 8, no. 30 (April 14, 1899): 118.

"Nýt hlutafélag" [New Company]. *Þjóðólfur* 57, no. 6 (3 February 1905): 21.

"Nýtt félag húsagerðameistara" [A New Society of the Architects]. *Þjóðviljinn* 1, no. 19 (November 21, 1936): 1.

"Nýung í húsagerð" [Innovation in Architecture]. *Norðurlandi* 6, no. 48 (June 8, 1907): 168.

O'Donnell, Sheila, and John Tuomey. *Í hlutarins eðli – The Nature of Things: Studio Granda.* Reykjavík: Kjarvalsstaðir, 1995.

Olving, Sven. "Education of Graduate Engineers in Sweden." *European Journal of Engineering Education* 2, no. 1 (1977): 105–14.

Oslund, Karen. *Iceland Imagined: Nature, Culture, and Storytelling in the North Atlantic.* Seattle: University of Washington Press, 2011.

Ostenfeld, Asger Skovgaard. *Teknisk Statik* [Structural Analysis]. Copenhagen: Gjellerup, 1900. Also translated into German as *Technische Statik. Vorlesungen über die Theorie der Tragkonstruktionen.* Leipzig: Druck und Verlag Von B. G. Teubner, 1904.

Ostenfeld, Christen. *Christiani & Nielsen: jernbetonens danske pionerer* [Christiani & Nielsen: Danish Pioneers of Reinforced Concrete]. Lyngby: Polyteknisk Forlag, 1976.

Overy, Paul. *Light, Air & Openness. Modern Architecture Between the Wars.* London: Thames & Hudson, 2007.

Ólafur Ásgeirsson. *Iðnbylting hugarfarsins. Átök um atvinnuþróun á Íslandi 1900–1940* [An Industrial Revolution of the Mind. The Battle for Industrial Development in Iceland 1900–1940]. Reykjavík: Bókaútgáfa menningarsjóðs, 1988.

Ólafur J. Engilbertsson and Pétur H. Ármannsson, eds. *Þórir Baldvinsson.* Reykjavík: Sögumiðlun, 2021.

Ólafur Kvaran. *Einar Jónsson myndhöggvari. Verk, táknheimur og menningarsögulegt samhengi* [Sculptor Einar Jónsson. Work, Symbolism, and Cultural-Historical Context]. Reykjavík: Hið íslenska bókmenntafélag, 2018.

Ólafur Rastrick. *Háborgin: menning, fagurfræði og pólitík í upphafi tuttugustu aldar.* [The Acropolis: Culture, Aesthetics, and Politics at the Beginning of the Twentieth Century]. Reykjavík: Háskólaútgafan, Sagnfræðistofnun Háskóla Íslands, 2013.

Ólafur Rastrick and Benedikt Hjartarson. "Cleansing the Domestic Evil – On the Degenerate Art Exhibition in Reykjavík, 1942." In *A Cultural History of the Avant-Garde in the Nordic Countries*, edited by Benedikt Hjartarson, 879–902. Leiden: Brill, 2019.

"Ölfusárbrúin" [The Bridge over the Ölfusá River]. *Ísafold* 18, no. 47 (1891): 187.

Ólöf Kristín Sigurðardóttir, ed. *Ásmundur Sveinsson.* Reykjavík: Listasafn Reykjavíkur-Ásmundarsafn, 2017.

Paavilainen, Simo. *Nordisk klassicism 1910–1930.* Helsinki: Finlands Arkitekturmuseum, 1982.

Pace, Sergio. *Un eclettismo conveniente. L'architettura delle banche in Europa e in Italia, 1788–1925.* Milano: FrancoAngeli, 1999.

Páll Eggert Ólason, ed. *Íslenzkar æviskrár frá landnámstímum til ársloka 1940. Vol. 2* [Icelandic Biographical Dictionary from the Settlement to 1940]. Reykjavík: Hið Íslenska bókmenntafélag, 1949.

Páll Líndal. *Bæirnir byggjast* [The Towns Are Built]. Reykjavík: Skipulagsstjóri ríkisins og sögufélag, 1982.

Páll Líndal. *Reykjavík 200 ára: saga höfuðborgar í myndum og máli* [The Story of a Capital: Reykjavík in Words and Pictures]. Reykjavík: Hagall, 1986.

Páll Ólafsson. "Um grástein og steypustein". *Reykjavík* 5, no. 15 (April 8, 1904): 59.

Páll Sigurðsson. *Úr húsnæðis- og byggingarsögu Háskóla Íslands* [Architectural History of the University of Iceland]. Reykjavík: Háskóli Íslands, 1986–91.

Páll V. Bjarnason. "Icelandic Architecture in the Concrete Era." In *XIV Nordic Concrete Congress & Nordic Concrete Industry Meeting*, August 6–8, 1992, 251–58. Reykjavík: Icelandic Concrete Association, 1992.

Páll V. G. Kolka. "Þingeyrakirkja" [The Church at Þingeyrar]. *Lesbók Morgunblaðsins* 32, no. 45 (December 24, 1957): 684–88.

Pedersen, Julius. *Statik* [Statics]. Copenhagen: Høst, 1881. German edition: *Lehrbuch der Statik fester Körper.* Copenhagen: Høst, 1882.

Pedersen, Morten. *Cementen.* Aarhus: Aarhus Universitetsforlag, 2019.

Pehnt, Wolfgang. *Die Architektur des Expressionismus.* Stuttgart: Verlag Gerd Hatje, 1998.

Perko, F. V. "Die evangelische Kirche in Innsbruck." *Beton und Eisen* 6, no. 2 (1907): 36–38.

Petersen, Carl. "Grundtvig-Kirken" [Grundtvig's Church]. *Berlingske Tidende* 168, no. 216 (August 3, 1916): 3.

Petersen, Mayntz. "Íslenzkt steypuefni" [Icelandic Aggregates]. *Tímarit Verkfræðingafélags Íslands* 1, no. 1 (1916): 13–16

Pétur H. Ármannsson. "The Development of Reykjavík in the 1920s and 1930s and the Impact of Functionalism." In *Nordisk Funksjonalisme*, edited by Wenche Findal, 45-62. Oslo: Ad Notam Gyldendal, 1995.

Pétur H. Ármannsson, ed. *Einar Sveinsson: arkitekt og húsameistari Reykjavíkur* [Einar Sveinsson: Architect and Builder of Reykjavík]. Reykjavík: Kjarvalsstaðir, 1995.

Pétur H. Ármannsson, ed. *Sigurður Guðmundsson Arkitekt* [Architect Sigurður Guðmundsson]. Reykjavík: Listasafn Reykjavíkur, 1997.

Pétur H. Ármannsson. "Reconstruction in Prosperity. An Introduction to Modern Architecture in Iceland." *Docomomo Journal: Nordic Countries* 19 (1998): 46–48.

Pétur H. Ármannsson. "Social Aspects and Modern Architecture in Iceland." In *Modern Movement Scandinavia: Vision and Reality*, edited by Ola Wedebrunn, 99–108. Copenhagen: Fonden til udgivelse af arkitekturtidsskrift, 1998.

Pétur H. Ármannsson. "Concrete's Furthest North." *Docomomo Journal: Bridges and Infrastructures* 45 (2011): 87–89.

Pétur H. Ármannsson. *Gunnlaugur Halldórsson architekt* [Architect Gunnlaugur Halldórsson]. Reykjavík: Hið íslenska Bókmenntafélag, 2014.

Pétur H. Ármannsson. "Salir Ásmundar [Ásmundur's Studios]". In *Ásmundur Sveinsson*, edited by Ólöf Kristín Sigurðardóttir, 172–83. Reykjavík: Listasafn Reykjavíkur – Ásmundarsafn, 2017.

Pétur H. Ármannsson. *Guðjón Samúelsson húsameistari* [State Architect Guðjón Samúelsson]. Reykjavík: Hið íslenska bókmenntafélag, 2020.

Pétur Hrafn Árnason and Sigurður Líndal, eds. *Saga Íslands IX* [The History of Iceland, Vol. 9]. Reykjavík: Hið íslenska bókmenntafélag-Sögufélag, 2008.

Pétur Hrafn Árnason and Sigurður Líndal, eds. *Saga Íslands X* [The History of Iceland, Vol. 10]. Reykjavík: Hið íslenska bókmenntafélag-Sögufélag, 2009.

Pétur Hrafn Árnason and Sigurður Líndal, eds. *Saga Íslands XI* [The History of Iceland, Vol. 11]. Reykjavík: Hið íslenska bókmenntafélag-Sögufélag, 2016.

Pétur Ingólfsson. "Bogabrúin á Fnjóská" [The Bridge over the Fnjóská River]. *Lesbók Morgunblaðsins* (July 3, 1993): 6–7.

Pétur Pétursson, Jens Sigurðsson, and Gísli Magnússon, eds. *Tíðindi frá þjóðfundi íslendinga árið 1851* [Reports from the National Assembly 1851]. Reykjavík: Prentsmiðja landsins, 1851.

Pétur Sumarliðason and Einar Laxness, eds. *Sjálfsævisaga: bernskúar Kaupfélags Þingeyinga: úr fórum Jakobs Hálfdanarsonar* [An Autobiography: The First Years of the Þingeyinga Cooperative. From the Belongings of Jakob Hálfdanarson]. Reykjavík: Ísafold, 1982.

Picon, Antoine. "Construction History: Between Technological and Cultural History". *Construction History* 21 (2005–06): 5–19.

Pieper, Jan. "Werke der 'Baumeisterin Natur' in Schilderungen der Romantik." In *Felsengärten, Gartengrotten, Kunstberge. Motive der Natur in Architektur und Garten*, edited by Uta Hassler, 136–53. München: Hirmer, 2014.

Piobb, Pierre. "Une Capitale en bois: Reykjavík." *Lecture Modernes* 2, no. 22 (October 10, 1902): 1353–60.

Poelzig, Hans. *Der zeichnerische Nachlass*. Berlin: Galerie Bassenge, 2014.

Poulsen, A [?]. "Om Puzzolan og Portland Cement" [On Pozzolana and Portland Cement]. *Tímarit Verkfræðingafélags Íslands* 14, no. 1 (1929): 1–6.

Poulsen, Ervin. *Betonkrav og –praksis. Normen, forskrifter, dokumenter og faglitteratur 1888–1988 i uddrag til brug i skadesager vedr. betonkonstruktioner* [Concrete Requirements and Practices. Excerpts of Norms, Regulations, Documents, and Literature 1888–1988]. Hørsholm: Statens Byggeforskninsinstitut, 1989.

"Póstskipið" [The Mailboat]. *Víkverji* 2, no. 1 (June 16, 1874): 118.

Putkonen, Lauri. "The Early Years of Concrete Construction in Finland." In *Tehdään betonista: Concrete in Finnish Architecture,* edited by the Association of the Concrete Industry of Finland, 8–19. Helsinki: Garamond, 1989.

Quantrill, Malcolm. *Finnish Architecture and the Modernist Tradition*. London: E. & F.N. Spon, 1995.

Rasmussen, Steen Eiler. *Nordische Baukunst*. Berlin: Verlag Ernst Wasmuth, 1940.

"Ráðhús Reykjavíkinga við Tjörnina" [The Town Hall of Reykjavík near Tjörnin]. *Morgunblaðið* 51, no. 8 (January 11, 1964): 1, 8, and 17.

"Reglur Verkfræðingafjelags Íslands um sölu og prófun Portlandsements" [Standard Specification regarding the Sale and Testing of Portland Cement]. *Tímarit Verkfræðingafélags Íslands* 1, no. 1 (1916): 3–6.

Ringbom, Sixten. *Stone, Style and Truth: The Vogue for Natural Stone in Nordic Architecture 1880–1910*. Helsinki: Suomen muinaismuistoyhdistyksen aikakauskirja, 1987.

Rögnvaldur Ólafsson. "Lýsing á hælinu" [Description of the Sanatorium]. *Ársrit Heilsuhælisfélagsins* 2 (1912): 7–19.

Rögnvaldur Ólafsson. "Um byggingarsamþykkt handa Reykjavíkurkaupstað" [On Building Regulations for Reykjavík]. *Ársrit Verkfræðingafjelags Íslands* (1914): 9–13 (translation into English on pp. 30–34).

Sacken, Eduard. *Katechismus der Baustile*. Leipzig: J. J. Weber, 1894.

Sartoris, Alberto. *Gli elementi dell'architettura funzionale: sintesi panoramica dell'architettura moderna*. Milano: Hoepli, 1941. Third Edition.

Schmal, Peter Cachola, ed. *Iceland and Architecture?* Berlin: jovis Verlag, 2011.

Schunck, Eberhard, Hans Jochen Oster, Rainer Barthel, and Kurt Kießl. *Dach Atlas*. München: Institut für internationale Architektur-Dokumentation, 2002.

Seelow, Atli Magnus. *Die moderne Architektur in Island in der ersten Hälfte des 20. Jahrhunderts. Transferprozesse zwischen Adaption und Eigenständigkeit*. Nürnberg: Verlag für moderne Kunst, 2011.

Seelow, Atli Magnus. "Verslunarhús Nathan & Olsen við Austurstræti. Hornsteinn Guðjóns Samúelssonar að nýjum miðbæ Reykjavíkur" [The Building of Nathan & Olsen in Austurstræti. Guðjón Samúelsson's Cornerstone in the New City Centre of Reykjavík]. *Saga. Tímarit Sögufélags* 50, no. 1 (2012): 9–21.

Seelow, Atli Magnus. "Exploring Natural Stone and Building a National Identity: The Geological Exploration of Natural Stone Deposits in the Nordic Countries and the Development of a National-Romantic Architecture." *Arts* 6, no. 6 (2017).

"Sementsverkjsmiðjan, móðir framtíðarbygginganna á Íslandi" [The Cement Plant, Mother of the Future Buildings in Iceland]. *Tíminn* 37, no. 140 (June 26, 1953): 1.

Shand, Philip Morton. "In Concrete. Third Series–IV". *The Concrete Way*, incorporating *The Road Maker* 5, no. 4 (January 1933): 195–208.

Shand, Philip Morton. "Concrete's Furthest North." *The Concrete Way*, incorporating *The Road Maker* 7, no. 6 (May/June 1935): 330–35.

Sigfús Jónsson. "The Icelandic Fisheries in the Pre-Mechanization Era, C. 1800–1905: Spatial and Economic Implications of Growth." *Scandinavian Economic History Review* 31, no. 2 (1983): 132–50.

Sighvatur Árnason. "Um samgöngur og vegagjörðir" [On Communication and Road Construction]. *Þjóðólfur* 35, no. 25 (1883): 75.

Sigríður Björk Jónsdóttir. "Einar Erlendsson og reykvísk steinsteypuklassík." [Einar Erlendsson and Concrete Classicism in Reykjavík]. Thesis in History, University of Iceland, 1995.

Sigurður Guðmundsson. "Three New Concrete Buildings in Iceland." In "In Concrete. Third Series–XXVI." *The Concrete Way*, incorporating *The Road Maker* 9, no. 2 (September/October 1936): 100–03.

Sigurður Gylfi Magnússon. *Wasteland With Words: A Societal History of Iceland*. London: Reaktion, 2010.

Sigurður Líndal. *Hið íslenska bókmenntafélag 1816–2016: Söguágrip*. [The Icelandic Literary Society 1816–2016. Historical Outline]. Reykjavík: Hið íslenska bókmenntafélag, 2016.

Sigurður Pálsson. *Mínum drottni til þakklætis: saga Hallgrímskirkju* [To My Lord in Gratitude: The History of Hallgrímskirkja]. Reykjavík: Hallgrímskirkja, 2015.

Sigurður Pétursson. "Um vegi og brýr á aðalleiðinni frá Reykjavík austur í Holt" [On Roads and Bridges Between Reykjavík and Holt]. *Ísafold* 27, no. 18 (April 4, 1900): 69.

Sigurður Thoroddsen. "Um steinsteypugerð í Reykjavík" [On Concrete Construction in Reykjavík]. *Tímarit Verkfræðingafélags Íslands* 40, no. 5 (1955): 78–80.

Sigurjón Baldur Hafsteinsson. "Icelandic Putridity: Colonial Thought and Icelandic Architectural Heritage," *Scandinavian Studies* 91, no. 1–2 (Spring/Summer 2019): 67-70.

Simonnet, Cyrille. *Le béton: historie d'un matériau: économie, technique, architecture*. Marseille: Parenthèses, 2005.

"Sómastaðir við Reyðarfjörð" [The Warehouse at Sómastaðir in Reyðarfjörður]. *Morgunblaðið* (April 5, 2004): 28.

S.P. [Sveinn Pálsson]. "Um kalkverkun af jørdu og steinum með litlum viðbæti um tilbúning skelia-kalks; samanlesit úr dønskum, þýðskum og ødrum ritum" [On the Effects of Lime on Earth and Stones, with an Addition on the Fabrication on Seashell-Lime; From Danish, German and Other Essays]. *Rit þess (konunglega) íslenzka Lærdómslistafélags* 9 (1788): 91–143.

Spur, Birgitta, ed. *Sigurjón Ólafsson: myndhöggvari*. [Sculptor Sigurjón Ólafsson]. Reykjavík: Styrktarsjóður Listasafns Sigurjóns Ólafssonar, 1985.

"Steinbær" [A City of Stone]. *Morgunblaðið* 2, no. 212 (June 7, 1915): 1.

Steingrímur Jónsson. "Knud Zimsen" [Knud Zimsen, Obituary]. *Tímarit Verkfræðingafélags Íslands* 38, no. 4 (1953): 95–96.

Stemann, Helga. *F. Meldahl og hans Venner* [F. Meldahl and His Friends]. Copenhagen: H. Hagerups Forlag, 1926-32. [5 Volumes].

Stewart, John. *Nordic Classicism: Scandinavian Architecture 1910–30*. London: Bloomsbury, 2018.

Straub, Hans. *Die Geschichte der Bauingenieurkunst*. Basel: Birkhäuser, 1975.

Sumarliði R. Ísleifsson, ed. *Iceland and Images of the North*. Sainte-Foy: Presses de l'Université du Québec/Reykjavík: The Reykjavík Academy, 2011.

Sumarliði R. Ísleifsson. *Deux îles aux confins du monde. Islande et Groenland. Les représentations de l'Islande et du Groenland du Moyen Âge au milieu di XIXe siècle*. Québec: Presses de l'Unversité du Québec, 2018.

Svava Jakobsdóttir. *Leigjandinn*. Reykjavík: Helgafell, 1969. English edition: *The Lodger and Other Stories*. Translated by Julian Meldon D'Arcy, Dennis Auburn Hill, and Alan Boucher. Reykjavík: JPV, 2006.

Sveinn Þórðarson. "Saga silfurbergsins" [The History of Iceland Spar]. *Náttúrufræðingurinn* 15, no. 2 (1945): 96–107.

Sveinn Þórðarson. *Frumherjar í verkfræði á Íslandi* [Pioneers of Engineering in Iceland]. Reykjavík: Verkfræðingafélag Íslands, 2002.

Sveinn Þórðarson. *Brýr að baki. Brýr á Íslandi í 1100 ár* [Bridges in the Past. 1100 Years of Bridges in Iceland]. Reykjavík: Verkfræðingafélag Íslands, 2006.

Sverrir Runólfsson. "Kalk og sement" [Lime and Cement]. *Ísafold* 5, no. 19 (August 5, 1878): 76.

Sverrir Runólfsson. *Æfiágrip Sverris Runólfssonar steinhöggvara* [Biography of Stonemason Sverrir Runólfsson]. Reykjavík: Prentsmiðjan Gutenberg, 1909.

Tegethoff, Wolf. "Art and National Identity." In *Nation, Style, Modernism. CIHA Conference Papers*, edited by Jacek Purchla and Wolf Tegethoff, 11–23. Cracow/Munich: International Cultural Centre/Zentralinstitut für Kunstgeschichte, 2006.

"Tilraunir og uppástungur ýmsra manna um bæjabyggingar" [Experiments and Suggestions by Several People on Farmhouses]. *Bóndi* 1, no. 2–6 (1851): 24–27; 42–44; 54–57; 71–78; 81–86.

Trausti Valsson. *Planning in Iceland: From the Settlement to Present Times*. Reykjavík: University of Iceland Press, 2003.

Tucker, David Gordon. "The History of Industries and Crafts in Iceland." *Industrial Archaeology* 9, no. 1 (February 1972): 5–27.

Tulkki, Pasi. "The Birth of Engineer Education in Finland." *European Journal of Engineering Education* 24, no. 1 (1999): 83-94.

Tuomi, Ritva. "On the Search for a National Style." In *Abacus* 1, 57-96. Helsinki: Museum of Finnish Architecture, 1979.

Tvinnereim, Helga Stave. *Arkitektur i Ålesund 1904-1907: Oppattbygginga av byen etter brannen 23 januar 1904* [Architecture in Ålesund 1904-1907: The Reconstruction of the City After the Fire on January 23, 1904]. Ålesund: Aalsunds Museum, 1981.

Valur Ingimundarson. *Í eldlínu kalda stríðsins. Samskipti Íslands og Bandaríkjanna 1945-1960* [In the Line of Fire of the Cold War: Relations Between Iceland and the United States]. Reykjavík: Vaka-Helgafell, 1996.

Valur Ingimundarson. *The Struggle for Western Integration. Iceland, the United States, and NATO during the First Cold War*. Oslo: Institut for forsvarsstudier, 1999.

Valur Ingimundarson. *The Rebellious Ally. Iceland, the United States, and the Politics of Empire 1945-2006*. Dordrecht: Republic of Letters, 2011.

Van de Voorde, Stephanie, and Roony De Meyer. "L'application innovante du béton armé dans la construction d'églises en Belgique. Béton sacré ou usine à prière?" In *Édifice & Artifice. Histories constructives*, edited by Robert Carvais, André Guillerme, Valérie Nègre, and Joël Sakarovitch, 587-96. Paris: Picard, 2008.

Van de Voorde, Stephanie, Sabine Kuban, and David Yeomans. "Early Regulations and Guidelines on Reinforced Concrete in Europe (1900-1950). Towards an International Comparison." In *Building Histories. The Proceedings of the Fourth Conference of the Construction History Society*, edited by James Campbell, Nina Baker, Michael Driver, Michael Heaton, Yiting Pan, Treve Rosoman, and David Yeomans, 345-56. Cambridge: The Construction History Society, 2017.

Van Hoof, Joost, and Froukje van Dijken. "The Historical Turf Farms of Iceland: Architecture, Building Technology and the Indoor Environment". *Building and Environment* 43 (2008): 1023-30.

Varas, María José, Monica Alvarez de Buergo, and Rafael Fort. "Natural Cement as the Precursor of Portland Cement: Methodology for Its Identification." *Cement and Concrete Research* 35 (2005): 2055-65.

"Verksmiðjan 'Mjölnir'" [The Mjölnir Firm]. *Þjóðólfur* 56, no. 3 (1904): 9.

"Verzlan á Íslandi árið 1866" [Trade in Iceland in 1866]. *Skýrslur um landshagi á Íslandi* 4 (1870): 334.

Vikurfélagið H.F. *Nokkur orð um vikur* [On Pumice]. Reykjavík: Vikurfélagið, 1952.

"Vífilsstöðum" [At Vífilsstaðir]. *Lögrétta* 4, no. 53 (November 17, 1909): 210.

Voigt, J. J. *Statistike Oplysninger angaaende den polytekniske Læreanstalts Kandidater samt Fortegnelse over dens Direktører og Lærere (1829-1902)* [Statistical Information Regarding the Candidates at the Polytechnic School and a List of Its Directors and Teachers]. Copenhagen: Schultz, 1903.

Voss, Knud. *Arkitekten Nicolai Eigtved 1701-1754* [Architect Nicolai Eigtved 1701-1754]. Copenhagen: Busck, 1971.

"Völundur." *Óðinn* 2, no. 12 (March 1, 1907): 92.

"Völundur." *Vísir* 12, no. 126 (June 6, 1922): 4.

"Vöruskrá" [List of Goods]. *Norðanfari* 3, no. 30-31 (1864): 62.

Wagner, Michael F. "Danish Polytechnical Education Between Handicraft and Science." In *European Historiography of Technology. Proceedings from the TISC-Conference in Roskilde*, edited by Dan Ch. Christensen, 146-63. Odense: Odense University Press, 1993.

Wästlund, Georg. "Betongteknikens historiska utveckling." [The Historical Development of Concrete Construction]. *Beton-Teknik* no. 1 (1946): 1-22.

"Það væri lengi..." [It would be long...]. *Þjóðólfur* 19, no. 14-15 (February 8, 1867): 58-61.

Þ. B. "Sigurður Pjetursson og byggingarannsóknirnar" [Sigurður Pétursson and the Building Research]. *Búnaðarrit* 15, no. 1 (1901): 3-14.

"Þinghúsið" [The House of Parliament]. *Þjóðólfur* 32, no. 29 (November 17, 1880): 114.

Þorleifur Þorleifsson. "Járnbrautin í Reykjavík 1913-1928" [The Railway in Reykjavík 1913-1928]. *Saga* 11, no. 1 (1973): 116-61.

Þorsteinn Gunnarsson. *Viðeyjarstofa og kirkja* [The Residence and Church at Viðey]. Reykjavík: Reykjavíkurborg, 1997.

Þorsteinn Gunnarsson. "Steinhlaðnar kirkjur á Íslandi" [Stone Churches in Iceland]. In *Kirkjur Íslands. Vol. 3* [Churches of Iceland], 52-58. Reykjavík: Hið íslenska bókmenntafélag, 2018.

Þór Magnússon. "Þingeyrakirkja. Byggingarlist kirkjunnar" [The Church at Þingeyrar. Architectural History of the Church]. *Kirkjur Íslands. Vol. 8* [Churches of Iceland], 270-72. Reykjavík: Hið íslenska bókmenntafélag, 2006.

Þórir Stephensen. *Dómkirkjan í Reykjavík. Byggingarsagan. Vol. 1* [The Cathedral in Reykjavík. History of the Building]. Reykjavík: Hið íslenska bókmenntafélag, 1996.

Þórður Atli Þórðarson. "Land án járnbrauta. Tilraunir Íslendinga til járnbrautvæðingar." [A Land Without Railways. Attempts of the Icelanders at a Railway Connection]. Bachelor Thesis in History, University of Iceland. September 2011.

Image Credits

INTRODUCTION

Fig. 1
Photograph by author, 2016.

Fig. 2
Photograph by author, 2016.

Fig. 3
Photograph by author, 2019.

Fig. 4
Photograph by author, 2016.

Fig. 5
Photograph by author, 2019.

Fig. 6
Photograph by author, 2019.

CHAPTER 1

Fig. 1
Icelandic and Faroese Photographs of Frederick W. W. Howell, Fiske Icelandic Collection, Rare & Manuscript Collections, Cornell University Library.

Fig. 2
Icelandic and Faroese Photographs of Frederick W. W. Howell, Fiske Icelandic Collection, Rare & Manuscript Collections, Cornell University Library.

Fig. 3
Icelandic and Faroese Photographs of Frederick W. W. Howell, Fiske Icelandic Collection, Rare & Manuscript Collections, Cornell University Library.

Fig. 4
Icelandic and Faroese Photographs of Frederick W. W. Howell, Fiske Icelandic Collection, Rare & Manuscript Collections, Cornell University Library.

Fig. 5
Icelandic and Faroese Photographs of Frederick W. W. Howell, Fiske Icelandic Collection, Rare & Manuscript Collections, Cornell University Library.

Fig. 6
Icelandic and Faroese Photographs of Frederick W. W. Howell, Fiske Icelandic Collection, Rare & Manuscript Collections, Cornell University Library.

Fig. 7
Norsk Teknisk Museum.

Fig. 8
Þjóðminjasafn Íslands – National Museum of Iceland, Mms-2378.

Fig. 9
Bornholms Museum.

Fig. 10
Photograph by author, 2019.

Fig. 11
Photograph by author, 2019.

Fig. 12
Photograph by author, 2019.

Fig. 13
Photograph by author, 2019.

Fig. 14
ETH-Bibliothek Zürich, Rar 5121. https://doi.org/10.3931/e-rara-3581.

Fig. 15
Tryggvidor, Wikimedia Commons, 2014. CC BY-SA 3.0.

Fig. 16
Royal Danish Library, DKB 145, mappe 4, 12115f.

Fig. 17
Royal Danish Library, DKB 145, mappe 4, 12115b.

Fig. 18
National Library of Norway.

Fig. 19
Þjóðminjasafn Íslands – National Museum of Iceland, Lpr/2006-244.

CHAPTER 2

Fig. 1
Private archive of author.

Fig. 2
Þjóðminjasafn Íslands – National Museum of Iceland, Mms-29519.

Fig. 3
Þjóðminjasafn Íslands – National Museum of Iceland, Mms-17323.

Fig. 4
Þjóðminjasafn Íslands – National Museum of Iceland, Lpr-2811-a.

Fig. 5
Photograph by author, 2019.

Fig. 6
Lbs, Tímarit.is.

Fig. 7
Wikimedia Commons, Public domain.

Fig. 8
Lbs, Tímarit.is.

Fig. 9
Lbs, Tímarit.is.

Fig. 10
Lbs, Tímarit.is.

Fig. 11
Lbs, Íslandssafn.

Fig. 12
Icelandic and Faroese Photographs of Frederick W. W. Howell, Fiske Icelandic Collection, Rare & Manuscript Collections, Cornell University Library.

Fig. 13
Icelandic and Faroese Photographs of Frederick W. W. Howell, Fiske Icelandic Collection, Rare & Manuscript Collections, Cornell University Library.

Fig. 14
Icelandic and Faroese Photographs of Frederick W. W. Howell, Fiske Icelandic Collection, Rare & Manuscript Collections, Cornell University Library.

Fig. 15
Þjóðminjasafn Íslands – National Museum of Iceland, GZ1-793.

APPENDIX

IMAGE CREDITS

Fig. 16
Danmarks Tekniske Universitet, DTU Historie- og samlingsdatabase, 4000.4.19.

Fig. 17
Photograph by author, 2019.

Fig. 18
Vegagerðin – Icelandic Road and Coastal Administration, Teikningar A-34c/b-33.

Fig. 19
Þjóðminjasafn Íslands – National Museum of Iceland, Pk/1997-5.

Fig. 20
Þjóðminjasafn Íslands – National Museum of Iceland, Lpr/2003-387.

Fig. 21
Lbs, Tímarit.is.

Fig. 22
National Library of Norway, https://urn.nb.no/URN:NBN:no-nb_digifoto_20200415_00015_NB_LED_63_15.

Fig. 23
Þjóðminjasafn Íslands – National Museum of Iceland, Pk-160.

Fig. 24
Þjóðminjasafn Íslands – National Museum of Iceland, Lpr-396.

Fig. 25
Royal Danish Library, DKB 1414, mappe 8, 53767b.

Fig. 26
Royal Danish Library, DKB 457, mappe 14, 53323a.

Fig. 27
Royal Danish Library, DKB 457, mappe 14, 53323b.

Fig. 28
Þjóðminjasafn Íslands – National Museum of Iceland, VS-262.

Fig. 29
Þjóðminjasafn Íslands – National Museum of Iceland, Pk/2005-66.

Fig. 30
Þjóðminjasafn Íslands – National Museum of Iceland, Lpr-1605-62.

Fig. 31
ÞÍ, Teikningasafn 15/5.

Fig. 32
ÞÍ, Teikningasafn 15/5.

Fig. 33
ÞÍ, Vita- og hafnarmálastofnun. Bréfasafn, B-BDB/2, Örk 1.

Fig. 34
ÞÍ, Vita- og hafnarmálastofnun. Bréfasafn, B-BDB/2, Örk 1.

Fig. 35
Photograph by author, 2019.

Fig. 36
National Library of Norway, https://urn.nb.no/URN:NBN:no-nb_digifoto_20160819_00120_bldsa_FAalb006_27

Fig. 37
Þjóðminjasafn Íslands – National Museum of Iceland, Lpr-3589.

Fig. 38
Photograph by Magnús Ólafsson. Þjóðminjasafn Íslands – National Museum of Iceland, Lpr/2003-399-31.

Fig. 39
Photograph by author, 2019.

Fig. 40
Photograph by Vera de Kok, 2017. Wikimedia Commons, CC BY-SA 3.0.

Fig. 41
Borgarskjalasafn Reykjavíkur – Reykjavík City Archives, Teikningavefur Reykjavíkurborgar. BF 135/14.

Fig. 42
https://www.gamlabio.is/.

CHAPTER 3

Fig. 1
Skógasafn – Skógar Museum, MVSD-96.

Fig. 2
Private archive of author.

Fig. 3
ÞÍ, Húsameistari ríkisins, Teikningasafn, C/276.

Fig. 4
ÞÍ, Húsameistari ríkisins, Teikningasafn, Safn A(D), Flokkur 44.

Fig. 5
Skógasafn – Skógar Museum, Kort-213.

Fig. 6
The Einar Jónsson Museum, sketchbooks.

Fig. 7
The Einar Jónsson Museum, sketchbooks.

Fig. 8
Photograph by author, 2019.

Fig. 9
ÞÍ, Húsameistari ríkisins, C/776, Landsspítali gamli.

Fig. 10
Photograph by author, 2019.

Fig. 11
ÞÍ, Húsameistari ríkisins, Bréfa-og teiningasafn, Safn A(D), Flokkur 21, Verkefni H-L, Örk 30.

Fig. 12
ÞÍ, Húsameistari ríkisins, Bréfa-og teiningasafn, Safn A(D), Flokkur 21, Verkefni H-L, Örk 30.

Fig. 13
ÞÍ, Húsameistari ríkisins, Bréfa-og teiningasafn, Safn A(D), Flokkur 21, Verkefni H-L, Örk 30.

Fig. 14
Þjóðminjasafn Íslands – National Museum of Iceland, ÞÞ-197.

Fig. 15
Þjóðminjasafn Íslands – National Museum of Iceland, ÞÞ-199.

Fig. 16
Photograph by author, 2019.

Fig. 17
Photograph by author, 2019.

Fig. 18
Borgarskjalasafn Reykjavíkur – Reykjavík City Archives, Teikningavefur Reykjavíkurborgar. BF 326/11.

Fig. 19
ÞÍ, Húsameistari ríkisins, Bréfa-og teikningasafn, Örk V 431.

Fig. 20
Lbs, Tímarit.is.

Fig. 21
Photograph by author, 2016.

Fig. 22
Private archive of author.

Fig. 23
Listasafn Íslands – National Gallery of Iceland, LÍÁJ 435. Photograph: Listasafn Íslands / National Gallery of Iceland / SG.

Fig. 24
Photograph by Michele Francesco Barale, 2018.

Fig. 25
Þjóðminjasafn Íslands – National Museum of Iceland, SÍS-351-2.

Fig. 26
Photograph by author, 2019.

Fig. 27
Icelandic and Faroese Photographs of Frederick W. W. Howell, Fiske Icelandic Collection, Rare & Manuscript Collections, Cornell University Library.

Fig. 28
Byggðasafn Dalamanna, 2011-2-230.

Fig. 29
Þjóðminjsafn Íslands – National Museum of Iceland, Lpr/2007-126.

Fig. 30
Photograph by author, 2018.

Fig. 31
Photograph by author, 2018.

Fig. 32
Photograph by author, 2018.

Fig. 33
Photograph by author, 2019.

Fig. 34
Photograph by author, 2019.

Fig. 35
ÞÍ, Húsameistari ríkisins, Bréfa- og teikningasafn, Safn A(D), Flokkur 42, Örk 181. Háskóli Íslands, sérteikningar.

Fig. 36
Photograph by author, 2018.

Fig. 37
Borgarskjalasafn Reykjavíkur – Reykjavík City Archives, Teikningavefur Reykjavíkurborgar. BF 210/14.

Fig. 38
Photograph by author, 2018.

EPILOGUE

Fig. 1
Þjóðminjasafn Íslands – National Museum of Iceland, BB1-5746.

Fig. 2
Photograph by Arlène Lucianaz, 2020.

Fig. 3
The Einar Jónsson Museum, sketchbooks.

Fig. 4
Photograph by author, 2016.

Fig. 5
Photograph by author, 2019.

List of Names

Aalto, Alvar (1898–1976) n
134

Adam of Bremen (before 1050–1081/85)
30, 31, 57, 191

Ahrens, Georg Daníel Edward (1852–1911)
53, 54

Ásgrímur Jónsson (1876–1958)
159, 160, 184

Ágúst Pálsson (1893–1967) n
176, 188

Árni Jóhansson (1867–1940) n
127

Ásgeir Ásgeirsson (1894–1972)
192, 199

Ásmundur Sveinsson (1893–1982)
196, 197, 199, 200

Baillie Scott, Mackay Hugh (1865–1945) n
186

Bald, Fredrik Anton (1845–1909)
50, 52, 53, 61, 68, 103, 127, 133

Bald, Valdemar (1872–1921)
61, 103

Bartholin, Rasmus (1625–1698)
46, 47

Bárður Ísleifsson (1905–2000) n
188

Bech, C. (s.d.) n
132

Becker, Gottfried (1767–1845) n
59

Benedikt Gröndal (1924–2010)
138, 141, 159, 182, 183, 184, 185, 186, 187

Benedikt Jónsson (1846–1939) n
127

Björn Jónsson (1802–1886)
40, 59

Brummer, Carl (1864–1953) n
136

Christiani, Rudolf (1877–1960)
70, 128, 131

Clemmensen, Andreas (1852–1928) n
136

Coignet, François (1814–1888)
87

Edison, Thomas (1847–1931)
75

Eigtved, Nicolai (1701–1754)
38

Einar Ásmundsson (1828–1893)
50

Einar Erlendsson (1883–1968)
122, 123, 124, 136, 143, 146, 176, 178, 187

Einar Jónsson (1874–1954)
9, 143, 144, 145, 146, 148, 161, 183, 193, 194, 197

Einar Sveinsson (1906–1973)
172, 176, 177, 188

Eiríkur Einarsson (1907–1969) n
188

Eiríkur Kúld (1822–1893)
53

Finnur Thorlacius (1883–1974)
122, 136

Forchhammer, Johan Georg (1794–1865)
36, 37, 58, 59, 60

Frezzotti, Oriolo (1888–1965)
161

Gesellius, Herman (1874–1916) n
182

Guðjón Samúelsson (1887–1950)
10, 20, 21, 26, 100, 133, 140, 141, 142, 143, 144, 145, 149, 150, 152, 154, 156, 157, 159, 160, 161, 162, 163, 164, 166, 167, 169, 170, 171, 172, 173, 174, 177, 178, 182, 183, 184, 185, 186, 187, 188, 195

Guðmundur Björnsson (1864–1937)
110, 134

Guðmundur Einarsson (1895–1963)
166, 186

Guðmundur Finnbogason (1873–1944)
69, 83, 128, 130, 183

Guðmundur Hannesson (1866–1946)
13, 15, 38, 48, 52, 54, 55, 56, 59, 60, 61, 62, 83, 128, 129, 130, 132, 136, 141, 164, 166, 182, 184, 185, 186

Gunnlaugur Halldórsson (1909–1986) n
133, 188

Guttormur Andrésson (1895–1958)
170

Gylfi Þorsteinsson Gíslason (1917–2004)
192, 199

Halldór Kiljan Laxness (1902–1998)
18, 22, 28, 119, 135, 154, 184, 197

Hallgrímur Pétursson (1614–1674)
108

Haukur Thors (1896–1970)
141

Helgi Helgason (1848–1922)
53, 54, 62

Hennebique, François (1842–1921)
88, 93, 97, 98, 99, 108, 131, 132, 134, 135

Herholdt, Johan Daniel (1818–1902) n
133

Hjörfur Þorklesson (s.d.) n
127

Hoffmann, Josef (1870–1956) n
134

Holm, Jørgen (1835–1916)
107

Hovdenak, Nils Olaf (1854–1942) n
126

Högna Sigurðardóttir (1929–2017)
195, 199

Indriði Einarsson (1885–1939)
159

Ingólfur Arnarson (c. 849–c. 910)
50

Ingólfur Arnarsson (1956–)
197, 200

Jakob Hálfdanarson (1836–1919)
67, 68, 83, 127, 130

Jantzen, Ivar (1875–1961)
70, 128

Jens Eyjólfsson (1879–1959)
122, 143, 154, 155

Jensen, Thor (1863–1947)
73, 74, 76

Jensen-Klint, Peder Vilhelm (1853–1930)
160, 185

APPENDIX

LIST OF NAMES

Jes Zimsen (1877–1938)
76

Jóhann Eyjólfsson (1862–1951)
54

Jón Gunnarsson (1900–1973)
166, 186

Jón Hjaltalín (1807–1882)
41, 46, 47, 59, 61

Jón Jónsson (1841–1883)
53

Jón Sigurðsson (1811–1879)
32, 59, 145, 175, 183

Jón Þorláksson (1877–1935)
28, 64, 70, 78, 79, 80, 81, 82, 83, 84, 85, 86, 87, 89, 91, 92, 93, 99, 101, 102, 106, 112, 126, 129, 130, 131, 132, 133, 136, 166, 184, 185, 186

Jónas Jónsson [frá Hriflu] (1885–1968)
138, 141, 149, 156, 159, 161, 172, 182, 183, 184, 185, 186, 187

Kirkerup, Andreas (1749–1810)
38, 59

Kiørboe, Frederik (1878–1952)
107, 108, 134

Klentz, C. (s.d.)
44, 60

Knud Zimsen (1875–1953)
69, 70, 71, 72, 73, 74, 75, 76, 77, 78, 82, 83, 93, 99, 101, 102, 112, 116, 118, 124, 128, 129, 130, 132, 133, 134, 178

Kolderup, Edvard (1847–1911)
85, 130

Krabbe, Thorvald Haraldsen (1876–1953)
65, 97, 98, 99, 101, 107, 108, 112, 113, 126, 131, 132, 133, 134

Kristín Sigurðsson (1881–1944)
143

Labat, Jean-Baptiste (1663–1738) n
58

Labonne, Henry (1855–1944)
64, 65, 66, 126

Lambot, Joseph-Louis (1814–87)
87

Lindgren, Armas (1874–1929) n
182

Macdonald, Margaret (1864–1933) n
186

Mackenzie, George Steuart
30, 31, 57

Mackintosh, Charles Rennie (1868–1928) n
186

Magnús Stephensen (1863–1917)
118, 127

Maillart, Robert (1872–1940)
111, 134

Meldahl, Ferdinand (1827–1908)
50, 51, 61, 103, 133

Monberg, Niels Christensen (1856–1930)
101

Monier, Joseph (1823–1906)
87, 88, 112, 131, 134

Mörsch, Emil (1872–1950)
88, 131

Nielsen, Aage (1873–1945) n
131

Nielsen, Johannes Magdahl (1862–1941)
107, 108, 109, 134

Norum, Karl (1852–1911) n
182

Nyrop, Martin (1849–1921)
140

Ostenfeld, Asger Skovgaard (1866–1931)
85, 130

Pedersen, Julius (1839–1910)
85, 130

Petersen, Carl (1873–1923)
160, 185

Petersen, Chr. (s.d.) n
132

Perret, Auguste (1874–1954)
122

Plesner, Ulrik (1861–1933) n
136

Poelzig, Hans (1869–1936) n
185

Reffstrup, Knud (s.d.)
93, 96

Ruskin, John (1819–1900)
160

Rothe, Alexander (?–1914) n
126

Rögnvaldur Ólafsson (1874–1917)
69, 70, 99, 100, 102, 107, 111, 112, 113, 115, 119, 120, 122, 123, 128, 133, 134, 135, 139, 140, 176

Saarinen, Eliel (1873–1950)
140, 143, 161, 182, 183

Sartoris, Alberto (1901–1998)
141, 182

Schiøtz, Carl (s.d.)
98, 99

Schytte-Berg, Hagbarth Martin (1860–1944) n
182

Shand, Philip Morton (1888–1960)
92, 131, 141, 182

Sigurður Guðmundsson (1885–1958)
141, 180, 182, 184, 186, 188, 195, 196

Sigurður Hansson (s.d.)
48, 54, 61, 72

Sigurður Pétursson (1870–1900)
67, 68, 69, 70, 78, 83, 84, 126

Sigurður Thoroddsen (1863–1955)
66, 89, 99, 126, 133, 188

Sigurgeir Sigurjónsson (1948–)
197, 200

Sigurjón Ólafsson (1908–1982)
197, 200

Sigvatur Árnason (1823–1911) n
126

Skúli Magnússon (1711–1794)
38, 59

Snorri Sturluson (1179–1241)
73, 108, 182

Sonck, Lars (1870–1956) n
182

Steinn Steinsen (1891–1981)
166

Suenson, Edouard (1877–1958)
98

Sveinn Pálsson (1762–1840)
35, 58

Sverrir Runólfsson (1831–1879)
41, 42, 43, 44, 45, 46, 47, 48, 60, 164

Sörensen, Poul (1873–1964)
70, 128

Teilmann, Charles (s.d.) n
59

Thuren, Christian Lauritz (1846–1926)
103, 106, 133

Trausti Ólafsson (1891–1961)
170

Tryggvi Gunnarsson (1835–1917)
73

Van Epen, Johannes Christiaan (s.d.) n
185

von Emperger, Fritz (1862–1942)
88, 130

von Ripperda, Udo (1859–1949) n
126

Wad, Gregers (1755–1832) n
59

Wayss, Gustav Adolf (1851–1917)
88, 131

Windfeld-Hansen, Ib (1845–1926) n
126

Winstrup, Laurits Albert (1815–1889)
38, 40, 59, 133

Þorgrímur Þorláksson (1732–1805) n
59

Þorsteinn Briem (1885–1949)
169, 186

Þórir Baldvinsson (1901–1986)
139, 177, 182

Ögmundur Sigurðsson (Sivertsen)
(1799–1845)
37

Ørsted, Hans Christian (1777–1851)
36

IMPRINT

Opening quotes: Jorge Luis Borges, "A Islandia," in *El Oro de los tigres* (Buenos Aires: Editorial Emecé, 1972), p. 145, trans. by the author.
Giacomo Leopardi, "The Dialogue of Nature and an Icelander," in *The Moral Essays (Operette morali) Vol. 1*, trans. Patrick Creagh (New York: Columbia University Press, 1983), p. 99.

Cover images: Sofia Nannini
Design and typesetting: Floyd E. Schulze
Project management: Franziska Schüffler
Copyediting: Bianca Murphy
Production: Susanne Rösler
Lithography: Bild1Druck, Berlin
Printed in the European Union.

Funding bodies:
Aalborg Portland Íslandi
Federbeton Confindustria
Steinsteypufélag Íslands – The Icelandic Concrete Association
Vegagerðin – The Icelandic Road and Coastal Administration
Þjóðminjasafn Íslands – The National Museum of Iceland has generously supported this publication by offering their archival reproductions free of charge.

© 2024 by jovis Verlag
An imprint of Walter de Gruyter GmbH,
Berlin/Boston

Texts by kind permission of the authors.
Pictures by kind permission
of the photographers/
holders of the picture rights.
All rights reserved.

Bibliographic information published by the Deutsche Nationalbibliothek
The Deutsche Nationalbibliothek lists this publication in the Deutsche Nationalbibliografie; detailed bibliographic data are available on the Internet at http://dnb.d-nb.de

jovis Verlag
Genthiner Straße 13
10785 Berlin

www.jovis.de

jovis books are available worldwide in select bookstores. Please contact your nearest bookseller or visit www.jovis.de for information concerning your local distribution.

ISBN 978-3-98612-027-6 (softcover)
ISBN 978-3-98612-071-9 (e-book)